# *Dustbowl to Paradise*

**Eastern Colorado to Frisco Colorado**

**Harold's Humorous History**

by

**Harold J. Rutherford**

**Ten Mile Publishing**

**9740 Peacock Street**

**Federal Heights, CO 80260-5749**

The many incidents described herein are based on actual experiences and events, to the best of the author's knowledge. In a few cases, two or more related events are combined into a single story. In other cases names are changed or last names are omitted. The author and publisher do not guarantee the accuracy or completeness of any information.

Library of Congress Catalog Card Number 00 091394
Rutherford, Harold J.
A history of the years 1927 through October 1941 in Colorado, largely biographical but also describing other people and interesting events of that time.

ISBN 0-9700307-0-3

Published by:
Ten Mile Publishing
9740 Peacock Street
Federal Heights, CO 80260-5749 U.S.A.

## WHY THIS BOOK?

The author has had a lifelong desire to tell of life in Colorado during the 1920's through the early 1940's, *as he saw it*.

Not your usual record of names, dates, politics, battles, etc., this is a history of trials and triumphs of ordinary people, as well as some very extraordinary people, many of whom were blessed(?) with very unique personalities! The Dustbowl and the Great Depression added up to a very difficult time in American history, but Rutherford brushes most of that aside as he shares *some* of his hilarious antics as well as those of his friends, neighborhood pets, and ranch animals.

Russell, the father of Harold, was a practical, hard working man, truly the provider, problem solver, and head of the family. Rutherford feels blessed by all the knowledge received from his dad. He shares details of some of his activities such as various construction projects, putting up hay, branding cattle, remodeling and repairing vehicles, etc.

From his mother Minnie, Harold inherited his sense of humor, storytelling ability, and optimistic outlook.

Even though the work was hard and the hours were long, Harold and his family found plenty of time for practical jokes as well as observing the humor that just seemed to be everywhere around them!

Thank God for good memories.

## ACKNOWLEDGMENTS

My thanks to those who have in one way or another contributed to this endeavor: My wife Lois, sisters Mildred Rutherford and Helen Davidson, daughter Danetta Aggus, granddaughters Robin Benson and Brittany Aggus, friends Becky Keran, Shirley Dehart, and Jean Olson.

A special thanks to old Frisco friends Sue Chamberlain, Howard Giberson, Harold (Chick) Deming, and Charles (Chuck) Chamberlain who shared their old photos and memories.

**Graphic Illustrations**
Danetta Aggus and
Brittany Aggus

**Cover Design**
Lisa Lynch

# TABLE OF CONTENTS

# PART I
# LIFE ON THE PRAIRIE

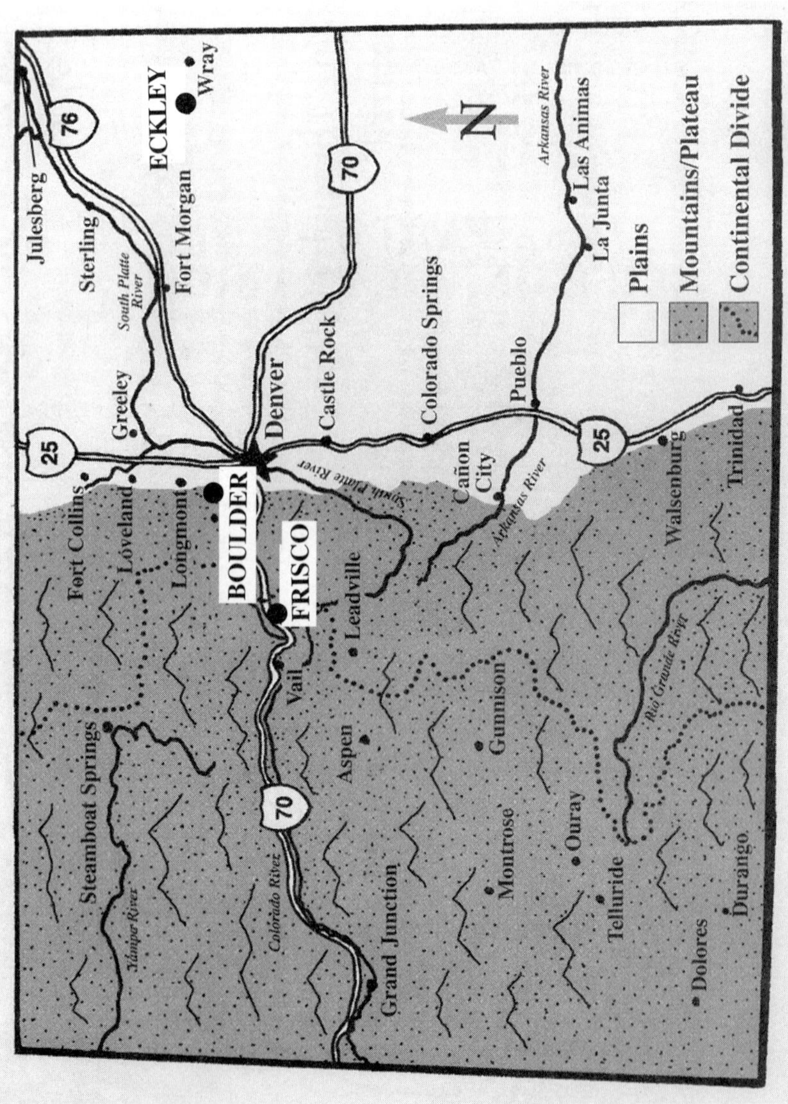
Julesberg
Sterling
South Platte River
Fort Morgan
ECKLEY
Wray
76
70
N
Greeley
25
Denver
Castle Rock
Colorado Springs
Pueblo
Arkansas River
La Junta
Las Animas
Plains
Mountains/Plateau
Continental Divide
Fort Collins
Loveland
Longmont
BOULDER
FRISCO
South Platte River
Cañon City
Arkansas River
25
Walsenburg
Trinidad
Leadville
Vail
Aspen
Gunnison
Steamboat Springs
Yampa River
70
Colorado River
Grand Junction
Montrose
Ouray
Telluride
Rio Grande River
Durango
Dolores

It all started in 1927. I was three years old and lived in Eckley, Yuma County, Colorado. My parents had named me Harold James. At least, I think my parents gave me this name when I was born, but I can't remember as I was rather young at the time.

My parents were James Russell Rutherford and Minnie Rutherford. I found out years later that the name Minnie was of Indian origin and meant "Laughing Water." There was no Indian blood in Mom, but she did a lot of laughing down through the years. She always saw the best in everything. I guess I inherited some of her humor and outlook on life.

In 1927 I had an older sister Mildred Fern and a younger sister Helen Lucile. There were two years between each of us kids. My brother Dean Russell would arrive in 1928 and bring up the rear.

Dad did carpenter work around the area and once a year he worked in the Eckley train depot so Carl Crane, the Depot Agent, could take a two-week vacation.

In 1899, Dad was only twelve years old when his father died in Riverton, Nebraska. He had one sister, LuRosa (pronounced Larose), who was five years old at the time. His older brother Samuel was seventeen and had already left home. Samuel had gone to Red Cloud, Nebraska, where he married at a young age.

After Grandpa died, Grandma did laundry, cleaned houses, kept the railroad depot clean, and did extra cooking when possible. Dad quit school and helped Grandma with her work. He also cut firewood for sale and logs for railroad ties. An agent at the depot taught him telegraphy in the evenings. When he was fifteen, he went to work for the railroad as a telegrapher. He soon got the name of being one of the best telegraphers on the Burlington line. His long hours of work from early morning till late at night had paid off.

In time Dad moved to more than one town along the Burlington route when better pay was offered.

Outgoing mail bags were hung on an L-shaped pole and, when the train came by, the conductor reached out and grabbed the bag with a pole without the train stopping. The incoming mail bags were thrown out from the moving train.

Occasionally robbers would go to the depot right after the mail came in to rob the depot. Dad said he always threw the money bag from the mail sack in the waste basket and threw some wadded paper on top. Dad was never robbed, but robbers came by and looked for the money bag several times while he was working.

In 1912, Aunt LuRosa married Emile Poulignot (pronounced Po-lin'-e-o) in Red Cloud, Nebraska. Uncle Emile was working on the railroad at the time. After about a year they moved to Woodruff, Kansas, and Grandma moved with them. In 1915 their daughter Ruth was born and Aunt LuRosa went to work part time in the telephone office since Grandma was there to look after Ruth.

Dad worked several places for the railroad system. He, along with Uncle Sam and his family, were in Texas for a time but finally settled in Eckley, Colorado. Uncle Sam homesteaded a tract of ground southwest of Eckley while Dad went to work as a depot agent. Dad decided inside work wasn't what he liked so he quit his job and went to work as a carpenter in Eckley and the surrounding area. In his spare time, he built himself a home in Eckley and worked as a depot agent only part time when he was needed.

In the meantime, Mom taught school several years in towns around Alma, Nebraska. Her brother Dean persuaded her to go with him to Sedro Wolly, Washington, for a couple of years. When she came back she couldn't find a teaching job so she went to Woodruff and worked in the telephone office where she first met Aunt LuRosa. Mom, Uncle Emile, Aunt Clari (pronounced Clara), and a neighbor sang in a quartet while Mom was in Woodruff and, in later years, Mom and Uncle Emile often sang in church whenever they were together.

Dad went to Woodruff to see Grandma, Aunt LuRosa, Uncle Emile, and their new baby Ruth. It was there in the telephone office that Dad met Mom.

A courtship of two years followed, involving many trips to and from Woodruff before Dad and Mom were married on December 26, 1917. They began their life together in Dad's house in Eckley where he continued to work as a carpenter. He put in a large garden including watermelons and cantaloupe. One year he put 108 cantaloupe in his storm cellar after he had sold and given away as many as he could.

Uncle Sam wasn't living on his homestead and the place was empty and available. Dad decided to sell their home in Eckley and take over the farm to see if he could make a living on it. After several years of crop failure due to drought and hail, Dad decided that he had better move back to Eckley and go back to work as a carpenter.

Eckley lies between Wray and Yuma in the middle of the sand hills, not too many miles away from where they had met in Woodruff.

The plains were beautiful in the springtime when the cactus, yucca, and sage brush were in bloom. White phlox and flowers we called pinkies came up in the springtime but withered when the hot summer sun hit them in the peak of the day. Each morning there was a fresh supply of flowers for the new day. During the summer sunflowers were abundant everywhere, but when the drought and dust storms took over there were no flowers to be seen anywhere, not even on the cactus plants.

## A TRIP TO NEBRASKA

In the late fall of 1927 bad news came from Grandma Fitzgarrald. Grandpa had had a serious surgery and wasn't expected to live very long. They wanted us all to come to their farm near Stamford, Nebraska, to see them, and they especially needed Dad to take charge of harvesting their 250 acres of corn.

Dad had just finished a carpentry job so it was a good time for us to head to Nebraska.

Seven o'clock in the morning found us loading Dad's Model T pickup with boxes and sacks holding our clothes for the trip. Since Helen was the youngest, she rode in the cab with Dad and Mom while Mildred and I pressed ourselves tightly against the cab in the pickup bed. Wearing our winter coats and piled with blankets we were warm as toast as we traveled the dusty roads towards Nebraska. Sandwiches, graham crackers, and jars filled with water eliminated the need for food stops along the way.

"Russell, how long do you think it will take us to make the trip?" asked Mom with a note of concern in her voice.

"Well, around ten hours if I drive around thirty miles an hour. Of course, we'll have to stop to stretch a little and to find an outhouse from time to time, but we should be there well before supper."

It was a beautiful morning. We could hear the meadow larks singing as we traveled along. We loved it when we went by trees because the engine noise echoed, becoming much louder. As we approached the farm Dad pulled his watch out of his pocket and said, "Not too bad, it hasn't been quite ten hours since we left Eckley."

Pandemonium reigned as aunts, uncles, and excited cousins descended on the Fitzgarrald farm. There were so many people that we had to eat in shifts and some shifts ate more than their share! After dinner we went to the barnyard to see some chickens, cows, horses and calves. I really suspect it was to check and see what was left of the livestock after the feeding frenzy.

Some of our cousins had come all the way from Michigan and others had arrived from nearby towns. A great aunt and uncle came all the way from Canada. They were joined by various and sundry double cousins of Mom, which did not necessarily refer to their size. When two siblings marry two siblings, their children are double cousins.

And then there was Aunt Clari who stood out from the rest of the crowd. Aunt Clari had never married which made her seem rather odd in a family bursting with offspring, but she made up for that with her funloving personality, not to mention her teaching and musical gifts. She was a very vivacious person.

My face lit up with joy when I spied my mother's baby brother, Lynn, now 21 years old. Uncle Lynn had visited us many times in Eckley and seemed to bring a holiday spirit with him even in troubled times. Most of the people left for the night but were back for breakfast the next morning when they discovered that there were, in fact, enough chickens for eggs and a leftover pig for bacon for breakfast and pork sandwiches for lunch. Even though they had completely drained the coffee supply the evening before, they found the coffee pot full again!

Deane Devars, my second cousin, was about my age of three years old. He had two wooden guns his Dad had made that shot rubber bands made from old tire inner tubes cut in about one half inch wide bands. A snap-on clothespin mounted on the back of the pistol made up the hair trigger. We stood up jars for targets and, boy, did we ever have a lot of fun, especially when Deane "accidentally" missed the jars and hit his napping dad, Guy Devars.

Guy was a rural mail carrier in Orleans, Nebraska. He told us that a year earlier the snow was so deep that he had to wear snow shoes to deliver the mail to all the farms. One afternoon while going from one farm to another he saw a big cowboy hat lying out in the snow. He picked it up and to his amazement, found a man's head under the hat. "What are you doing out here in the deep snow?"

Well," the man replied, "me and my brother was going over to a farm to work when this here snow storm come up and this is as far as we got."

I'll be glad to help you get out of the deep snow, but where is your brother?"

With a woeful look on his face the man said, "Mister, he is riding the horse."

"Horse? Where in tarnation is the horse?"

Tearfully he choked out, “My brother is riding the horse and I am standing on my brother’s shoulders!” Guy swore that this was the truth and if we could have seen how deep the snow was we wouldn’t question whether it was true or not.

Meanwhile, back at the farm with all of its organized chaos, stood a haystack that was about half used up, off the top no less, standing close to the barn. Leading the charge, I led my cousins and Mildred to the top of the barn loft and jumped out onto the beckoning haystack. We continued with our sport until Great Uncle Rich came by and terminated the fun, shaking his head and mumbling in a deep voice as he walked away.

Hearing the problem, Uncle Lynn came out of the house and set a post in the ground with a brace front and back, then fastened a pipe from the barn to the post and hung three rope swings with wood seats from the pipe. He tied a heavy rope from the top of the post to a shed, a little higher than I could reach on the high end. They hoped the ropes course and swings would keep us out of trouble for the next thirty minutes and, because it contained a small degree of danger, this was the place we spent much of our time while we were there on the farm.

One evening Dad turned the windmill on to pump water into a great big water tank at the edge of the pasture for the cows to drink out of. The fence came up to the tank on opposite sides so that half of the tank was in the pasture and the other half was in the barnyard where the windmill was. A pipe from the windmill emptied water into the tank along the inside edge, causing the water to circulate around in the tank.

The water current had to be put to good use so when the cousins produced five celluloid ducks as gifts to my sisters the water fun started. We put the ducks in the water where they would ride around the tank. When they arrived back near the pipe, the water would duck them and then they would pop back up and go around again. I watched them for a time and decided my mouth organ, which had been presented along with the ducks, should join the ducks in the tank. Into the water it went where it immediately sank to the bottom. Anxiously I watched for it to appear and much to my relief, the current brought it back to our side of the tank, still on the bottom.

My baby sister Helen was too little to see the ducks in the water tank, so it was up to our big cousins Lavone (aged 11) and Garrald (9), to enable the smaller ones to participate. Garrald found a hoe and stood on the side of the tank so that every time my mouth organ circled around to our side he would try to retrieve it with the hoe. Cousins Lavone and Deane along with Mildred were trying to hold him up and help him keep his balance when Great Uncle Rich came out of the house and raced to the tank. We were immediately ushered into the house and the ducks were confiscated. Later Uncle Lynn went out and retrieved my mouth organ and, much to our dismay, we were not to get the ducks back till we promised never to go near the water tank again. We were not sure if that promise was just for that day, but as we moved on to other amusements that did not present a real problem.

Many people from my grandparents' church brought horses and wagons and helped with the harvest.

During the harvest Dad kept a tool box fastened on the side of the corn sheller so he would have tools to use when the sheller or other equipment broke down. Occasionally workers would borrow tools and forget to return them, forcing Dad to go look for another tool or find the person who used the tool. This, of course, shut the work down till Dad could find the needed tool and make necessary repairs.

Dad, resourceful person that he was, found a unique solution to this dilemma. "I simply placed a big bull snake in the bottom of my toolbox and from then on my tools were always there when I wanted them."

Late fall and early winter found us still at the Stamford, Nebraska, farm. The days got colder and colder and we couldn't play outside. Grandpa was in bed most of the time.

Before we knew it, Christmas came and Santa brought Mildred and me each a tablet and a box of six crayons for Christmas. I also got a little car and the girls each got a doll. The dolls soon became mountain roads when stuck under a rug. My car drove miles and miles over their faces. Girls sure can be loud when they are upset!

Soon after Christmas the crops were all up and Uncle Lynn, who had been away to college, decided to stay home and help take care of the farm. Dad went back to Eckley, but Mom and us kids stayed for another month.

## HOME AGAIN

On a cold snowy morning Uncle Lynn took us to the train station in Oxford in his Model A coupe. I rode on a shelf behind the seat against the rear window which rapidly became cold as we traveled through the wintery landscape. I thought I would freeze before we got on the train. The train was warm, making it hard to keep awake till we arrived in Eckley late that night.

Dad met us at the door of the train. I held onto his pant leg as he carried Helen to the pickup. Mom and Mildred followed behind us. It was snowing hard and there were several inches of snow on the ground. As we walked along our breath could clearly be seen.

In the cold pickup we bundled up and waited while Dad retrieved the rest of our boxes and bags. It was sure nice to go into a warm house and get into my own bed.

The following days were cold and stormy on the eastern plains. Mom would gather us kids around her, tell us stories and recite poems. She seemed to know millions of them! We never tired of them and loved it when she sang to us and taught us songs.

We moved into a two-story frame house, with traces that only hinted of a previous color of white. We were only two lousy doors away from my Aunt Eliza and Uncle Sam and their girls, girls, girls!

Some of the girls were much older than Mildred and me but the leftovers were close to our ages. Margie was Mildred's age (seven), Charlotte (Toddy) was nine, Beulah was eleven and Juanita was thirteen. We played with them a lot except that, actually, the girls played together while harassing me all the day long.

There was a vacant shed-like house between our two houses that contained lots of old clothes, perhaps from an old dry goods store, as well as a couple of old dilapidated show cases. This made a perfect place for a gang of kids to play store.

Every once in a while the girls would run out to invite me in for a cup of so-called tea, which was really just a cup of water from a dirty teapot. When I had my kite in the air, I didn't have time for such trifling things.

One time my kite took a dive and came down on a shed at the back of the vacant building. "Can someone come and help me get my kite off the roof?" I hollered. About the third time I called I got a smirky answer, "You got it up there, you can just get it down."

Then, suddenly the whole company of girls came out to help me. I thought this was certainly not the usual pattern, but I needed my kite. They helped me climb on top of the shed, but as soon as I got up there they left in a cloud of dust.

I threw my kite down off the roof and yelled, "Please help me down." No answer, and it was getting hot on the tin roof. I yelled again and again. Still no answer. I screamed as loud as I could, hoping Mom would hear me and come to my rescue and the girls would get into trouble. Still no answer. Drastic action had to be taken. There was a garden on one side of the shed. I just closed my eyes and jumped off the roof into the garden hoping I wouldn't get hurt landing in the soft dirt. I squashed two tomato bushes and skinned my knee on some sticks that held up the tomatoes. I bled real red blood.

When Dad was home, he would help me fly my kite after having retrieved it from the phone lines.

One day he said, "We must find a better place to fly your kites. It isn't a good idea to fly your kites around the electric and telephone lines."

Much of the time the wind was so strong that we didn't try to fly a kite, but one time Dad got it high up in the air when the wind broke the string. The kite went sailing over in a pasture way beyond our neighbor's farm yard. Although we searched for some time, we never found it and, seeing my crestfallen face, Dad put his hand on my shoulder and said, "Your mother can take you to the store and buy you a nickel's worth of string. Then she can take you to Mrs. Birdsill's to get some more string, and I'll bring home some sticks to make a new kite."

Whenever we bought groceries, the store clerk would tear off a piece of paper from a big roll, lay it on the counter, and wrap up the groceries we purchased. He then would take string and tie it around the package. We saved the string from these packages, the only problem being that we would have to tie the pieces together to make a long line. When we bought groceries the grocery clerk would sell me quite a little string for one penny and a lot more for two pennies. If I needed kite string I always managed to buy at least two cents worth. I covered the sticks on my kite with the paper from the store packages.

Mrs. Birdsill saved the string from her groceries especially for me and wrapped it around a nail in her pantry. We visited her and she gave me the string that she had saved. I spent a whole day tying the pieces of string together.

Dad taught me to always run into the wind when launching my kite. "This creates wind to make your kite fly. If you run

***Uncle Sam's girls. Back row, left to right, Clellan, Ellen, Hazel, and Artheretta. Front row (the leftovers), Beulah, Margie, Toddy, and Juanita.***

away from the wind the kite may fly, but when you stop running the kite will settle back to the ground for lack of wind. Sometimes the wind rolls so I put a tail on the kite to keep it from rolling and diving towards the ground. We can't see the wind, but many times when the wind rolls the kite will follow the roll. Then we need to add some more length to the tail."

Dad also told me that when there wasn't any wind, which seldom was the case, to pick up some dried grass or dried leaves and get a short distance from a building and hold it up as high as I could and drop it. It would usually move slightly in the direction the wind was blowing, so I would know which way to run. If there wasn't any wind on the ground there was usually enough wind to keep a kite in the air if you got it higher than the top of the houses around you.

I just about used up a cedar fence post cutting kite sticks off of it. To keep the fence from falling down Dad had to replace the post, well almost. When the weather was fit I always had a kite in the air. Dad made a little wire carrier and a little parachute about a foot in diameter so the wind blowing the parachute would pull the carrier up the kite string and when it arrived at the kite it had a little lever that would bump the kite and release the parachute. As soon as the parachute dropped, the carrier would come back down the kite string. The carrier worked perfectly, but it was a good thing that the Department of Defense never made use of our invention on parachutes as they seldom opened when they came down.

I usually built a kite with two sticks forming a cross. Then I tied a string around the ends of the sticks to form a frame, and then covered the string and sticks with paper, overhanging the string about an inch, and glued the paper together with flour and water paste. Most of the time I tied my kite string to the kite where the sticks crossed. I had to make a little hole in the paper to run my string through. If I tied it to the bare sticks the wind would blow the paper away from my sticks.

When Dad helped me make my kite he tied a string from one end of the cross brace to the other, leaving enough slack to bring the string three or four inches away from the kite. Then he did the same for the vertical stick and used the kite line to tie the two strings together where they crossed. This worked real well. When we launched the kite the height could be regulated by where we tied the strings where they crossed.

Sometimes I wanted the kite to go straight above our heads and other times I wanted the kite to go away from us and not so high. I made several kinds of kites including box kites, but I liked star kites and cross kites best.

I launched my new kite and shortly after I got it aloft Mom called and said, "Harold, I'm going down town as soon as we eat lunch. Bring your kite down and come into the house." I had the string nearly wound up when the kite took a nose dive into the corner of the porch hanging onto a shingle. I couldn't get it loose and I couldn't reach it so I looked around for something to stand on. I located a tub on the opposite side of the porch. It had a little water in it, but I turned it over and dumped the water out. I tried to drag it, but it hung up on some uneven floor boards so I turned it on its side and rolled it along. I had to correct the roll several times because the tub was wider on the top and wouldn't roll straight.

I was almost to the porch corner when I spied Helen's doll lying on the floor right in my path. I yelled, "Helen get your doll out of my way." She didn't answer so I yelled again and this was my last call. I suppose she was over playing with Uncle Sam's million girls and didn't want to leave. The tub was going so good I didn't dare hold it back. I rolled it right over the top of the doll smashing the face and one arm. At the corner I turned the tub on its top, stood on the bottom, and used the rake to rescue my kite.

Half a day later Helen came for her doll. I had never heard so much screaming before in my life. Mom came running out to the porch where Helen showed her the doll and said, "Look, Mom, what Harold did to my best doll."

Mom, with a very alarming voice called, "Harold, I want to talk to you."

I wanted to ignore the call, but I could tell by her voice that I was in trouble. I answered innocently, "What do you want, Mom?"

"Come around to the porch right now."

I went around to where Helen was holding her doll and Mom was holding the arm and head. "Mom, I didn't want to hurt the doll, but it was in my way when I rolled the tub to the corner of the house. I called Helen to come and get her doll before I got to it, but she wouldn't pay any attention."

Mom said, "Come into the house and you can sit on a chair till your Dad gets home. You'll have to explain to him how this happened."

I still don't think it was my fault the doll got run over, but Dad was able to repair it, kinda. He couldn't save the hair, but he made her a new face out of plaster and Mom made a bonnet for the top of her head. She looked like she was ninety years old so the girls renamed her Grandma. I'm not saying what I called her.

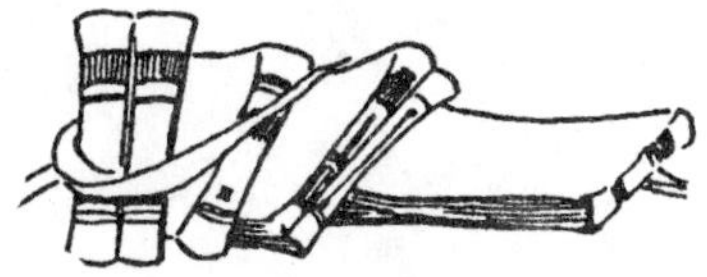

***Harold, Helen, and Mildred on front porch where I smashed Helen's doll.***

On April 29, 1928, Dad took us kids to Mrs. Birdsill's for a couple of days. I didn't object as it was not good kite weather. We didn't understand what the occasion was till we arrived back home. Quietly, Dad ushered us into the bedroom and there was a brand new baby.

"Mom, where did you get the baby?" I asked as I climbed on the bed to get a better look. Imagine my unbelievable joy to find out it was a brother named Dean Russell. I sure did want him to grow up fast so I wouldn't have to play with the girls all the time.

Sometimes, with joy comes sorrow. Soon after Dean was born Mom received a letter from Grandma telling us that Grandpa Fitzgarrald had died. Sadly Mom said, "I would so like to go home, but I can't since I have the baby to care for. I'm thankful I was able to spend most of the winter at home with the folks. It will never be the same."

Us kids felt sorry for Mom because she was so sad.

## REAL PILOTS DON'T CRY

In the evening after a very uneventful day, Uncle Sam, Aunt Eliza and several of their girls came over to our house.

The girls, as usual, gathered together to play. Suddenly a voice rang out from the upstairs bedroom, "Harold, would you like a ride down the stairs in the bathtub?"

You may be picturing in your mind a built-in bathtub, complete with stylish indentations for soap and shampoo. Well, we didn't have those modern conveniences in our house. The tub Mom bathed us in was metal, and oval in shape. A boy of five could fit in it quite nicely.

The girls' plan was like music to my ears. Naturally they decided that I would be the one to make the first trip down. If I arrived at the bottom without any blood showing and was still alive, then the rest might consider the trip, possibly with me as the pilot.

This would take a lot of planning and engineering and I didn't think the girls gave enough thought to the adventure ahead, but I was willing to cooperate.

They carried the tub up the stairs and placed it at the top of the last step. The narrow enclosed stairway went down most of the way where it made a ninety degree turn to the left and then emptied out into the kitchen. Toddy, the nurse, was wearing Dad's white hankie around her head and was placed at the turn with a pillow in case I was unable to negotiate the turn and crashed. She had a bottle of disinfectant and two first aid bandages.

Helen was parked in the kitchen with a pillow in case I overshot my landing and continued out into the kitchen. Mildred and Margie held the airship while I boarded.

"Hey, how am I going to make the curve?" I asked. "Simple," replied Margie, the air traffic controller, "lean to one side and if it doesn't turn the right direction, lean the other way and you'll go around the curve perfectly."

An expectant hush fell over the crowd as I was seated in the ship and, as the adrenaline rushed to my inexperienced brain, I yelled what I deemed to be the perfect words of wisdom, "Let her go!" I headed out into the unknown.

At first the ship seemed to go slowly, then it picked up speed. My heart was beating fast as I approached the curve. Expecting a quick response, I leaned out to one side but the ship didn't respond. I quickly threw myself against the opposite side expecting instant results but the ship was slow to follow my command. As we approached the curve we sideslipped into the wall, removing a nice piece of wallpaper. The drop was a little sudden and almost disastrous, but we completed the curve and shot out into the kitchen, just missing Helen with the pillow, and plowed into a chair that had been strategically placed to stop the ship before it ran into the kitchen cabinet under the sink.

As I stepped out of the ship, I was suddenly confronted with a gang of girls. I thought I would have a welcoming committee, but, no, just a bunch of noisy, laughing girls. They grabbed the ship and disappeared back up the stairs, now knowing that it was a survivable ride. I wanted to shed tears, as my unpadded seat hurt so bad, but, real pilots don't cry. I rubbed my sore spot and climbed back up the stairs.

Something must have taken place while I was climbing up the stairs. They all wanted to take a ride, but now they wanted a command pilot. Mildred and Helen were selected for the next trip and I was asked to be the command pilot, as no one but me had ever flown this trip before. Guidelines were now imposed. First, the command pilot would have to take the blame for any trouble we might encounter and second, if we got into trouble with the management, the command pilot would have to take sole responsibility.

"Harold you get in front," Mildred directed. She sat in back with Helen kinda on her lap and a pillow in front of Helen against my back. Helen's legs came around me with one pointed shoe partially imbedded in my pants pocket. Although we were top heavy and overloaded I was sure we would be able to get her off the runway, but I wasn't sure how it would work when I banked for the sharp turn.

Once again Nurse Toddy was placed at the curve with the first aid supplies. The pillow and chair were again placed in the kitchen to act as a stopping wall. Margie and Beulah were positioned on each side of the ship with Juanita in the back.

As command pilot, I fearlessly yelled, "Let her fly!" They pushed with all their might and, boy, did we take off! Mildred started laughing and Helen screamed right in my ear. We flew down the stairs to the curve where I leaned to the side as I was instructed, but the ship again was slow to respond. Then I must have over controlled. The ship went up the wall and fell back into a spin.

The passengers fell out of the ship, but I continued on out into the kitchen. I sailed past the pillow and into a chair, knocking it over, and continued on to the sink where I stopped with a deafening crash. Mildred had a scratch on her leg and Helen had a bump on her head. Mildred limped to the kitchen and Helen crawled backwards down the stairs from the turn and climbed on a chair, still holding her pillow and crying with joy and excitement.

The welcoming committee arrived immediately after the crash. I lost my job as command pilot. Mom shut down the Airline Flying Service and those who wanted to get a ride would have to look to other airlines.

One day Margie came to our house and wanted Mildred to go to the store with them.

Mom stepped outside for a minute and when she came back in she said, "It's windy out, but there is no sign of any dust clouds today. Mildred can go and take Harold, but I want you girls to be sure he stays with you."

To make certain that the girls would stay together Mildred and four of Uncle Sam's girls buttoned one side of one girl's coat to the other side of another girl's coat till they were all fastened together making a circle. Then they put me inside the circle and headed to the store.

Trouble was not far away! If I walked close as I could to the girls in front they would holler that I was walking on them. If I held back a step the girls in the back would walk on me, or just kick me along. Really, five girls didn't make a very big circle!

We didn't go very far until I said, "I'm going to go back home. I didn't want to go to the lousy store anyway." With this, I crawled under their coats and got out of the mess. This caused a big shakeup in the girls' operation.

"You can't go back by yourself, you have to stay with us. Mom said so." I didn't pay any attention to what they were all saying at once. I started home, but someone caught my coat and held on. I unbuttoned two buttons and let them have the coat. Beulah retrieved my coat and took me back home and then she went on to the store with the girls.

Early one Sunday morning we took our food and went to Olive Lake a couple of miles from Wray to a family reunion with my Dad's side of the family. Some of the families that we knew very little about were the VanSickles, the Wentworths, and the Rawsons, and there was a number of people that us kids didn't even know their names. Uncle Sam's and Uncle Emile's families were there too.

The tables were located at the top of a steep hill. The road was solid sand and those who tried to drive to the tables couldn't make it up the hill. They had to drive their fancy cars several miles around and come in from the back side. Dad stopped at the foot of the hill, turned around, and backed up the hill. I was sure proud that our Model T pickup made it up the hill even if we did have to go up backwards.

After the meal us kids dug around in the sand looking for Indian arrows. Every one of us found at least one arrow head. We were less that twelve miles from Beecher Island in the Arickaree River. This is where a famous battle between Indians and a group of civilian scouts took place September 17 and 18, 1868.

One day Dad came home early from Boggs' lumberyard. Dad and Mom talked together quietly for awhile, then they told us that our grandmother Artheretta Abbott Rutherford, Dad's mother, had died in her sleep. (The name Abbott is our connection to the Scottish Clan Macnab. Rutherford is a Scottish name also.) Grandma had lived in Wray with Aunt LuRosa and Uncle Emile. As we had no phone, Aunt LuRosa had called Boggs' lumberyard to give Dad the sad news.

As the rest of us prepared to make the trip Mom arranged for Mrs. Birdsill to keep Dean and Helen. Ed Weeks, a Realtor and friend, drove us to the funeral at Wray in his brand new Model A Ford. I was sure excited when I got to ride in the front seat of that brand new car with Dad and Mr. Weeks.

"I notice you drive about forty miles an hour," Dad said.

"For sure," Ed replied, "the car can go sixty or a little more, but I don't think we should drive over forty on a gravel road."

Grandma was buried in Eckley.

***Before the cyclone hit.***

## DUST STORMS AND CYCLONES

Saturday was a shopping day in Eckley for the town people and farmers. It seemed to me that the shopping day was mostly visiting. One sultry Saturday afternoon Mom took us kids downtown where we met Ellen Gilbert, one of Uncle Sam's older girls, and her family of three girls at that time. They lived on a farm southwest of Eckley and came to town every other Saturday for groceries. We usually traded at Sewell's Grocery Store, but they traded at Catchpole's Grocery so we met them there.

Anxiously we watched as the sky grew dark and one of those eastern Colorado storms came up. In hushed whispers, so as not to frighten the children, the feared word spread through the crowded store: CYCLONE! The storm was coming from the west and some of the farmers who had their horses and wagons in town drove to the east sides of the buildings in hopes that their horses would not get hurt by debris flying around in the driving wind. They gathered all the tarps and blankets they could find to cover the backs of horses.

The store had the usual Saturday crowd until the storm hit; then everybody out on the streets headed for the nearest shelter. As the cyclone approached it started to rain and hail. Some of the hail stones were as large as baseballs. One man tried to run across the street when a big hailstone hit him on the head, knocking him out. Two men who were standing in the front of J. Pounds Hardware store ran out and carried him into the store. He was bleeding badly. When the hail abated they took him up the street to the doctor, where his wound was sewn up.

A lady got her team of horses in under a roof overhang on the east side of the hardware store and stayed with them all through the hail storm. She had hoped the overhang would give enough protection for her and the horses, but it was only enough to protect the horses' heads. Her hands and arms were bleeding where the hail hit her as she held the horses.

The twister descended with a deafening roar of wind, hail, thunder, and violent flashes of lightning as it passed through town. One crash of thunder was followed by another crash. The thunder exploded almost before the lightning flashed. The wind was terrible. Everything loose blew around and the sky was filled with all kinds of trash. Cars were overturned, windows broken, and many outhouses were moved or destroyed. The ground was covered with hail. It looked like winter. Adding to the din of the wild storm were the frightened cries of children and the stomping and neighing of the terrified horses.

As the lightning and thunder abated, signaling the passing of the cyclone, the people stepped out into the falling rain to take up where they had left off before the storm hit. Two houses were torn to pieces, with one house missing the entire roof. The storm missed our cousins' farm, but all the farmers around the north, west, and east of Eckley lost their entire crops. The corn was just starting to tassel when the hail completely destroyed it.

As we went to town we had walked by a cornfield with the corn towering above my head, but when we went back home it was lying flat on the ground and only showed in places where the hail hadn't covered it.

The west windows in our house were broken. Dad put burlap sacks over two windows and boards over another window till glass was available. All of our windows were covered with hail screen, but when there were large pieces of hail with a driving wind the hail broke through the screen. There were very few trees in town, but what trees we had were stripped of their leaves and small branches.

In the 1930's, the dust storms were very bad. The winds started in the very early spring and blew all spring and summer. A lot of the time the wind blew so hard it was hard to walk. A windstorm would come up and blow for several days and then stop for a few days and then it would come again. There was no rain or snow but the sand drifted around just like snow. Black clouds of dust formed just like a snow storm. Sometimes the dust got so thick it was very dark during the day and at times the visibility was near zero. Once in awhile the storms would bring orange dust from Oklahoma while the dirt from Texas was gray. One of the reasons the dirt and dust storms were so bad was because farmers had plowed up land all over the country to increase their production. When the drought came, the crops died and the exposed soil started to blow away.

Oftentimes the lights in the school would go out because the wind blew the light wires together or down. Then it was too dark to study so our teacher, Margaret Earnest, would take a heavy rope and lay it on the floor in a big circle, tying the ends together. Then all the kids in her class would get inside the circle and hold on to the rope with both hands. She then led us out into the wind and dust, walking from one kid's house to the next, till all the kids were home. Sometimes she used her car to take some of us home that lived farther away, but other times it was so dark and dusty that she couldn't see to drive. Sometimes a couple of men in town assisted with this chore.

Farmers were unable to raise crops because they were hailed out or dried out. The dirt and dust storms were so bad farmers were having trouble finding enough pasture for their cattle. Some farmers sold their cattle at a loss. Many cattle died from breathing so much dust. Tumbleweeds would pile up along the sides of fences causing the sand to drift over the top of the fences. Back roads were blocked in some places. The road grader would have to be called time and time again to plow the sand off the roads.

Mom would take flour sacks, dampen them, and use clothes pins to fasten them around the sides of the windows to keep some of the dust out. When we ate, Mom would have to wipe dirt out of the dishes before food was put in them. When dishes were set on the table with food in them Mom covered the dish with another dish to keep the dust in the air from settling on the food. Sometimes Mom would take wet rags torn into triangles and tie them around our faces to keep us from breathing so much dust on our way to school.

During the summer many changes took place in our extended family because of the worsening economy.

Uncle Sam drove the county road grader which was headquartered in Yuma. To save on travel time and expenses he loaded up his family and moved to Yuma. Sadly, shortly after they moved, Aunt Eliza died. Although we were no longer close neighbors, Uncle Sam would stop by to see us whenever he came to Eckley to plow sand off the roads. These trips, by this time, were becoming quite frequent.

Work was getting very hard to find because the farmers didn't have the money to pay for it. Dad had a number of jobs where he did the work with the understanding that the money would be paid by a bank loan when the next crop was harvested. The bank went broke and many farmers were unable to buy more seed to plant again. Consequently, some farmers were unable to pay for work Dad had already done.

We moved from our two-story house to a small three-room house on the north side of town, probably for cheaper rent.

Uncle Emile, Dad's brother-in-law, fired the boilers that generated the electricity for Wray. He and Aunt LuRosa decided to move to Boulder hoping to find a similar job at the University of Colorado and prepare for my cousin Ruth's college years. He drove a truck till he was able to get a job at the university. His truck-driving job brought him through Eckley quite often and he would stop at our house for lunch or dinner and a short visit.

Things were getting very serious and with a family to feed Dad did any kind of work that could be found.

Dad had a friend named Frank Boggs who owned the Eckley Lumber Yard and whenever his customers needed help Frank called Dad to do the work. Sometimes Dad would take Mildred and me to the lumberyard when he wanted to talk to Mr. Boggs. There was a great big clock hanging on the wall in the office. The pendulum swung a good six feet from side to side. The ticking echoed in the large room with high ceilings giving you a lonely feeling. It swung so slow I wondered if it was going to stop, but it never did.

Mr. Boggs bought part of his lumber in large unplaned pieces called rough lumber. The lumber was cut into the needed sizes and planed as it was sold. The saws and planers were run by gasoline engines. It was hard for one person to cut and plane lumber without help, but many times Dad worked by himself to save on labor. Boggs got a job furnishing some lumber to build several large chicken houses. Dad cut up the lumber order and was to build the houses.

While Dad was running the saw the sawblade became pinched so tightly in the green wood that it almost stopped the saw. Dad moved behind the board to push harder to get it to go on through. Suddenly the saw kicked the board back out of Dad's hands, hitting him in the side, laying it completely open. Two men who saw the accident rushed Dad to the doctor. It took a number of stitches to close the wound and Dad couldn't work till it was healed up. The wound required more surgery than was possible in that small town, so Dad had to wear a binding or corset around his waist the rest of his life.

It was a dark dreary day. Dad, doing light duty work, had a short time job in Eckley. I was working on one of my eternal projects, this time making a new kite. Right after lunch dark clouds covered the sky. Looking up I saw white churning clouds moving very rapidly. The wind came up and I thought we were going to have another windy afternoon.

I yelled, "Mom, come out here and look at the clouds."

Mom came outside and looked up. She said, "I hope there isn't going to be another cyclone this afternoon," and went back into the house.

Following her into the house I said, "Mom, I need some flour and water paste. I've got my kite ready to put the paper on."

Mom made me enough paste to glue the paper to the kite. After I glued the paper on my kite I went back outside to check on the wind. I looked again at the sky and decided I'd better leave the kite inside.

Suddenly it got real quiet, there wasn't a breath of air moving. I took my cap off and when I pushed my hair back, my hair clung to my hand from static electricity. Mildred followed me out and I held my hand over her head and her hair rose up to my hand. When I moved my hand away her hair fell back down. I told her, "It feels like the end of the world is coming." It was getting dark in the middle of the afternoon!

Dad came roaring up in his pickup and shouted, "You kids run into the house, it looks like we're going to have a cyclone, I'll be right behind you."

I ran into the house and yelled, "Mom, Dad said there is a cyclone coming." Mom rushed to the window and looked out.

Dad said, "I saw a funnel cloud as I came in the gate," as he and Mom stared out of the window.

"Look," Mom said, "there's the funnel cloud, but it seems to form and then vanish." They stood at the window and watched. You could see it coming down out of the sky and then going back up. It got closer and larger. Suddenly a high wind hit the house. The windows buzzed and rattled. We could see boards, straw, and all kinds of debris flying in the sky. When the end of the funnel struck the ground, dirt would fly up into the sky. It was moving rapidly towards us! There was a big crash of thunder and immediately there was another murderous crash! Lightning snapped and flashed and the thunder crashed again! The lightning kept up a steady shimmering and flashing. It started to rain and hail and the wind became hurricane strength. Besides a terrifying roar, we could hear objects hitting the house. Sometimes the house would shake. Helen and Dean started to cry. Mom picked them up and held them on her lap.

Dad shouted above the roar, "Minnie, we are right in the path of the cyclone, put coats on the kids and grab a couple of candles for light and get ready to go to the storm cellar." We put our coats on and stood waiting at the back door. The storm was coming from the west and the rain, mixed with hail, pounded the west side of the house. On the east side there was hardly any rain falling next to the house, but just a few feet away it was pouring down rain and hailing hard. Dad ran to the storm cellar which was not over thirty five feet from the house and raised the door. He dashed back to the house, grabbing Helen and me by our hands and we ran to the cellar. My shoulders were wet from the rain.

Dad said, "Stay here and I'll be right back." Returning to the house he grabbed Mildred by the hand and ran to the cellar with Mom following, carrying Dean. Dad didn't close the cellar door because he was afraid we might become trapped inside if the chicken house blew down on the door. The wind grew in intensity. We could hear a lot of banging and thumping followed by loud crashing outside. Dad, with Mildred at his heels, went up the steps to where they could see.

Dad yelled, "The chicken house just exploded." Our clothes line was fastened to the house and ran to the chicken house. It seemed to hold onto the chicken house like a kite in the air when all of a sudden it broke loose and pieces flew everywhere. The roof landed not far from the house, upside down, but the rest of the building was scattered several blocks away out into the pasture. The chickens were very lucky as we didn't have any at that time. The roar from the hail and wind was so loud I could hardly hear what Dad said.

We heard another crash and Dad said, "Our outhouse just hit the ground in front of the cellar, in pieces." The thunder was terrifying and one crash would sound followed by another explosion before the first crash had stopped echoing. Lightning kept up one flash after another. Sometimes you could hear a snapping sound in the house when the lightning flashed. My legs didn't want to hold me up. I wasn't cold, but I kept shivering and goose pimples covered my arms. The sky was filled with pieces of wood torn from buildings. It was dangerous for anyone to be outside. A river of water started running right in front of the cellar door. With the chicken house gone Dad reached up to close the door when it just flew away.

Dad said, "Minnie, if the rain doesn't stop shortly, we will have to go back to the house. When the water starts to come into the cellar it won't take but a few minutes till the cellar will be filled." We stood at the bottom step waiting to go back to the house. Dad stood about halfway up the steps watching the storm.

Little by little the rain and hail diminished and the lightning and thunder moved on east of us. The wind died down and the hail all but stopped, but it was still raining hard. There were drifts of hail as high as the top wire of the fence where junk and bushes blew against the fence.

Dad went outside and then came back into the cellar and said, "The cyclone has moved on, we can go back into the house." Dad carried us kids to the house one at a time. Then he helped Mom wade through the water.

Dad had to build us a new outhouse. The two west windows of the house were cracked so he again covered one window with boards and one with gunny sacks till glass was available.

Many people, including us, existed mostly on beans and bread.

One time Dad came into the house and said, "Minnie there is a truck in town selling corned beef for twenty cents a pound and cabbage three heads for a dime. He just arrived from Denver. Do we have enough money to buy some of each?"

Mom went to the cupboard where she picked up a glass toothpick holder and dumped the contents out on the table. Dad counted the coins several times and then he said, "Maybe we can borrow some pennies from the kids and get us some meat, there isn't enough money to buy over one meal here."

I got my money and Mildred got her money and gave it to Dad.

Dad said, "I sure hate to use you kids' money, but I'll give it back to you before long." Mom took Dean and went uptown with Dad. When they came back they brought each of us kids a stick of peppermint candy.

During the winter we burned cow chips in our heating stove for warmth. Dad, Mildred, and I went out into the prairie where the Whittenburgs pastured their milk cows. Dad took two gunny sacks and tied one corner of each sack together and filled them with cow chips. Mildred and I each took a sack and only partially filled ours. Some times our search for chips took us over a mile from the house. When the sacks were full we carried them to the house. We carried a piece of sage brush to turn the cow chips over before we touched them because a rattle snake could be curled up by a cow chip. When it was cold they would curl up against a fresh cow chip while it was still warm.

Sometimes Dad was able to bring home some scraps from Boggs' lumberyard and once in a long time he brought home a pickup load of corn cobs when he worked for a farmer. Our kitchen stove used kerosene which was not hard to get.

The last winter we were in Eckley Mildred and I took our gunny sacks and went to the pasture for cow chips since Dad was in the mountains. We took it upon ourselves to try and keep enough chips for heat during the winter, but Mom had to buy a little coal to help carry the warmth through the winter nights.

During the drought, jack rabbits were forced to expand from their areas and spread out into the pasture lands. When money was tight, men would hunt coyotes because the pelts would bring a good price. In time, nearly all of the coyotes were killed off allowing jack rabbits to multiply like wildfire. They ate up pasture and small crops causing a big loss for farmers. Something had to be done to control the rabbits.

Organized drives were set up in many areas. They drove the rabbits into large fenced enclosures where they were slaughtered. Sometimes there would be several hundred people on a Sunday afternoon drive. They would get over a thousand rabbits in one afternoon. The rabbits were shipped to Denver where the furs were sold and the meat was ground up to make chicken feed and fertilizer.

# PART II
# LIFE IN TRANSITION

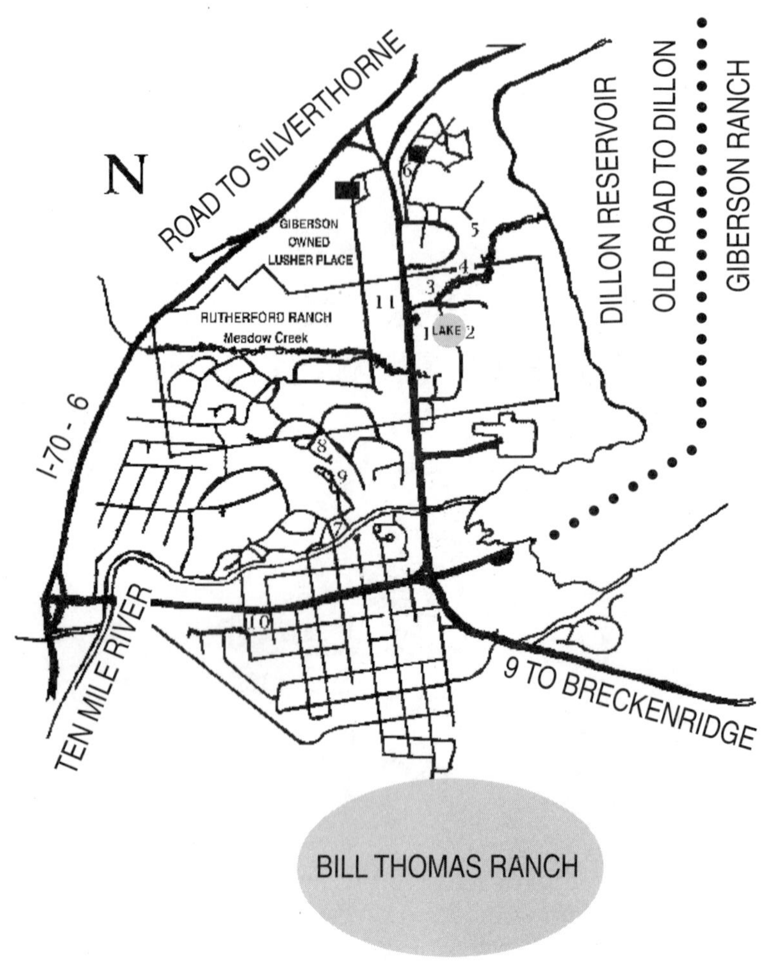


1. - A & W Rootbeer
2. - Rutherford Ranch
3. - Big Spring Hatchery
4. - Little Spring
5. - Lusher Place (House and Barns)
6. - Holiday Hotel
7. - Walter Byron Park
8. - Pond in the Woods
9. - Frisco Beaver Ponds
10. - Frisco School and Historical Park
11. - Walmart Store

## DAD GOES TO WORK IN SUMMIT COUNTY

In the early spring of 1932 Frank Boggs came to Dad with a job offer. He said, "Sometime back I received a letter in the mail from a Mr. Bill Thomas giving away a free lot on a mountain ranch close to Frisco, Colorado, if I would build a cabin and occupy it part of the time. I went to Bill's Ranch and talked to Bill and we looked over the different spots of land. I chose one site that was nearly covered with trees. I also bought a rundown cabin close to my lot. I want to remodel the cabin to live in while I am building my cabin. I need to hire someone to remodel the cabin and there will be two or possibly three months of work. Next year I want to build a new cabin on the lot and sell the old cabin. Do you want to take the job?" he asked.

Without a moment's hesitation, Dad said, "I will gladly take the job and I can be ready to go as soon as I make arrangements for my family to get by while I'm gone."

Excitement tinged with sadness surrounded the preparations for Dad's departure.

In a few days Frank Boggs picked Dad up at home. They loaded Dad's tools and a box of his clothes in Frank's pickup. Dad kissed us all goodbye and they left for the mountains.

The parting was hard, but there was joy in the fact that Dad would have a paying job. Dad was to make fifty cents an hour, big money!

Living on the prairie, I couldn't picture what a mountain was like, but I tried to build one in our back yard. I took a fire shovel and our little red wagon and went to the front yard, which was nothing but sand, where I filled the wagon with as much sand as I could pull and took it to the back yard to make a mountain. Every day I would do a little work on the mountain.

One day Mom looked at my mountain and said, "Harold, the mountains where your Dad is working are higher than our house and they drive cars on top of them." This didn't discourage me and I kept on adding to my mountain. I finally got it so high that I had to throw the sand on top with a regular shovel. It wasn't till after we received a picture of Buffalo Mountain Dad mailed us that I realized I couldn't build a mountain.

## WE VISIT GRANDMA AND UNCLE LYNN

The coming of spring found us preparing for another trip. Mom said, "When school is out we'd better plan on visiting Grandma in Beaver City, because it will be a lot harder after we move to the mountains." Grandma Fitzgarrald and Uncle Lynn had left the farm and moved to Beaver City, Nebraska.

We were an excited bunch as we rode the train to Oxford, Nebraska, where Uncle Lynn picked us up.

It was real hot in Beaver City, but there were no dust and dirt storms. The trees in Grandma's back yard were filled with strange birds. Some of the birds were jays, catbirds, woodpeckers, cardinals, cedar waxwings, and some birds whose names I never learned. Sometimes I would get up early in the morning just to see them and hear their strange songs.

On Saturday evenings we went to a park in the center of town where there were swings and teeter-totters. There was a large wooden floor for concerts and shows with chairs and wooden benches for people to sit on. We played on the swings till the local brass band started their weekly concert. We were so proud when Uncle Lynn played his trombone with the band.

Grandma had an RCA record player with a picture of a dog inside the lid looking into the end of a horn, which was the speaker. Grandma had a record of Harry Lauder singing Scottish songs with his Scottish accent, also a record of a German singer called Madam Schuman Heink who sang so beautifully. We played the records so much we just about wore them out. Since we had a Scottish background I suspect that was part of the reason we played the record with Harry Lauder so much.

Barns always had a special fascination for me and imagine my delight when I discovered one next door. Carefully opening the door I peered in. There were no animals, but there was some hay in part of the loft and a bunch of boxes piled up in another corner. Looking around I saw a guitar and some other kind of instrument that I had never seen before.

When I finished checking it out, I returned home and inquired about the instruments in the loft. "Boy, I sure would like to have them, do you think they would sell them to us?" I asked.

Uncle Lynn said, "I don't know whether they would sell them or not. They'll be gone for a while and I have no idea when they will return."

When we went to Grandma's church the next Sunday I told my Sunday School teacher about the instruments and she asked, "Did you ask Jesus if you could have them?" I thought to myself

I hadn't asked Jesus about the instruments, so as soon as we got home from church I ran over to the barn where no one could hear me and asked Jesus to let me have the instruments.

"I wouldn't have to have the big one, just the little one with the round back."

One evening Uncle Lynn went over to the barn with me and looked them over. "One is a guitar and the other is a mandolin," he declared. I was so excited when Uncle Lynn told Mom that he would talk to the neighbors as soon as they came home.

He said, "If they aren't keepsakes and if they don't want too much for them, I will buy them for the kids, but they will have to be repaired and probably need new strings."

In late August Uncle Lynn took us to the train in Oxford, Nebraska.

Back in Eckley we could do nothing but cry when we looked at the barren ground and millions of three cornered stickers growing around our back door. We couldn't even go outside without our shoes on. The sand had drifted around our water pump and filled a tub that we kept at the pump. We had some flowers growing there when we left, but now they were buried in at least two feet of sand. We were gone just a few weeks but the sand had sifted in the back door and we had to use a shovel to get most of the sand out before we used the broom. Hot winds were blowing every afternoon, but the dust had stopped for the time.

Despairingly Mom said, "I don't think I can live another year through these hot winds." I immediately ran around behind the house and asked Jesus to stop the hot winds so Mom wouldn't die. I was really afraid!

Fall came and school started again for Mildred and me. Helen was not old enough to go to school and Dean was only four years old. Mom had been a school teacher before she and Dad were married, so she taught Helen her first grade at home, the same as she had for Mildred and me.

One weekend Mom's cousin and her two girls, Jean and Shirley, stopped in on their way back to Denver from a trip. While they were there Aunt Amelia took a bunch of coins out of her purse and had each of us kids take three coins out of her hand and then she gave each of us additional coins. The totals added up to the same amount for each kid.

I told Helen that I would let her have my turns riding around the outside of the house in our little red wagon, for her quarter and

I would give her a dime and two pennies back. She agreed to this. I then gave her three more pennies for one nickel. This gave her more coins. I gave Mildred a nickel for five pennies. Then I gave Dean three pennies for his nickel and then I gave him one dime and four pennies for his quarter. I was in the process of loaning the use of my windup train for the next week to Dean for four more coins when Mildred and Jean decided I was taking advantage of Helen and Dean and told Mom. Mom confiscated my money and gave it back to Helen and Dean.

She said, "You can pull Helen around the house five extra times a day for the next several days." The time was to be determined by her. Dean got the privilege of running my train for the next two days. Mom kept my money till after our company left.

## MAJOR FOOTBALL INJURY

In the fall of 1932, school was going great guns for us kids with a little learning thrown in. I joined a group to play football during activity periods. One of our teachers acted as coach, although we had never heard the word at that time. Our football field was vacant land on the east side of the school which was, naturally, inhabited by a colony of prairie dogs and an occasional rattle snake.

In a game early in the school year, I received the ball and dodged one lone guard, giving myself an open field to the goal line. Hoping to make it to the Dustbowl (since we had no Orange Bowl), I ran as fast as I could, ending my football career when I stepped into a prairie dog hole!

When I stood up an unbelievable pain hit my ankle and I saw that it was rapidly swelling. The pain was so intense that afternoon in class that I couldn't concentrate on my school work.

After school I limped home and Mom put my foot in a bucket of hot water.

The next morning a neighbor, Charlie Fostabend, took his daughter, Evelyn, Mildred, and me to school. My ankle didn't seem to hurt too much if I didn't put my weight on it, but by the time school ended for the day I could hardly step on it. We lived nine blocks from school, four blocks of sidewalk and the rest on sandy ground. I had walked about three blocks when my ankle got to hurting so bad I sat down and rested for awhile. When I tried to continue I found I couldn't put my weight on my foot. There was no way out of it, I had to get home, so I crawled on my hands and knees the rest of the way home in mostly sand, but there were lots of stickers and sand burrs in it. When I finally reached home I don't know which hurt the most, my ankle or my hands and knees filled with stickers.

I didn't go back to school for several weeks. I soaked my foot in a bucket of hot water for an hour twice a day, but it didn't seem to be getting any better. The doctor in Eckley didn't have an x-ray machine so Mom asked Frank Boggs to take us to the doctor in Wray, where the doctor told us I had torn the ligaments in my ankle. The doctor applied a heavy bandage and I was not to put any weight on it till I came back in a couple weeks.

When I was able to return to school I couldn't go out to play for a month to allow for the healing time. Needless to say the prairie dog field was off limits and the road to the Dustbowl was forever buried.

## MARBLES

It all started when two boys came into the school room arguing over a marble that was made out of black agate. It had belonged to one kid and the other kid had grabbed it and dropped it into a hole in a concrete foundation. (The wind had carried the building off several years earlier leaving the exposed foundation next to the school gym.) The hole was about one and a half inches in diameter and down into the concrete about sixteen or eighteen inches. Two or three older kids had tried to get the marble out, but nothing seemed to work.

An enterprising teacher, Elmer Burkhardt, made a spoon out of wire, but when he would get the marble part way up out of the hole it would fall back down. He finally gave up and then the school janitor, Mack Cain, also tried but soon gave up. While Mack Cain and Mr. Burkhardt were discussing the problem I grabbed a quick look, using Mr. Burkhardt's mirror to reflect the sunlight down into the hole. Then I said to Mr. Burkhardt, "I think I can get it out."

"You kids don't touch it," he said. "I doubt that we will ever be able to get it out." By this time there were a lot of kids watching.

When school took up I said, "Miss Earnest, I know how to get the marble out of the hole, but Mr. Burkhardt wouldn't let me try."

She said, "Harold, come up to my desk and tell me how you plan to remove the marble."

I ran up to her desk and said, "Pour a little sand in the hole and take a stick and move the sand around till the marble comes out on top of the sand, then pour a little more sand into the hole and do it again and continue doing it till the marble is at the top of the hole."

She excused me from class so that I could go and try to remove the marble. In a few minutes I had the marble out of the hole and gave it to my teacher. She gave me a quarter and showed the marble to all the class and told them how I got the marble out. I was sure proud, not to mention rich!

I bought clay marbles, five for a penny, and covered them with red-orange Indian Paint. Mildred and I would go to the railroad track where we found some colored rock, or possibly it was partially burned coal. I'm not sure what it was, but it was called Indian Paint. It didn't stay on the marbles very long, but they sure did look good for a while. I tried using crayons on the marbles but it didn't stay as long as the Indian Paint did. When I got the "commies" colored I sold some of them three for a penny. I made enough money that I could buy glass marbles for a penny apiece.

Playing marbles and flying kites were two of the sports that I did a lot of since football was ended for me.

There was a marble contest at school that ran from noon till afternoon recess. I entered with about thirty other kids separated into groups near the same age. There were ten kids in my group and when recess period was over everyone was eliminated but Dale and me. First prize was a silver dollar and second prize was a box of chocolate candy.

It was my turn to play when Miss Earnest appeared and said, "Harold, the bell has rung, come on in, I don't want to mark you tardy."

I had never been tardy and I didn't want to be tardy now, but then in a minute or two, I might win the game. We had a big circle, around ten feet in diameter marked on the ground with a little circle in the center where each contestant put in one marble. I could try to shoot the marbles out of the little circle or I could shoot at my opponent and if I hit him I would win the game. We could move our marble around the big circle to any place we wanted as long as the distance was the same from the outside ring, but no one wanted to move into a position that would leave his marble close to the opponent after he shot. With the teacher's pressure, I didn't take time to move around to the opposite side where I would be only a few inches from Dale's marble when I shot at it. If I missed him my marble would be nearly across the circle from him. That shot would have been easy but, not having time to move around, I shot across the big circle narrowly missing

Dale and stopped about three inches from him. Dale shot and hit my marble, ending the game. Dale received first prize plus the marbles that were left in the little ring in the center. I got second prize. I rushed back into my class and Miss Earnest kept the box of candy on her desk till after school.

## AN ANSWER TO PRAYER

Fall was progressing nicely, my ankle was almost completely healed and the candy from the contest was long gone. It was a crisp afternoon when a freight truck stopped in front of our house. This was an unusual occurrence in our small town so we anxiously awaited the freight man at the door. He came up with a large package in his arms. "Who sent us a package and what could it be?" we wondered. I caught my breath when I spied the name of the sender: Lynn Fitzgarrald! Eagerly we tore the box open and there they were, the guitar and mandolin!

Although they both needed some repairs it was like a hundred Christmas Days in one moment.

We had Charley Hess, a carpenter who worked part time for Dad, repair the mandolin. I took lessons at school and soon played in the beginners' orchestra till we moved to the mountains. At the same time, Mom was teaching Mildred how to play the pump organ Mom had bought when she was sixteen.

Charlie did some work on the guitar, but it needed more expertise than Charlie could give so he didn't try to repair it. When Helen was a little older the folks had new strings put on the guitar for Helen to use. It was hard to finger and Helen was soon the proud recipient of another guitar.

## DAD WORKS ON BOGGS' CABINS

While all of this excitement was occurring on the prairie, Dad arrived in Frisco and went right to work making repairs on the cabin for Frank Boggs.

By midsummer the cabin was remodeled and Dad found work at Dan Mogee's ranch near Dickey, which was between Dillon and Breckenridge. Dan Mogee was of Scottish heritage the same as Dad. I suspect that is why they got along so well. Dickey was a railroad junction where trains from Breckenridge could be switched to head either to Dillon or to Frisco. This is near where the water from Iron Springs empties into the Blue River.

When Dad finished the carpenter work at Dan Mogee's ranch, he worked a short time for various ranchers around the area.

While Dad and Frank Boggs were in the mountains working on the cabin, Frank, Bill and Dad made permanent marks for Frank's land by marking a tree, going from the tree to a big rock, to a steel stake they drove in the ground, to another tree, and back to the tree where they started. This was called a meets and bounds description of the plot of land.

In the fall Dad came back to Eckley for the winter months.

***Frank Boggs' new cabin, 1933***

When spring of 1933 arrived, Dad and Frank Boggs returned to Bill's Ranch to build the new cabin. The cabin took shape and by midsummer the cabin was completed. Dad did carpenter work at a couple of places in Dillon and when haying season started he went to work at Dan Mogee's ranch cooking for hired hands till haying season was finished and then he again returned to Eckley with Frank Boggs.

An Eckley school professor, Mr. Sullivan, bought Frank Boggs' old cabin. The Neinnemans, Niemoths, McKees, DeSellens, and Rev. Dexheimer, vacationers from Denver, were neighbors of Frank Boggs. They all had taken Bill up on his offer of free ground.

□□□

Dad again returned home from Frisco and brought ore samples and rocks from the mines. Seeing the pretty rocks and ore samples sure made us all want to move to the mountains as soon as possible. Dad had several rocks of iron pyrite which looked like gold, lead cubes, blue green rocks which were copper, silver, and a number of other kinds of rocks that all came from mines in Summit County.

Dad said, "It's the most beautiful spot in the world. We'll move up there as soon as I can get enough money to make the move."

## BILL THOMAS

Bill Thomas was born in 1882 and had a brother Walter and a sister Nellie. His parents had come from Wales. Bill was a small boy when his folks purchased a hotel in Frisco. Bill, Walter, and Nellie went to school in Frisco while their parents, John and Jane, ran the hotel. When the mines shut down, the Thomas family sold the hotel to Mrs. Evelyn Mix. She had the hotel torn down and rebuilt on Bill's Ranch naming it Ophir Lodge for the mountain southeast of the lodge.

Bill was married to Minnie Thomas for many years, but she had moved to Breckenridge before we ever met Bill.

Bill's brother Walter had died before we met Bill. He had suffered lung damage caused by gas in World War I.

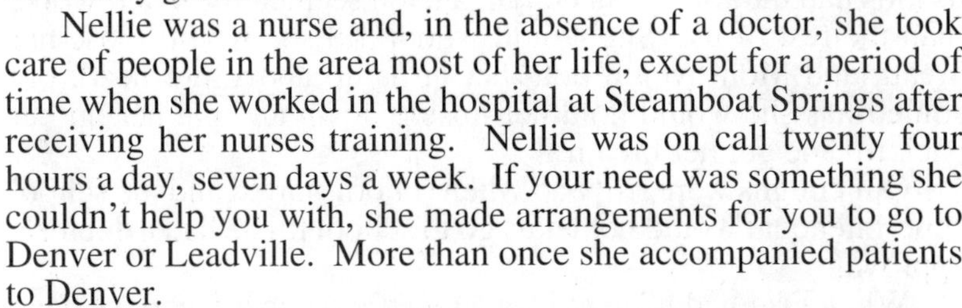

Nellie was a nurse and, in the absence of a doctor, she took care of people in the area most of her life, except for a period of time when she worked in the hospital at Steamboat Springs after receiving her nurses training. Nellie was on call twenty four hours a day, seven days a week. If your need was something she couldn't help you with, she made arrangements for you to go to Denver or Leadville. More than once she accompanied patients to Denver.

Once when she was accompanying a patient to Denver they were involved in an auto accident on Loveland Pass. Nellie suffered a broken leg and severe knee injury. People had to do without her for quite some time which was a big frustration for them as well as for Nellie.

Their mother, Jane, was a very small lady. She probably didn't stand much over four and a half feet high with cowboy boots on. She also had committed her life to helping people, from delivering babies to cutting wood. When we met her she lived with Bill and Nellie on the ranch.

Before Walter died he had given Bill his car. Bill didn't want to drive the car, but since he had it he decided to try it out. Shortly after he received the car he drove to Frisco to get his mail. (In those days, not over five or six cars went through Frisco on any given day.) After the mail arrived he backed out into the main street and was hit by a car coming up the road. No one was hurt, but Bill would never drive again.

Bill was one of a kind. He could remember and tell stories better than anyone I ever knew. Whenever you were talking to Bill he soon would be reminded of a story.

## DAD GETS TICK FEVER

In the spring of 1934, Dad went back to Frisco with plans to move the family as soon as school was out. However problems came up with unexpected consequences.

Dad had been hired to do some work on the Buffalo ditch headgate and the flume on Chief Mountain. It was there that he was bitten by a poisonous tick. Tick fever (Rocky Mountain spotted fever) brings on a high fever and besides the fever Dad developed a bad infection on his back where the tick had bitten him. Dad stayed at Ophir Lodge during his high fever time where Nellie Thomas nursed him back to health. He had his own very small room. When he was over the fever he moved to Dan Mogee's ranch, but was very weak and unable to work all day.

Meanwhile, back on the prairie, all was not well. All four of us kids had the whooping cough. Helen seemed to have it worse than the rest of us. She would whoop till she would loose her breath and Mom would hold her arms up above her head, but sometimes she would hold her upside down and pat her on her back till she got her breath.

Our coughs were still bad when school started and the school superintendent would not let us go to school till he had a doctor's approval.

When Dad had been at Dan Mogee's ranch a few days, Dan said, "Russell, since you are trying to find something to do while recovering, maybe you would feel like panning for gold. You can use my pan and there's plenty of lumber around here to build a sluice box. I have a mine claim in Iron Springs Drainage at the north end of my big meadow. I think there is a lot of gold there and you are more than welcome to work the claim."

Dad immediately came to life and said, "That's a good idea and if I don't feel like coming back to the house to rest, I could stay in that old cabin at the end of your meadow." Dan used the cabin for hay hands to stay in during haying season. With all the details worked out Dad built a sluice box twelve feet long and Dan helped him set it in a good spot at the foot of the hill below Iron Springs Pass. This was perfect for Dad.

Dad dammed up the spring water forming a small lake. When the lake was full of water he would open the dam and the water would rush down the mountain through the sluice box he had made. While the water was running down the hillside, Dad straddled the stream and used a small pick to stir up the sand and rock in the fast flowing water. The water would carry small rocks, sand and mineral deposits through the sluice box, dropping the fine sand and minerals in the bottom of the sluice box and, after the water passed, Dad would remove all the wood cleats in the box. He would then have several days of panning the sand for gold that had collected in the box. He placed quicksilver (mercury) in the gold pan and the gold would stick to the mercury. He managed to get a couple ounces of gold and took it to a refinery at Malta, close to Leadville, where he was given cash for the gold.

At that time gold was worth $32.00 per ounce. Dad also saved many little rubies, about the size of a match head and smaller, that he had found in the sand in the sluice box.

In the late summer, Dad was feeling much stronger and caught a ride to Denver and then another ride to Eckley with Mr. Catchpole, who owned a grocery store in Eckley.

## THE SILVER STREAK ZEPHYR

During the whooping cough summer a new streamline train called the Zephyr was to go through Eckley on the Burlington line at a high rate of speed at six o'clock in the morning. When the great day arrived, over four hundred people gathered at the Eckley Depot to see the train go by.

We couldn't join the crowd because of our whooping cough, but since we only lived four blocks from the railroad track we were all at the windows watching. Around two thirty in the afternoon the whistle could be heard as the train approached town! Excitement gripped the few remaining diehards as the Zephyr drew near. Would it only be a blur as it flew by? Would the details of that marvelous train be forever etched in our memories?

Could it be? No, not as the prestigious silver streak passing through town at a high rate of speed, but an ordinary old steam engine puffing black coal smoke going along at a very slow speed pulling the Zephyr. What a letdown!

The Zephyr had broken down about halfway between Yuma and Eckley and a steam engine was sent from Yuma to pull it to Chicago.

## DAD WALKS TO FRISCO

When Frank Boggs was ready to return to Eckley from Frisco, he decided he would help Dad, not realizing that Dad had intended to leave his tools in Frisco. He went to Dan Mogee's and loaded up Dad's tools and brought them to Eckley when he came. Meanwhile, back in Eckley, Dad soon found there was no work available. The hot days were hard on him in his weakened condition and after a lot of thought Dad and Mom decided he should leave immediately for Frisco where work was waiting. Since money was in short supply, Dad decided to walk and hopefully catch rides most of the way.

Dad made arrangements with Rowland Hanson, a trucker, to move our belongings to Frisco as soon as school was out the following spring. The plan was for us to ride to Denver with my school teacher, Margaret Earnest. We would then meet Rowland in Denver and ride on with him to Frisco. Rowland would be paid $15.00 plus gas, oil, food and lodging for the round trip.

By this time Dad's tools had been returned to him in Eckley. This would make the trip back to Frisco more difficult, but he selected the tools he would need the most and built a tool box just big enough to house them. Mom made a small sack out of canvas for Dad's clothes.

Dad gave Mom instructions regarding what to take to the mountains and what to sell, including the pickup which needed work. Dad had a wide leather belt that he fastened to the tool box and a cord he could use to tie his clothes bag to the tool box. In the end of the toolbox was a space for food, coffee, a couple of cups and a pot to boil water in to make coffee.

Daylight came after a sleepless night for Mom and Dad. When lunch was over Dad kissed us all goodbye and, putting the strap over his shoulder, he stepped out of the house into the hot sun and walked to the railroad siding where there was a freight train waiting for orders to leave. He climbed into an empty boxcar and it wasn't long till the train pulled out heading towards Denver. The train arrived very late in the evening in Denver after many stops. Dad went to the home of one of Uncle Sam's daughters and stayed for the night.

When morning came Hazel took Dad to the west end of Denver where he started walking towards Frisco. Dad walked till nearly noon when a car came by and took him several miles west of Silver Plume. This was a great lift, but there were still a lot of miles ahead for him. A rain storm stopped travel for over an hour during the afternoon, but Dad had traveled far enough to arrive at an area of dense trees, which was his tent during the rain storm. When the storm ended Dad set out on a fast walk up the road towards Loveland Pass. Just before dark he stopped for the night at a large culvert that carried water from a small stream under the dirt road.

When daylight came, Dad heated water in the pot he carried to make coffee. Hot coffee and cold sandwiches made his breakfast. He shouldered his satchel and tool box and with a lot of determination headed towards the top of the pass and to Frisco. Hour after hour he followed the road which was not much more than a trail, stopping from time to time to rest and look at the beauty around him. Late in the afternoon he arrived at the top of Loveland Pass. The view towards the west was obscured by some low-hanging clouds, but the rest of the mountains were silhouetted against the blue sky.

"The view is out of this world," he thought, but also he was pleased that he had arrived at the top and it would be easier traveling downhill to the timber where he would spend the night.

His back throbbed where the infection from the tick bite had been so he shifted his tool box and satchel of clothes to the opposite shoulder and pressed on. One hour passed, then another. Darkness was approaching in the high mountains.

"I need to find a spot to spend the night," he thought as he stepped off the road and leaned up against a big spruce tree to rest. He looked up into the sky at all the millions of stars. His mind carried him back to Eckley and his family and how much he hated to leave them, and how long it would be till they could all be together again. Minnie had probably just put the kids in bed and all would be quiet except for the coughing that would be going on. He hoped little Helen would get better quickly as the cough seemed to have affected her more severely than the rest. His heart hurt thinking of all the work Mom would have to do in the weeks and months till they would be united in the coming spring.

"I'll bet it's a terrible hot night there," he said to himself. About that time a chill went up his back and he came back to the reality of where he was. It was cold, dark, and strangely quiet and he had no place to make camp. He finally found a large fallen tree and crept in against the trunk, pulled his coat over his shoulders and went to sleep.

At daylight he built a little fire and made a cup of hot coffee. He pulled a sandwich out of the end of his satchel and, using a forked stick, he toasted the bread. After his breakfast he headed on down the road. He was losing altitude rapidly after leaving the mountain summit.

As he walked along he saw a movement in the spruce trees. He stopped and watched for a minute and discovered there were several birds about the size of small chickens. Their legs were covered with feathers and as it was late summer some of the brown birds were already starting to turn white. "Ptarmigan," he said to himself as he watched them. "Now I know they turn white in the winter."

Dad's heart leaped with joy at the sight he saw when he rounded a curve and before him, framed with spruce trees stood Buffalo Mountain! It already seemed a place of comfort as it beckoned to him. This gave him the much needed strength to continue to the valley floor and Frisco.

He said to himself, "Today I will be back in Frisco, I'll never leave this beautiful area again." After a long rest he picked up his tools and satchel and, placing the strap over his shoulder, continued on.

As he hurried along the sky suddenly darkened. He hadn't gone very far before a few drops of rain started falling. He looked up at the side of the mountain and saw that it was partly obscured by the heavy rain moving down towards him. The rain got heavier and heavier and soon it was a downpour. Looking for some sort of shelter he discovered that he had to go some distance to get into some large trees where he could get out of the rain.

He was wet, boy, was he wet! When the rain stopped, he stepped out from under the big branches of a spruce tree, and looking up, saw the clouds were parting and the sun was about to come out. A typical late summer day, he thought, as he looked at the white clouds vanishing against the blue sky. He opened his satchel and took out his last set of clean, dry clothes. Just as he finished buttoning his shirt he heard a car coming. He grabbed his tool box and satchel and ran towards the road.

The pickup stopped and a man yelled out, "What'ya doing up here in the rain storm?"

Dad replied, "I've been traveling towards Frisco from Eastern Colorado for the last several days."

"Climb in, Mister," the driver said, "I live in Dillon and I have been working up here. I left some tools here yesterday so I came back to pick them up."

"Boy, I'm sure glad to see you! I had just about decided I would have to walk all the way to Frisco," Dad said as he climbed into the pickup.

A thirty minute ride instead of an eight hour walk and the driver stopped in front of Erickson's Garage in Dillon. Dad stepped out of the pickup and thanked the man for the great lift. When Dad picked up his tools and his satchel from the back of the pickup he realized he had left all of his wet clothes lying on a log when the pickup had approached. "A small sacrifice," he thought.

Back on the road Dad walked to Frisco and not a car passed him going either way. He stayed with Bill Thomas that night and the next day he walked to Dan Mogee's ranch at Dickey.

He did carpenter work at various places during the late fall and winter. He stayed at Dan Mogee's ranch most of the time. When spring came Frank Boggs came back to his cabin where Dad did some more work for him.

## FRISCO, HERE WE COME

Finally the time arrived to make the move to the mountains!

It was mid May 1935 and school was out. We motored to Boulder with Margaret Earnest, my school teacher. We saw our first traffic light when we went through Fort Morgan. This was really exciting to us kids as we had never heard of such a thing before.

We stayed about a week in Boulder with Aunt LuRosa, Uncle Emile, and Ruth. The second morning we got up to find a light rain had started during the night. It seemed like an unreal world watching white clouds drifting along the foothills called "Flat Irons," showing the tops of the peaks above the clouds. It sure was a beautiful sight.

Our adventure continued when we went to Denver and spent a week with Mom's cousin, Amelia James. Amelia's dad, Stephen Fitzgarrald, had been Lieutenant Governor of Colorado in the early 1900's.

Before dinner one evening, while the adults were occupied, us kids went into the back yard where there was a little half moon shaped fish pond. Helen wanted to let her celluloid doll swim in the water. The doll wore a swimming suit and had a spring in it and when you wound it up the arms would go round and round. Mildred wound it up and put it in the water. It took right off swimming across the pond. Helen jumped up and down and laughed and laughed, but didn't understand the concept that we could catch the doll at the far end of the pond. She watched a minute as the doll swam out into the pond. Suddenly she reached out to grab the doll and into the pond she went, head first. When she stood up the water was up around her neck. As soon as her mouth was above the water she started screaming to the top of her lungs. Trying to keep her quiet so as not to interrupt the adults lengthy and boring ancestral analysis, Mildred and I got her out of the pond by the time Mom arrived. Helen was nearly scared to death. She shrieked and howled, but stopped suddenly when she was informed about our evening's outing to Elitch Gardens, a local amusement park.

After dinner it was off to Elitch's with Aunt Amelia and her daughters, Jean and Shirley, and Jean's husband, Clyde Kellogg. What a treat! It was impossible to understand what it was like till we were there. We spent all evening riding on the kids' rides. We sure did have a lot of fun. This is where we had our first taste of cotton candy.

The neon signs in downtown Denver and the thousands of traffic lights made a lasting impression on us. There was so much to see and do, but we could hardly wait to see Dad and the mountains where we would be making our new home!

Several days later it was time for us to continue our journey to the mountains. Amelia took us to West Alameda Avenue and Federal Boulevard where we were to meet Rowland. Mom said she was a little nervous about Rowland being there, but we just had to trust the Lord. It had been nearly three weeks since we left Eckley and not a word from Rowland. With no phones it was nearly impossible for a talk. When we got there Rowland was waiting with his stake-bed truck filled with all of our belongings. Mildred, Dean, and I rode in the back of the truck, where we could see inside the cab and where Mom could see us. Helen rode inside the cab with Mom. She had been sick off and on since we had left Eckley. Mom thought it was too much excitement for a little girl of eight.

It was a clear, warm day and we marveled at the beauty of the mountains and the beautiful green forests as we traveled along. Our trip took us up Highway 285 through Morrison, Bailey, Fairplay, Alma, over Hoosier Pass to Breckenridge, and to Frisco. There were high banks of snow on the sides of the road when we arrived at the top of Hoosier Pass, where we met Dad and Frank Boggs in Frank's pickup.

After a tearful but joyful reunion, we played in the snow for awhile. When we left we rearranged our seating. Mom, Mildred and Dean rode in Frank's pickup. Helen, Dad, and I rode in Rowland's truck. We traveled through Breckenridge and continued on through Frisco to Bill's Ranch and Boggs' cabin.

Dad had just finished building a fireplace in the cabin a short time earlier. Frank started a fire in it as soon as we got there.

It had been warm all day, but by the time we arrived at the cabin the sun had set behind the mountains and it had grown chilly. Frank put a log on the fire and it was nice and warm when we sat down to eat. The smell of the burning wood added to the coziness of the small but comfortable room.

After dinner Mildred, Dean, and I went to bed in the crow's nest or loft, which was a partial attic made into sleeping quarters with one end open into the room. In cabins it was usually reached by a portable ladder as it was in this case. Mom, Dad, and Helen slept in the one and only bedroom. It sure was nice to lie down in a nice bed and just relax. It had been a very long, but exciting day. Mildred and Dean were soon fast asleep, but not me, I could hardly wait till morning! It was late in the day when we arrived at Boggs' cabin, but I had seen enough to know that this was, as Dad said, the most beautiful place in the world.

*Giberson barnyard: Mildred Giberson on Popcorn, Chick Deming in center, Bill Thomas on right.*

The following morning we went to the Giberson Ranch about two miles below Frisco. At Giberson's we met Mollie, Wib, their daughter Sue, and their boys, Glenn, Howard, and Kenneth. They also had another son, Jim, who lived in Frisco with his wife and son Tommy who was Dean's age.

***Sue Giberson and her horse Bird at the Giberson Ranch***

Leaving Giberson's we continued about a mile into the back country to the Lusher Place.

This was to be our home for the next year and a half. There was a two-room house with a shed on the back and a small porch on the front. There was a large hay barn, a machine shed, and a large horse barn with a great big hay loft just waiting for a handful of kids with great imaginations.

We got our drinking water from a spring about a quarter of a mile from our house, but water for cooking, bathing, and laundry came from Meadow Creek which was about fifty feet from the house. We cut dead trees for wood for cooking and heating.

***House and horse barn on the Lusher Ranch; Peak One, Victoria, and Royal Mountains in the background.***

***The Little Spring, the source of our drinking water both at the Lusher Place and Rutherford Ranch.***

# PART III
# LIFE IN PARADISE

## EARLY DAY MILK DELIVERY

As soon as we got settled, Mom wanted to visit with Mrs. Boggs at their cabin on Bill's Ranch. Mrs. Boggs had planned to arrive from Eckley shortly after our arrival. Mom made plans to leave early one morning for the two-mile trip, so she could have a full day's visit. Us kids thought this would be great, especially the walk through Meadow Creek Ranch and Frisco. We didn't know at the time that Meadow Creek Ranch was our future home!

Walking was our only mode of transportation. We left home around eight in the morning and, after crossing creeks and skirting ponds which dotted the forest, we arrived in Frisco one hour later. Mom stopped in the store to make arrangements for a post office box. While we were waiting Bill Thomas came down the road riding a horse and carrying two small cream cans with one on each side of the horse and fastened to the saddle horn with leather straps. Bill stopped at the store and picked up his mail.

We talked with Bill for a few minutes when he said, "I guess I'd better get my milk delivered." He climbed back on his horse and rode off to the street north of Main Street. He rode to the first house, got off the horse and took one cream can off the side of the saddle and filled the jar that was sitting beside the front gate. When it was full, he led his horse to the next house where he did the same thing. Mom was anxious to get on over to Mrs. Boggs, but I wanted to stay and see Bill deliver the milk as I had never thought how milk got to people after it left the cow. After he left the milk at the third house, he got back on his horse and rode for about a block where there was another stop. By this time Mom's persistence was so great I was compelled to go with her on over to Bill's Ranch. I hated to leave, but this proved to be one of the great days in my new life.

A neighbor family of the Boggs arrived that morning to spend the summer at their cabin. They had a boy my age, Dale Ninneman, and he had spent the previous summer at Bill's Ranch. He knew all the places to go and what to do and what not to do. We spent most of the day at a lake that Bill had built a couple years earlier. It covered several acres and was filled with fish, but Bill did not allow any fishing there. This being the case, we went to the upper end and had a great time catching frogs.

The frog catching team was rudely interrupted when my sisters arrived on the scene. We both had our hands full with our best catches for the day when, after much shrieking and screaming over our catch they told us that Mrs. Boggs had made some sandwiches for lunch. Dale went with us back to the Boggs' for lunch.

After lunch Bill Thomas came by and took us to see his barn, milk house, and his home where we met Mrs. Thomas, Bill's mother.

At the milk house we were introduced to Nellie who was just getting ready to churn some cream. Dale, Mildred, and I helped churn the butter. She put the cream into a three gallon crock and covered it with a top that had a hole in the middle of it. There was an X-shaped paddle that fit nicely in the crock with a handle protruding out of the lid on top. We stood there and stomped the plunger up and down for about fifteen minutes until the butter was formed. Nellie gave us a glass of buttermilk. Dean and I loved it, but Mildred, Helen, and Dale turned up their noses.

***Taking a ride on popcorn.***

While we were still in the milk house, Mrs. Thomas brought us each a slice of hot bread, buttered with some of the butter we had just churned. It sure was good. I liked to hear Mrs. Thomas talk with her Welsh accent. I had never heard anyone talk with an accent before and hers was so strange that sometimes it was hard for me to understand what she was saying.

Helen wanted to go to the toilet so Mildred headed back to Boggs' cabin with her.

Bill took us to the upper pasture where he showed us Popcorn, his donkey. He said, "I bought Popcorn from Chuck Chamberlain two or three years ago. I sure like her, but she is as contrary as a mule and lives up to the reputation of being a stubborn donkey.

"Come over some time and ride her, all the kids in Frisco have ridden her one time or another. I have a saddle for her and if you go up in the hills I have a pack saddle to carry the supplies."

"I'll be glad to come over and ride any time when you are

around and not too busy," I replied eagerly.

My excitement abated somewhat when my new friend reported on his dealings with Popcorn. "I rode her last summer. Once she threw me off when I rode her from the corral to the barn and then she had the nerve to stand there and laugh at me."

I then asked Bill, "Can I go with you when you deliver milk, sometime?" The thought entered my mind after I had spied several milk cows feeding in the pasture on the other side of the narrow gauge railroad.

"I'll be glad to take you anytime," he said. "I take the milk to town on Monday and Thursday. The customer puts out a jar or a milk bottle for me to fill with milk. If there isn't any container on the porch or out by the gate, I know they don't need any milk till the next time I take milk to town."

He continued, "I go around to the customers once a month and collect my money. I used to take a little butter and cheese around, but that didn't work very well. I let them come to my house when they want butter, cream, or cheese, or they can order it when I am delivering milk.

"Sue Giberson also delivers milk in Frisco, but there are enough customers for both of us."

Mildred caught up to us where Bill was showing us a cabin and continuing a story that he had started several hours earlier along with a fresh dip of snuff. "Mom is ready to go back home," Mildred stated, completely ignoring the snickers that were punctuating Bill's continued story.

We headed back to Boggs' cabin, where Mom was already standing in the yard tapping her foot. It wasn't one of her ground shakers, but it was rapidly getting there.

I tried to hide my collection but Mom said, "Leave those frogs here; you can catch some at our place." With a great amount of reluctance I turned the frogs over to Dale just knowing that there would never be as good a bunch again. Dale took the can of frogs and said he would take them back to where we had caught them.

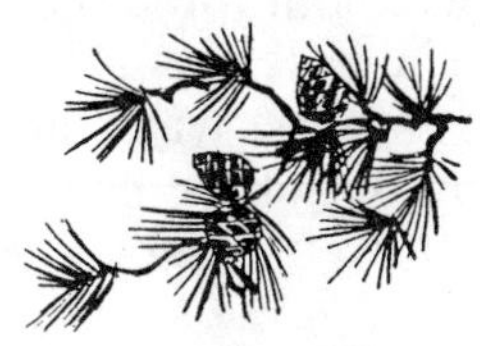

*The Frisco Spring*

## THE FRISCO SPRING AND POST OFFICE

When we arrived back at Frisco, Mom wanted us to see the Frisco Spring which she had heard about from Mrs. Boggs. The spring had a little house built over a spot where the water was boiling out of the ground. The house had a hexagon roof and six sides with six posts holding up the roof. The roof was covered with hand-split shakes. Five sides were enclosed up about three feet from the bottom leaving one side open to go in and out.

A low wall was built around the spring with a hinged wooden cover which was opened to gain access to the water. A rope was tied to the handle of a bucket, going up through a pulley at the roof and down to a loose end on the floor where it had a big knot tied to keep it from ever going back through the pulley. A solid steel flatiron was tied to the bucket handle to cause the bucket to turn on its side and sink into the water. The hole was about three feet deep and the water came up to within six inches of the top of the ground where a ditch ran out of the hole carrying the water to Ten Mile River. It was about three feet from the cabinet top to the top of the water. The hole was about three feet by four feet. You could look down into the water and see three spots where the water was bubbling out of the ground. It never ran dry and maintained the same flow of water the year around. It never froze.

When we arrived at the spring there were several people getting water. Of course each one of us had to have a drink of the ice cold spring water. There was a big dipper hanging on a nail on a corner post. Most of the people in town didn't have a well, so they came to the spring to get drinking water. It usually took two trips, one in the morning and one in the evening, to take care of their needs.

You could go to the spring almost anytime all summer and fall and find a group of people standing there visiting. It seemed to me that this was our daily newspaper delivered in person. The other news service in town was at the Frisco Post Office where there was usually a gathering just before mail time.

The automated mail service in the 1930's in Frisco actually consisted of a train, a cart, a sled, an ancient car, and assorted people, ancient and young, among whom was Chick Deming.

A cart was pushed up to the depot, leaving the outgoing mail and picking up the incoming mail. Some of the time the Demings used an old Overland Whippet car to haul the mail. In the winter

***Mrs. Chamberlain and her grandson Chuck***

***Chick Deming***

time they used a sled to move the mail to the Post Office.

Charlie Masterson, a retired miner, helped Mr. Wildhack get the mail before the Demings took over the job.

When a picture of Hoover Dam came out on a stamp, Lillian MacMasters received a letter with the new stamp on it. She let everyone in the store know that she had the new stamp. Charlie, with a grin on his face and a sparkle in his eye said, "Let me see your Dam stamp." He knew that Mom and Lillian would take him to task for saying "Dam." Everyone in the store got a laugh out of Charlie's mischief.

Lillian MacMasters' husband had died from the effects of poison gas during World War I. She had two sons, Glen and Millet, the ages of Dean and me. They lived in Colorado Springs but came to Frisco as soon as school was out in the spring and stayed till school started in the fall. One year they stayed till after Christmas and several times they stayed till Thanksgiving. Mrs. MacMasters was a poet and wrote many poems during her lifetime.

One time when Chick Deming showed up at the post office with the old car to haul the mail, Mr. Wildhack grabbed him by the shoulders, spun him around in front of him where they could communicate eye to eye and in a stern and gruff voice said, "Chick, you have to be sixteen years old before you can haul mail, just how old are you anyway?"

"Well, I've been driving for several years," Chick replied.

"I don't care how many years you have been driving, it's a federal regulation."

"Well, I'm over sixteen, what can I do to prove it?"

"If you say so, I guess that is good enough."

Chick was the youngest of five boys and two girls. His dad died when he was two years old. A brother, Clyde, died in his teens. Nellie Deming worked at about everything to keep the family together till the boys were old enough to help.

In the late summer of 1935 Louis Wildhack sold the post office and store to Guy Cannam. Soon after Guy and Nell Cannam arrived, Nell was trying to meet every one and at the same time trying to expand her knowledge. Bob Deming, the oldest boy, had lost his eye in an accident and had just received his new glass eye. One day, we heard Nell ask him, "Bob, can't you see just a little bit out of your glass eye?"

Bob, not wanting to make her look stupid said, "Just a little bit, and just a little fuzzy." Nell told everyone who came into the store that Bob could see a little bit out of his glass eye.

The Demings continued to haul the mail to and from the depot till the trains quit running. Ardel Deming would listen for the train whistle as it neared Frisco. She, or one of the boys, would be at the depot when the train arrived. On Monday, Wednesday, and Friday the train would travel from Denver through South Park and over Boreas Pass to Breckenridge. Leaving Breckenridge the train would go through Dickey to Dillon. At one time it continued to Keystone. With a short stop in Dillon the train would back up to Dickey, then head to Leadville going around the end of Ophir Mountain, through the south part of Bill's Ranch and to the Frisco Depot, arriving in Frisco around 4:30 or 5:00 P.M. After another short stop it would continue on towards Curtain, Kokomo, Climax, and Leadville.

Tuesday, Thursday, and Saturday the train would travel from Leadville to Denver going the same route, except when it arrived in Dickey it would stop and backup to Dillon, then return to Dickey, Breckenridge, and Denver.

Meanwhile, back at the spring, as soon as we all had our second turn drinking spring water we headed home.

Dad made me a fishing pole out of a long willow stick. I didn't have a reel, but I could throw my bait into the creek. Dad wanted me to use his good pole and reel when he was at work, but I liked to have my own pole even if it was only a willow pole with a line tied onto it. I caught fish all summer long.

When Meadow Creek was low in the late summer, I was just above the house where the creek was wide and shallow, running over and through baseball sized rocks. I spotted a German brown trout working his way up through the rocks. His back was out of the water part of the time. He didn't seem to be in a big hurry. I ran to the house and yelled, "Come and help me. I think we can catch a big fish." Out of the house came the whole herd ready to help. We ran back to the creek and he was still there feeding in the ripples. After looking at the situation we decided that Mildred should go to the creek bank twenty five or thirty feet below the fish and take a long heavy willow pole and if the fish started downstream she would hit the water in front of him and scare him back up the creek and Dean and Helen would do the same if he tried to go upstream. When they were all set I put a worm on my line and cast in the water a short distance above him. He swam upstream and grabbed the worm. I jerked and the battle was on. He went upstream and when Helen and Dean splashed the water in front of him he headed back downstream.

About the third time he went upstream I tried to pull him out. My line broke. I waded out into the creek and tried to hit him with my pole. He finally got tired. He tried to hide under the bank, but the bank didn't cover the water over three or four inches. He stuck his head under the bank and left most of his body hanging out. I took what was left of my line and wrapped it around and around his tail and tied it to a stick. I was afraid I would lose him if I tried to pull him out so Helen ran to the house for Mom. When these situations come up Mom was the best one to call for help if Dad was gone.

Mom came out and just stood there laughing. She finally got down on her stomach on the bank and reached down into the water, grabbing the stick and threw the fish out on the bank. He was twenty inches long.

When winter froze ice on the creek I caught fish through the hole in the ice Dad made for us to get water. We put a board over the hole and covered it with snow. The next time we wanted to get water or go fishing, all we had to do was scoop the snow off the board and remove it. The water wasn't frozen.

Knowing that he was preventing a lot of potential problems, Dad made a saw horse for me to saw wood on. He brought home a new buck saw and showed me how to cut wood the right size to go into our cook stove. You can't imagine the number of dead trees that fell in my path that first day I wielded the saw.

Every day for my work chore, I would cross the creek on a little bridge Dad built and bring some more small dead trees to the house to cut up. Each day I cut up a little more wood than we burned. The girls stacked the extra wood by the shed for winter.

It was three miles to Dillon through the timber where Dad did carpenter work. He would leave by six o'clock in the morning and get back home by five thirty in the evening. Several times during the summer Mildred and I walked to Dillon with Dad. We stayed till Dad finished his day's work and walked home with him. Many times we saw deer either going or coming from Dillon.

At the spring where we got our drinking water we saw beaver swimming around in the ponds they had built on Meadow Creek. One time we saw a muskrat eating on some grass roots he had carried out on the bank. He didn't seem to notice us as long as we kept a short distance away. One time when I was fishing with Dad he motioned for me to come over to where he was.

When I got to him he said, "Look over on the bank on the other side of the pond. There is a mink eating on something." At first I thought it was a black cat, but when Dad spoke it dove into the water and swam under water across the beaver pond and climbed out on the beaver dam and disappeared. Cats don't do that and you can't make them do that! We soon learned that mink lived around the ponds. The mink are slim and shaped like an ermine or weasel. They are a little smaller than a house cat and usually are dark brown with white on their neck and chest. They are very vicious carnivores with partly webbed feet. Their fur was very valuable in the 1930's and 40's.

Most of the time Dad worked six days a week. When he was home for a day, Mom would make up lunches and we all would hike somewhere. Some of the mines were still intact and we would go see them. Once we hiked up North Ten Mile Creek to the Square Deal Mine. It wasn't working, but the mill was still there and it looked like it had just shut down the night before. Ben and Mrs. Staley were there and Ben showed us all around and gave us a couple of ore samples from the mill.

We hiked up to Lily Pond on Buffalo Mountain on another occasion, but that was a hard trip for Mom.

One Sunday the Gibersons invited us all to go down to Rock Creek six miles below Dillon to their placer mine for the day. Every year they had to do some work on the placer. We stayed all day and there were at least four or five people using gold pans. Mollie Giberson and Mom made sandwiches, cookies, and took Kool Aid and milk for drinks. It was a fun time for all. I am afraid to tell you how many people were in the Gibersons' Roosevelt car for the trip to Rock Creek and back home. It was at least twice the amount specified in the manufacturer's hand book.

There was never a lack of opportunity for entertainment after our chores were done. There was an old buggy without a tongue in it at the horse barn. This was the kind of equipment I was looking for, having previously earned my pilot's license several years earlier. I moved the buggy around to where we could get it to run down a gentle slope towards the gate at the Lusher Place. It had a foot brake on it so I could stop it when I arrived at the gate. I turned it by pushing on the axle with my feet in the direction I wanted to go. Nearly every day we would ride down the gentle slope to the gate.

Once in a while there is a trip that pilots don't want to talk about. This was one of them. Wind sheer must have contributed to this mishap as the buggy didn't turn as well as I expected and it went into the creek just below the house into about three feet of water. We sure got wet, but then we probably could stand a bath anyway. Dean and the girls tried to help me get it out of the creek, but we just couldn't get it to move.

Having failed in our attempt to get it out before Dad got home we asked for his help. Dad took one look and said, "It will take a horse to get it out of the water. I will go by Gibersons' in the morning and tell them of the mishap and when we get it out I don't want you kids playing with it again.

Glenn Giberson came up with a horse and pulled it out. He kindly suggested that we shouldn't play with the buggy as we could get hurt. This ended our fun on the buggy. I didn't care as it was an awful lot of work to push it back up the slope to the barn just to ride it back down. It took such a short time to go from the barn to the gate that I didn't even have time to get my breath before it was time to push it back up the slope towards the horse barn.

The Gibersons had a retired horse they called Whiskers. One weekend they brought Whiskers up to the Lusher Ranch with several other horses and left them for a time. They put a saddle and bridle in the barn so we could ride her. We only rode when Dad or one of the Gibersons was around, but, boy, did we ever have fun riding. One time all four of us kids got on her at the same time. Mildred was in front and I brought up the rear. I had to hang on to the horse's tail to keep from falling off the rear end which happened more than once. Most of the time we rode her with only a rope tied to the halter and no saddle. She sure was a good horse to have around kids. They also had a saddle horse called Bird that was Sue's horse. They brought Bird to the Lusher Place from time to time. I got to ride her every once in awhile.

Howard Giberson had a horse that he trained to teeter-totter on a heavy plank. The horse would follow every command and of course loved it when he was petted and given a bite of a favorite something to eat. Several times when Howard was training his horse us kids hiked to Gibersons' to watch the horse perform.

## CAMPING TRIP BEHIND BUFFALO MOUNTAIN

During the summer Dad went on a camping trip with Wib Giberson and his visiting brothers Win (a preacher and dentist), and Leige. Also Bill Thomas, Dan Mogee, Grove Alder (Dad's friend from Eckley), and Frank Boggs. They rode horses and took a pack horse and Bill Thomas' donkey, Popcorn, to carry supplies. The trip took them up Meadow Creek behind Buffalo Mountain, over Eccles Pass and into South Willow Creek drainage, over Red Buffalo Pass and a short distance down into Gore Canyon. This was indeed a most beautiful trip.

As they traveled behind Little Chief and Little Buffalo Mountains they came to a large open meadow where North Ten Mile trail meets Meadow Creek trail. Dad guessed the open area to be over a mile wide and possibly two miles long, disappearing against the mountain. At one time it had been timbered, but now it showed the remains of a forest fire. A lot of stumps stood about ten to twelve feet high, scarred and blackened by the fire. The trees were cut down after the fire when the snow was ten to twelve feet deep. Many of the stumps were so large, they appeared to have been from virgin timber. At one time there was a vast logging operation working in the area.

***Eccles Pass in the distance.***

Meadow Creek wandered lazily through the grassy area and on towards the cliffs, where it terminated above timberline in a deep blue

***West side of Buffalo Mountain***

lake. Willows lined much of the banks of the creek where native trout lived in many of the small pools of water. The trail had been marked by stakes placed in the ground every so often. When the trail went above timberline it was marked by little piles of rocks placed one on top of the other.

As they rode along they came upon a large herd of domestic sheep in this beautiful, almost flat meadow. The sheepherders' camp was composed of a covered wagon, which had two mules tied to one back wheel, and a couple of small tents standing nearby. Several dogs could be seen near the sheep and at the far end of the herd was a rider on a black horse. I have an idea this is where Mr. Young pastured his sheep.

The party moved along through the open meadow and up the side of the mountain which by now was above timberline. When they got to the steep hillside, they led their horses. Five trails came together here: Meadow Creek trail, North Ten Mile Creek trail, Officers Gulch trail, Gore River trail sometimes called Pack trail, and South Willow Creek trail. The markers brought them to a saddle in the cliffs called Eccles Pass, also sometimes called Meadow Creek Pass. The view was breathtaking. The back side of Buffalo Mountain was nearly straight up and down. The Gore Range with its white snow peaks was silhouetted against the deep blue sky. As the men looked down into South Willow Creek small blue lakes dotted the steep side of the mountain. They looked like sapphires against the red rocks. The canyon was filled with a deep green forest dotted with occasional outcropping rock that appeared red in color at the top of the mountain and gradually changed into black as it disappeared into the canyon floor. Looking across to the north you could see the side of Red Peak, appropriately named because of the red color. The men were awestruck as they looked and looked at the beauty, almost beyond human comprehension.

Finally Wib took the lead and they walked single file down the steep grade into the canyon. The trail took them to South Willow Creek drainage. When they crossed the creek, little more than a trickle of water, there was a nice green meadow with a large downed tree close to the water. This was a perfect place to eat a late lunch. The men loosened the cinches on the saddles and removed the bridles from their horses and led them to the green grass.

Wib said, "I'll pile up some rocks and start a fire for coffee."

"I'll go to the creek for coffee water," volunteered Leige, his brother.

Dad got the coffee going and passed out sandwiches. Win gave thanks for the food and the privilege of making the trip.

When lunch was over Dan picked up the waxed papers and put them in a paper sack and said, "We may need these papers to start a fire when we camp for the night."

The horses were led to the creek for a drink and then they were ready to start up another mountain. Bill watered the pack horse and then he went over to Popcorn. Popcorn was just finishing eating the sack full of waxed papers!

***Red Buffalo Pass, also known as Wilkerson Pass.***

***Head of Gore Canyon near Red Buffalo Pass.***

Bill said, "I didn't think to watch Popcorn, I might have known she would clean up all the papers and garbage."

The trail gained altitude rapidly. They soon came to a place where the side of the mountain was as steep as the face on a cow. A narrow trail had been cut into the side of the mountain. Each rider led his horse along the trail. Wib was ahead with Dan next, then came Popcorn carrying the cooking utensils and some of the food. Next came the pack horse carrying tarps, sleeping blankets, and the rest of the food. The rest of the gang followed single file.

At a place in the trail where it was impossible for one horse to pass another, Popcorn got tired or sick and lay down on the trail. All attempts to get her back on her feet were to no avail. Bill was bringing up the rear. He left his horse and after some time managed to crawl around one horse, between the feet of another horse and finally got up to Popcorn.

"Get off your lazy butt and go on down the trail," Bill yelled. Popcorn just lay there and acted like she had lost her hearing.

Bill gave her a swift kick and again yelled, "You dumb old jackass, get up. Can't you see you are holding us all up?" Popcorn swung her head to the side and put one ear back and then stretched her feet out over the side of the trail, causing everyone to about panic. Where she was lying, a mountain goat would have had goose pimples trying to walk along the trail.

Wib said, with a grin, "Bill, I think she would get up if you would apologize for calling her a dumb old jackass." Everyone had a good laugh over this. Bill tried to take off the pack saddle, but the buckle on the cinch was on the underside. He pushed and pulled with no luck.

Dan Mogee, watching the ordeal, finally said, "Bill, if I can get up to you, maybe both of us can take the pack saddle off of her."

Bill responded, "I don't think we can. If she moves she'll fall off the trail and take our food with her." An hour passed and Popcorn was still resting.

Wib said, "I'll go on ahead a little piece to where the trail widens out and leave my horse, and then I can come back and help do something."

"A good idea, I will go with you and we can leave the horses and maybe somehow we can get her up," Dan said. In a few minutes they came back to the trouble at hand. Dan and Bill, working together, finally got the cinch loosened to where they could unbuckle the pack saddle. Once the saddle was off they were able to move Popcorn just enough to free the load. They unloaded all the contents and carried it a short distance ahead on the trail.

Bill once again yelled at Popcorn, "Get up off your duff or I will push you over the side." To add action to his threat he kicked Popcorn one more time causing Popcorn to slide a few more inches closer to the edge. Popcorn, with a grin on her face pulled her feet back and stood up, finally! Bill grabbed her halter and pulled a little. She followed right along as if nothing had ever happened. It wasn't long till everyone was off the bad part of the trail. Popcorn was loaded up again and ready to travel. About five steps and she stopped again. They tried to pull her, but she just stiffened her legs. They removed the load and the food was put on two other horses. The pots and pans were tied on the pack horse. Again they started up the trail. Popcorn walked right along and all seemed fine. About an hour passed and the pans must have shifted a little. One pan started banging against another pan as the horse walked along. This was a chance for the pack horse to let everyone know she wasn't going to carry the pans. At the first sound she shied and jumped to the side scaring the horse in front of her. The pans were removed and Dad took them with him on his horse.

After this was worked out, they went to the top of Red Buffalo Pass without any more problems. At the top of the pass you could see down into the bottom of Gore Canyon with the silvery Gore River winding its way through the canyon floor, a view that one wanted to look at forever. They continued on down the trail into the canyon to where they were a little lower than timberline in the spruce trees to a place called Hardscrabble.

This is where camp was made for the night. After dinner the evening was filled with talk, stories, and laughter. By the time the stars were coming out, the camp chatter had dwindled down to just Wib and Liege talking. They soon drifted off to sleep.

Daylight found the gang up and ready for breakfast made by Dad and Dan. Sunburned faces, stiff legs, aching backs, and a multitude of other pains were soon forgotten as they all looked at the beauty around them. From camp they walked down the canyon to see a waterfall. It didn't seem like it was a long trip down, but it sure was a long way back up to camp. In the afternoon they checked out a rose quartz outcropping near camp. Wib had a prospector's pick with him and they were able to pick loose some samples for souvenirs. In the evening they had a big supper of warmed up roast beef with cut up carrots, potatoes, turnips, and onions. Another evening was filled with stories and laughter. One by one they all drifted off to sleep thinking they had died and gone to heaven when the quiet of the night was punctuated with a loud yell, "It shouldn't have to happen to a dog." Liege crawled out from under his covers and feeling around in the dark knocked over the lantern. He tried to light it but finally set the job aside and took off to the timber in the dark. It was one of those really dark nights. You couldn't see a foot in front of you. The only way you could move without hitting a tree was to feel your way with your hands extended out in front of you. He didn't return in a reasonable length of time so Wib took a flashlight and went to look for him. Liege had tripped over a fallen tree and was crawling back on his hands and knees so he wouldn't fall again.

"What is your problem?" Wib asked as he approached him.

"I shouldn't have eaten that second helping of applesauce," Liege groaned. "It sure did give me the trots."

"If you have to go again use my flashlight. You could kill yourself out here wandering around in the bowels of the night in the dark," Wib said.

After breaking up camp the next morning they went up to the top of Red Buffalo Pass where they spent most of the day looking around. Dad, Wib, and Liege hiked up to a point on the side of Red Peak. From that place you could see forever! Several of the men took pictures. In the late afternoon they went down into South Willow Creek and camped for the night.

Morning arrived for a smiling but tired crew. Back in the saddle they rode to where the trail was just a shelf cut around the side of the mountain. This is when Popcorn found herself at the back of the group as they walked single file leading their horses along the narrow trail.

After crossing Eccles Pass they continued downhill into the large meadow where the sheep were when they came up. They crossed the meadow and entered the forest again. Dad noticed the horses were acting a little strange. They would all turn their ears forward listening at the same time. Dad's horse would shake his head, snort and walk partly stiff legged. Suddenly a Canadian lynx cat jumped out of a tree and disappeared close to the trail they were on.

Arriving below the Buffalo ditch on the Forest Service road Bill Thomas, Dan Mogee, Frank Boggs, and Grove Alter stayed on the Forest Service road to Frisco and to Bill's Ranch. Dad and the three Gibersons left the road and entered the Lusher meadow on the west arriving around five in the afternoon. Mom had hot coffee and cinnamon rolls for them to eat. They told as many stories as they could while they ate their snack and then Wib, Win, and Liege continued on home.

***Dad and the three Giberson brothers as they arrive back at the Lusher Place. Mom and family waiting on front porch.***

One Sunday we discovered smoke rising high into the sky west of Chief Mountain. Dad took one look and headed to Gibersons'. Wib was a fire warden for Arapaho National Forest for many years. There was a fire west of Frisco close to where Vail Pass road turned off from the road to Leadville. Wib rounded up his boys, several Deming boys, and Dad. It was just getting started so they were able to put it out before the large trees began to burn. A camp fire had been left burning and set the small trees and brush on fire.

***Fish for Supper***

Every so often, Gibersons had a potluck dinner and most of Frisco would come. Of course Bill and Nellie Thomas went and sometimes Dan Mogee and several people from Dillon came. The house was full, even though they had a large living and dining room. We laughed, sang songs, and played cards for the evening.

On one occasion Hattie Lund arrived with a three-gallon coffee pot. She walked in the living room and held up the pot and said, "I want you all to know I brought the pot." This, of course brought a number of laughs and some funny remarks.

One morning Dad let me use his fishing pole to go fishing. He wanted me to catch enough fish for supper. We dug a nice can of fish worms and I went to a beaver dam a short distance from the house. Every few minutes a fish would grab my line. It wasn't long till I had six fish. One for each member of the family. Dad was home for the day, so Mom took a picture of Dad, Dean, and me.

## HAYING ON THE LUSHER MEADOW

The first fall we were on the Lusher Place Wib Giberson and his boys, Glenn, Howard, and Kenneth, with Chick Deming and other hired help came to the ranch to put up their hay. They had seven or more horses to do the necessary work. They had two mowers, one following the other going around in a large rectangle. After a couple of days of mowing they added a couple of men raking the hay in windrows, still keeping the mowing going on.

Then a buck or bull rake was added to run down the windrows and pick up big loads of hay and move it in front of the stacker. Two horses were used on the bull rake.

Gibersons also had an old Buick car remodeled with the seat, steering wheel, and controls turned backwards. The bull rake was then mounted over the back wheels for better traction. It moved along much faster than the horses. They also had an old Dodge converted to a buck rake, but usually used it at the home meadows rather than at the Lusher Place.

Two horses were used to push a plunger up the stacker. At the top the hay would drop on top of the stack. This operation took a good driver and a well trained pair of horses to keep the plunger from going too high and pushing it off the top of the stacker, or stopping too short and leaving some hay on the stacker as the plunger came back down. Two or more men worked on the hay stack placing the hay around on the stack, making the sides straight up and down. When the stack was as high as they wanted, they would round the stack off, making the highest point in the middle of the stack and sloping off to the sides to shed rain and snow from sinking down into the stack.

It wouldn't take too long to put the hay up if there had been no rain. However one afternoon after they had the haying going in full swing it rained just enough in the afternoon to close the operation down. The half-wet crew brought all the horses into the barn where they removed the harness. The horses were given a bite of grain and turned out to pasture in the meadow.

Just before haying started one morning, some range cattle had broken into the meadow and were put into a corral that surrounded the horse barn. They were there several days when they were moved to another pasture, but they had left a lot of fresh cow manure all around in the barnyard. Most of the piles were close to the front entrance to the barn.

Howard, feeling his oats, picked up a stick and retrieved a healthy amount of manure on it. He aimed and threw it at Glenn, who was standing just outside the barn. He hit him on the belt buckle.

"Oh, so you want to get funny," Glenn yelled. "I'll show you how to throw manure!" He picked up a flat piece of wood, just the right thing for the job in front of him. He scooped up some manure and took after Howard who had disappeared around the corner of the barn. As he rounded the corner he got another plop of manure on his shoulder. Glenn threw his load at Howard, who now was stooping over to get another load. Glenn hit him in the seat with a powerful blow. Glenn ran back around the barn and scooped up another load as he entered the front of the barn. All was quiet, then he heard slow, sure footsteps coming around the side of the barn. Glenn raised his load and, as his mark appeared, he threw and hit him right in the side of the head. This would have been perfect, only it wasn't Howard, it was Chick Deming, who was helping with the haying!

"Boy, are you in trouble now," Chick hollered as he picked up a board and scooped up a nice load. He looked around, but there was no one in view. He sneaked around the edge of the barn door where he saw a figure he presumed to be Glenn and he threw, hitting Kenneth who had been up in the hay mow putting hay down for the horses to eat in the morning while they put the harness on them. He hit Kenneth right in his stomach, just above the belt, he was covered from his chin to his knees.

"Just wait till I get through with you, you will be sorry," Kenneth hollered, as he picked up a stick and headed towards some ammunition. By now it wouldn't have made much difference if he had gone right out in front of the barn where there was lots of ammunition. He collected a load and was about to fire at Howard when he received another direct hit from Chick. He took off after Chick, who tried to hide in the barn, but as he entered the barn, Glenn, who had hidden in the barn with a big scoop, hit him in the face. After a little running around and many misses Glenn caught Howard right in the chest. Glenn stood there with his mouth wide open laughing as hard as he could. Just at that time someone fired with a direct hit and got Glenn right in the face with his mouth wide open. I never saw a man trying to spit without closing his mouth, but Glenn tried. He coughed a couple times and headed for the creek. This ended the fight.

Wib Giberson, who was standing a short distance away observing the fun said, "Boys will be boys, but they still have the chores at the house to do."

I was glad I was too young to be involved in the fight, and it probably helped that I was standing next to Wib.

Next morning the haying gang arrived at the ranch around seven in the morning with clean clothes on. It was a beautiful morning without a cloud in the sky. After getting the horses in the barn and harnessed they were off to the field. It was just what they wanted, a clear, dry and warm day, perfect for putting up the hay. By mid-morning the hay was all dried out from the recent rain, so they started stacking. I went out close to the stacker to watch the process. Boy, the hay sure did smell good. I hated to see the haying season come to an end.

When evening came I headed to the horse barn to see if there was going to be another fight. Everyone seemed jolly, but too tired for any extra sport.

## FALL AND WINTER IN FRISCO, 1935

School started in Frisco with eight kids present: Ben Cluskey, Darrel Bailey, Chuck Chamberlain, Neil Westlake, Tommy Giberson, and our family, Mildred, Helen, Dean, and me. Dad walked to and from school with us until we learned the route, over a mile and a half.

Our teacher, Ann Elliot, was very nice. Unfortunately, Ann became very sick in the early spring and Ada Altland from Dillon finished the year for her. Mrs. Frank Olson was the school janitor. She kept the place clean and dusted. She would get up early in the morning and build a fire so when we all arrived at school it was warm inside. She shoveled a path to the street in the snow during the winter months.

In October during deer season Dad went hunting on Salt Lick Gulch north of the Lusher Place. The first morning he shot a four-point buck. Sunday afternoon we went up and carried the meat down to the house. Nights were cold so Dad hung the meat up in the hay barn. Mom canned most of the meat for the winter months. Dad tanned the hide and cut the leather in strips to restring an old pair of snowshoes he bought in Dillon. He made a piece for your foot to fit in out of the leather.

When Halloween came, snow came with it. Bill Thomas drove his horses to Frisco pulling a bob sled with sleigh bells on the harness. When the horses would trot the bells would jingle. It made you think of Christmas early. That afternoon Bill gave a ride up and down the street to everyone who came to the store.

Two weeks before Christmas Dad took us kids out to find a suitable Christmas tree. We went up the Forest Service road just above the Buffalo Ditch and close to the creek we found the perfect tree for our Christmas. This was the first time we had ever had a Christmas tree. We made paper chains out of heavy green and red paper and decorated the tree with the chains. There was over two feet of snow on the ground when we walked to the school program. It was a real Christmas to us kids.

On the Saturday before Christmas Mrs. Olson and Mrs. Staley gave us candy when we stopped at their houses before we headed home.

## HOMEMADE SNOWSHOES AND SKIS

After Christmas, while we were still on school vacation, I decided to make myself a pair of skis and a pair of snowshoes. I found an old wooden barrel in the grain room of the barn that had collapsed in times past. I took the two best looking pieces from the sides to make my skis. They were about three and a half feet long. Mom gave me some paraffin wax she had left from canning jam. I used a hot iron to melt the wax onto the bottom of my skis, making them slick. I looked around for suitable material to build bindings. I found some discarded and partially rotted pieces of harness with buckles on one end.

I used my Dad's pocket knife to drill holes in the sides of the skis where they would balance on my foot. It took me two or three hours *per hole* to drill into the hard wood. I took screws and fastened the leather bindings on the skis.

There was a nice slope from the house to the creek for me to practice using my skis. Dad packed the snow with his snow shoes for me and then I was ready for the trial run. I put on the skis and slid down the slope. It worked perfectly, if I could have kept from falling, but by the end of the day I could slide down without falling. I had to stop often to repair my bindings; the leather straps kept pulling off of the screws. Dad gave me some washers to put on each side of the leather and this helped a lot. I decided I needed a pair of snowshoes to walk up the hills and then I could use my skis to slide down the hills.

I took a couple of worn-out bushel baskets and removed the bindings around the middle of the baskets. I put them in the spring overflow and let them soak for a couple of days. Once they were wet, I tied them into the shape of a bear paw snowshoe. When they dried I took some old insulated electric wire and laced the snowshoes. Whenever I crossed a strand of wire I made a loop around the wire. This made a solid set of snowshoes. Dad gave me a piece of deer leather to make my bindings. I finally finished my work and took the snowshoes out to give them a trial run and they worked fine. I walked to a hill across the Lusher meadow carrying my skis. I made several trips up the hill and back down with the snowshoes. I then tried out my skis. After several attempts I was able to ride down the slope without falling. When I fell on the skis I usually pulled my binding off. I carried a small screwdriver and my knife to cut off the strap and make a new connection. I sure did have fun. I made at least eight or nine trips to the slope to ski when I decided I needed a steeper hill. I knew where there was a steep hill north of the Lusher gate. I left my skis at home and snowshoed to the hill. It was steeper than I had envisioned. I packed a trail down the hill hoping no more snow would fall till I could come back. By this time the snow on the level was over three feet deep. I went back home and waited till the next Saturday to go back to the hill.

In the middle of the week we had a snow storm that left an additional eighteen inches on the level. When Saturday came I took my snowshoes and went back to the hill. There had been so much snow I couldn't see where I had packed the snow down the Saturday before. The snow was hard to walk in. It seemed to cling to my snowshoes. I was going to pack a new trail down the hill, but I had hardly gone halfway down the hill when one side of my snowshoe broke. I tried to fix it enough to get home, without success. I finally took them off and tried to walk home, but the snow was up to my waist and I couldn't go anywhere. I worked my way up to a tree and broke a branch off the tree and tied it to the snowshoe with my handkerchief. It didn't work. When I would take a step my snowshoe would turn sideways from the weight of the pine branch and then I would step down in the snow up to my knees. I was making some headway when I completely broke the snowshoe. I broke a good sized branch off a tree and using my hankie and my snowshoe binding I fastened the branch to my foot. I made it a short distance, but it was so heavy I could hardly take a step so I discarded the tree branch.

"How am I going to get back to the house?" I almost panicked when I thought of the distance I had to go. I was wet to my knees and my arms were wet to my shoulders. I had lost one of my gloves when I was at the tree. Finally I took the snowshoes off and using them on my hands I was able to crawl on the snow and make a little progress. I still was sinking into the snow over a foot. I had to stop often to get my breath and warm my hands. I think about two hours passed before I could see the house. It still took me nearly another hour to get home. I was wet all over when I stepped on the porch.

Mom came to the door and said, "I was getting uneasy when you didn't return for lunch. I don't want you kids going so far from the house till you get better skis and snowshoes."

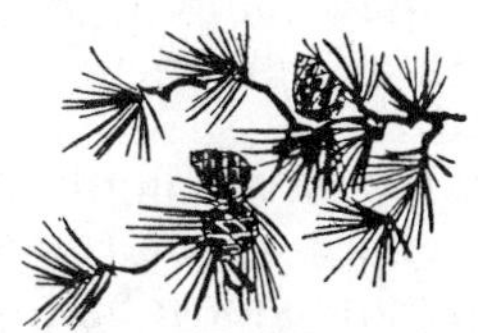

*Don't cross the tracks.*

## MILDRED WINS A SCENTED RIDE TO DENVER

Mildred won the Summit County spelling contest in the late winter 1936. She received a free trip to Denver on the narrow gauge railroad, joining sixty-two other contestants at the Olin Hotel for a week of fun, sight seeing and, of course, the State Spelling Contest. There was one kid from each county in the state competing in the contest.

In March Mildred boarded the train in Frisco and on the second day she arrived in Denver, going through Breckenridge, over Boreas Pass, through South Park to Denver. The train consisted of one coach, one baggage car, several engines, and one rotary snowplow. An extra engine was required to help push the snowplow through the deep snow over Boreas Pass during the winter.

There had been a big snowstorm that continued for over a week, and when the storm ended there were huge snowdrifts on the tracks and the roads. The main routes to Denver were on the railroad, over Hoosier Pass which had been closed for nearly a week, or to Kremmling and then over Berthoud Pass to Denver. Loveland Pass was only a summer road, and mostly a trail over the top. Travel was slow but, if you did encounter a snow slide, the train would make it through. The rotary snow plow had a big job to do. Every time they came to a large drift it would take from a few minutes to several hours to clear the tracks and move on to the next snow drift.

Mary Williams, the County School Superintendent made the journey with Mildred. The storm had ended by the time they left Breckenridge, and when the storm had passed it was clear and cold.

The temperature went far below "0." It was somewhat hard to tell just how cold it got as most of the thermometers had left their regular abode and had gone to warmer areas, most likely inside the house by the kitchen stove.

When the prolonged storm ended, the wildlife, as always, would leave their shelters and go out to look for food. Some of the wild group consisted of rabbits, mice, weasels, wolves, coyotes, foxes, elk, deer, skunks, bobcats, Canadian lynx, and many other animals. The temperature did not make any difference, they hadn't eaten since the storm had started.

The skunks, being one of these animals, took out in the deep snow looking for something to eat. Their warm bodies soon melted snow on their stomachs and legs making their fur wet. When they came across the railroad tracks their wet fur would freeze to the iron tracks.

## I CAN JUST PICTURE THIS

*A skunk frozen to the iron rail by the fur on his stomach. "Let go of me or you will wish you had," growled the skunk. Not a word from the iron rail.*

*"I am very easy to get along with, who do you think you are, to hold me like this?"*

*The iron rail remained silent.*

*The skunk said, " You can't eat me, so let me go." Still not a word from the iron rail.*

*"I'm getting mad now," growled the skunk, "if you don't let me go, you will wish you had." The angry skunk let go with his unique aroma and shouted, "Now I'll bet you will let me go."*

*A couple of coyotes caught a whiff of the skunk and one coyote said to the other, "Can you stand a skunk for breakfast?"*

*"You bet, I'm starved, I'll eat anything. Let's go." The coyotes followed the smell and soon found the skunk held fast to the iron rail.*

*"This will be easier than I planned," the smaller coyote said. The coyotes looked over the situation, neither one wanting to get too close to the railroad track.*

*"It's all yours," said the larger coyote. "I'm afraid the track will get hold of me and I can't get away. One time my Uncle Sid was hunting along the track and he decided he would see what the rail tasted like. He gave it a lick and the rail held him right there. He was there for hours, he couldn't howl or anything. Finally the rail let him loose, but his bark and howl have never been the same. Let's forget this food and go down to the creek and see if we can get breakfast there."*

*"This smell is so bad I couldn't eat him on an empty stomach anyway," the smaller coyote answered. They left the skunk and headed towards the creek bed.*

*Time went on and the skunk finally gave up and laid down on the rail. His body warmed the fur enough to free him. Mumbling words not printable, the skunk continued on his way through the snow.*

This is not the case for most of the skunks as they are stuck fast till the train comes and runs over them. Mildred said they ran over at least ten or twelve skunks before they arrived in Denver. The train had to go to the trainwash before it stopped at Union Station for people to get off. Mildred said the smell was still terrible.

Mildred didn't win in the State contest, but she finished in the top ten.

## SPRINGTIME IN THE ROCKIES

On April 22, 1936 it snowed over 24 inches during the day and over a foot the next day.

It was one of those unusual winters. The snow was high as the eaves around most of our house, but on the west side the wind drifted the snow back two feet away. There was a lot of snow during the winter, so when spring came the runoff filled the rivers to overflowing. We had to walk to Gibersons' ranch, cross Ten Mile River on Gibersons' bridge and walk up the highway to Frisco. The Ten Mile River was running over the top of the bridge by Mrs. Olson's home in Frisco, hitting its crest around midnight and receding till afternoon when it started to rise again. Backwater filled the area around the junkyard and over to the Frisco ponds. Travel over the bridge was stopped for over six weeks. Dad was afraid the bridge would wash out before the runoff was over, but it seemed to handle the high water. However the next year the north approach had to have a lot of work done. At that time they put in new stringers (main beams) and a new deck.

Each year Miss Badger gave a quarter to the kid who brought her the first mayflower (anemone) in the spring. Usually after the first flower was found, it wasn't but a few days till there were hundreds of them, along with other spring flowers blooming as soon as the snow melted off.

When summer came, Guy and Cora Devars with their two kids, Deane and Phyllis, came from Orleans, Nebraska, and spent several weeks with us. They pitched a tent by the gate to sleep in and ate their meals at the house. Deane and I slept in the hay loft of the horse barn.

We took several trips to neighboring towns with my cousin Deane and me insecurely placed in the trunk with the lid propped open. This afforded us the opportunity to see where we had been and also to entertain ourselves without being bothered. You can imagine our delight when we spotted a roll of toilet paper in a bucket in the trunk. We lost many flying banners as we traveled through Breckenridge until once when the car stopped at the side of the road and an adult brought to an abrupt end our banner parade through town. The folks in the front thought that this was a mostly friendly town because so many people waved as our car passed by. It wasn't until the flutter of the toilet paper caught Guy's eye in the rearview mirror that he finally realized the cause of the friendly waves. So much fun in so little time!

On one trip we went to Leadville where we wandered around town to see the sights and over to Malta to see the ore smelter. We drove up by the Matchless Mine, the famous silver mine that made millions of dollars for Horace Tabor. There was a small house, not much larger than a one-car garage, on the property besides the mining buildings. The little house was where Baby Doe, Tabor's second wife, starved and froze to death while waiting for silver prices to rise again. She had been found just a few months before we were there. We collected some pieces of ore from the dump. We also walked up to the mine shaft and dropped some rocks into the hole to hear them crash in the bottom. It was after we let a rock drop and it took forever to hit the bottom that we realized how very deep the shaft was. Guy, realizing the danger, herded all of us kids away from the hole. The whole area was filled with numerous shafts and tunnels and no warning signs were posted of the danger.

One afternoon while us kids were playing in the barn loft we heard Cora scream. We ran down the stairs and to the house. Mom came out of the house and then we saw Guy, carrying a bucket, come out of the willows by the gate.

Mom called out, "Guy, did you hear a scream?"

Guy laughed as he walked up to the house and said, "No biggie. Cora sneaked down to the creek to take a bath. I saw her go so I took some ice we had left over from freezing the ice cream and put it into a bucket of water. After it set a few minutes I slipped down to the creek and up behind her. She couldn't hear me with the sound of the water going over the beaver dam. She didn't know I was around till the water hit her bare back as she sat on the creek bank. I guess that would explain the scream." He laughed and laughed as he thought about it.

In a short time Cora showed up in her bathrobe.

She said, "I am going to drown him the first chance I get." All went fine till we were finishing supper when Cora accidently spilled her glass of water on Guy's lap. For a minute I was afraid there was going to be a full fledged water fight, but then it finally died down and we all finished our ice cream before Guy left for the tent.

## BIG BLAST ON JULY FOURTH

On the Fourth of July just after daylight there was an earth shaking boom that rattled the windows and echoed through the canyon. The folks were up, but us kids were still asleep. My cousin Deane, my brother Dean, and I were sleeping in the horse barn hayloft. We were up and out of there without any shoes or socks on. Brother Dean didn't even take time to dress. Guy, Cora, and Phyllis arrived at the door about the same time as we did. Dad opened the door just as another big blast rocked the peaceful summer morning followed in a minute by another blast that rattled the windows. Dad and Guy decided that it had to be a huge dynamite blast.

Dad said, "I would think it was something that could be attached to one of the mines around here, but the morning of July Fourth I rather think it was done for fun." With this settled we were all ready for pancakes.

In the afternoon us kids walked to Gibersons' and there we found out that the noise was dynamite that Chick Deming, Chuck Chamberlain, and one or more of the Giberson boys had shot off on top of the Piston Hill in Frisco. It was hard to believe that it was so loud at the Lusher Place coming from nearly three miles away. This turned out to be an annual function every Fourth of July that had been started by John Deming, Chick's dad, when he was a young man. The Deming and Giberson boys, with the help of others, kept this patriotic function going over the years.

In later years, Chick, Chuck, and Glen MacMasters continued the Fourth of July celebration until Elmer Swanson came to Frisco. Then he continued the fun with the help of his son Eddie, Hank Bradon, Glen MacMasters, and me.

One day we went to Breckenridge and to Tiger with our cousins. There was a partially sunken dredge in a lake at Tiger, having been abandoned several years earlier. We walked out on the dredge to get our pictures taken. There was a dredge working between Alma and Fairplay. Also a dredge was working three shifts between Breckenridge and Dickey on the Blue River.

***Dredge near Breckenridge. The tailings which are behind the dredge are river rock. The buckets that dig deep into the river bottom on the left are hoisted out of the water showing the dredge is shifting its location. An enclosed conveyor belt dumps the tailings at the rear.***

The dredge was a large boat which sat on a lake which it had created in a stream. It had a continuous bucket chain on the front that dug deep into the lake bottom, picking up bucket loads of rock and sand from the bottom of the lake. The rock and sand were processed, taking out gold, silver and several other metals. The tailings were then dumped in a pile behind the boat with a conveyor belt. The dredge moved forward digging the lake in the front and filling it up in the back. It would move forward very slowly, sometimes only a few feet a day. The only way to get on the dredge was by a gangplank, which was a narrow movable platform forming a bridge from the bank to the dredge. The rock piles can still be seen between Breckenridge and Frisco.

## SUMMIT COUNTY ANNEXED TO THE U. S.

On August 8, 1936, we went to Breckenridge for the annexing of over 1,300 square miles of "No Man's Land" to the United States. The area annexed was "peak to peak" (top of Loveland Pass, Hoosier Pass, Fremont Pass, and down the Blue River to near Green Mountain Reservoir). The land was missed during the survey for the annexation of the Louisiana Purchase. A Breckenridge ladies group found that this portion of Summit

County had never belonged to the U.S. and they immediately made plans for the annexation.

The United States Secretary of the Navy, Governor Edwin C. Johnson and other dignitaries were there for the occasion. All legal transactions were reaffirmed. The celebration was one of the biggest events to ever hit Summit County.

They had games for all different ages, and a big marching brass band from Denver added to the excitement. There was singing and of course the usual political speeches to celebrate the occasion. I was so excited while we all stood in the hot sun, after a cool morning rain, saluting the flag. Suddenly I felt faint, everything started to whirl around. I couldn't see very well and I couldn't keep my balance. I remember trying to keep standing up by hanging onto someone in the row in front of me. My legs gave out. As soon as I hit the ground I was all right, but Mom wouldn't let me play any games the rest of the day. A doctor was found in the crowd and checked me over and said I was all right. I probably got too excited with all the clamor of the event. How embarrassing!

Ken and Betty Chamberlain with their son Charles (Chuck) had come a long way since they lived in Kaiser where Ken operated a Caterpillar for a mine in Tiger. Betty worked for the mine-owned store. The mine shut down and the Chamberlains moved to Dillon where Ken hung out a mechanic's sign.

The Chamberlains bought lots in the lower part of Frisco where they built a one-room house and a small chicken house. When they were working on the new home, Chuck rode his donkey, Popcorn, yes, THE Popcorn, all the way to and from Frisco. After two years in Dillon they moved to their home in Frisco. There they had room for a cow and about two dozen chickens. A year after they moved to Frisco Chuck sold Popcorn to Bill Thomas for $15.00. He took the money and bought his mother a new washing machine which operated with a Briggs and Stratton gasoline engine.

Ken soon looked around for a place where he could have a mechanic's garage and living quarters. He rented a log building west of the Wortman Hotel. They remodeled the upstairs and moved in. They put in a gas pump and remodeled the bottom for a garage. They lived there a short time when the building was advertised for sale for taxes and Ken was able to buy the property.

## BILL THOMAS HIRES DARREL BAILEY

Bill Thomas gave room and board to a kid named Darrel Bailey to help him with the chores. The Bailey family had been richly blessed with many children, so when the opportunity arose for Darrel to leave home, the event was celebrated by both Darrel and his dad. Darrel's dad brought fresh vegetables to Frisco, Dillon, Kokomo, Robinson, and sometimes Slate Creek, going from door to door with his truck. He arrived from Denver every Tuesday afternoon. Staying all night at Mrs. Olson's, he would deliver in Frisco on Wednesday. This gave Darrel an opportunity to see his dad every week. If anyone wanted anything from Denver, Mr. Bailey would buy it and bring it up for a small charge.

During the summer the Bailey family stayed in one of Mrs. Olson's cabins at the Ten Mile River Bridge for a couple of weeks. There were twenty or twenty-one kids in the family.

Mrs. Olson's husband, Frank, had died before we arrived in Frisco. She was the school janitor and had several rentals which she rented whenever she could. She was a great person. Every kid in town liked her. She was of medium height, slender, and wore her long black hair in a bun. She always wore canvas shoes and had very long feet.

One time at school she was watching us kids put our skis on before we headed home and said, "I don't have to wear skis or snow shoes, I just wax the bottom of my shoes."

One of Darrel's chores was to deliver milk in Frisco. When school started Darrel rode Popcorn and delivered the milk before he went to school. Bill took several bales of hay and a five gallon bucket for water to the school and left them behind the outside toilets. When Darrel got to school he would feed and water Popcorn, put a halter on her and tie a rope from the halter to a tree. This gave Popcorn room to walk around and eat whenever she wanted to. The only drawback to this arrangement was that Popcorn would walk around and around and around the tree till she was nose to trunk against the tree. During the most severe part of the winter Darrel would leave Popcorn at the ranch and carry the milk to town. He delivered twice a week so it wasn't a daily chore.

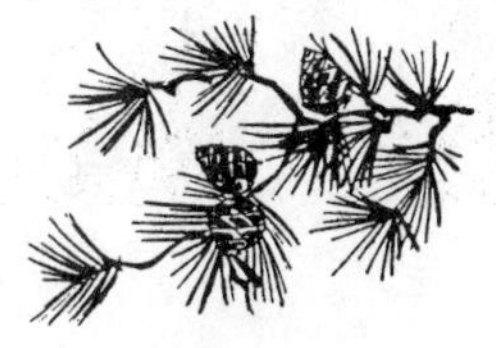

***The Matchless Mine ruins in Leadville***

# PART IV
# THE RUTHERFORD RANCH

*Meadow Creek Ranch, our new home.*

When school started in the fall of 1936 we had over a mile to walk through willows, aspens and evergreen trees to Frisco and across the Ten Mile River bridge by Mrs. Olson's. The aspen trees had just started turning to yellow with tinges of red, orange, and gold. When the sun set behind the mountains it was still shining on the slopes of the mountain tops. It sure was beautiful. I doubt that an artist could actually put this beauty on paper. Oftentimes I would stop and look at this beautiful sight. We saw deer nearly every day and once we saw several elk.

Our new school teacher was Miss Julia Wilson. She was a lot of fun and mingled with the people from Frisco. Right after school started she went to a potluck party at Gibersons' and met Otto Limpke from Alma, Colorado. They got married at Christmas but had to keep it a secret until school was out because, at that time, a teacher could not be married. We had a school picnic at the end of the year. A discussion came up about Miss Wilson's gaining weight over the winter and Tommy Giberson suggested she might be pregnant. Everyone was embarrassed, as we had not yet been told she was married.

In the fall of 1936 Dad purchased the vacant ranch called the Prestrud Place or Meadow Creek Ranch. Close to the house there was a beaver dam lake consisting of about four acres. Meadow Creek ran into the ranch on the west end and continued down through the middle of the ranch close to the east end where it turned north and ran into the Lusher Place. The creek was filled with small beaver dams. One large dam at the west end had a small stream flowing out of it and sort of paralleled the main channel of the creek. It had swamps and beaver ponds on it all the way to the Big Spring where it went underground into the Big Spring lake. We called the area between the creeks the island. It was a natural place to have for a pasture for the milk cows for overnight feeding.

The ranch house had been vacant for a number of years and all the doors, windows, and all of the flooring in the kitchen had been removed. There was a deep hole under the milk house and shed. The corner of the milk house had settled down in the hole for over a foot. Dad made a long pry pole from a lodgepole pine tree and put one end under the corner of the milk house and extended the other end out across a big rock. He persuaded Mom to sit on the end of the log raising the milk house up where it belonged. Mom sat on the log till Dad braced the corner. Later Dad laid a rock foundation under the shed.

***Who weighs the most?***

We papered all the rooms with orange or blue building paper. Dad put up shelves from the floor to the ceiling in two locations in the kitchen to act as kitchen cabinets. Mom made curtains to cover them. Dad built an outside toilet and then our efforts had to be turned to cutting wood for the soon approaching winter.

We got our drinking water from the Little Spring across the creek on the north side of the house. Cooking water, bath, and wash water came from Meadow Creek. Water was heated in a reservoir on the back of the cooking stove. It was my job to keep the reservoir filled with water from Meadow Creek. I also went to the spring for drinking water. Dean and the girls kept the wood box by the kitchen stove full of wood and kindling.

We didn't have electricity. We used kerosene lamps. One lamp was a large Aladdin lamp with a large mantle. It gave a very good light. We set it on a library table in the center of the living room so all the family could sit around it and have reading light at night. We had other lamps that sat in bowls with adjustable reflectors behind them. The bowl had an arm that fitted into a wall bracket. There were several brackets or hangers that we fastened on the wall in different locations in different rooms. This way we could move these lights to different places in the kitchen and living room. The bedrooms had kerosene table lamps. Lanterns served the barn and the milk house.

We sawed wood into stove lengths and then split the larger logs into stove-size pieces. Dead trees were in abundance around the ranch, so by late fall we had enough wood cut and piled up for all winter. We split pitch stumps for cold winter nights. The stumps burned slower than other fire wood and gave more heat. On a cold winter night we would put a stump in the stove just before going to bed. In the morning there would be enough hot embers in the stove to start the morning fire without kindling. The room would be fairly warm, providing you had never been exposed to some kind of circulating heat with which to compare.

The winter was filled with lots of fun. The Demings gave us several skis where one half of the pair was missing. We paired them up and made three pair of skis. Of course, they didn't match, but they were a far cry from the barrel skis I had built the year before. There was a hill at the back of the house where we were able to learn to ski, or at least be able to handle the skis. I built a small jump about one third of the way down the hill. I went down over the jump many times before I was able to ride down without falling.

After a big snow storm Dad would pack our trail to Frisco with his snowshoes. Where our trail crossed open areas the trail would often be lost with new or blowing snow. To take care of this we stuck willow stocks every thirty or forty feet in the snow. We walked right along the left side of the willows on top of our old trail going to town and on the right side of the willows going home. When Dad made two round trips to Frisco with his snowshoes, the fresh snow would pack well enough for us to walk on the snow without the aid of snowshoes.

When spring came our packed trail didn't melt nearly as fast as the unpacked snow. As the snow melted, in some places the trail was several feet higher than the unpacked snow beside it.

In the spring we skied to school rather than walk on the trail; however, the skis didn't pack the snow solid enough to walk on.

One Saturday Mildred and I went to Gibersons' to get a half gallon of milk. It cost ten cents a quart. When we left the Giberson house we went up a hill to a fairly level area that continued with a gradual climb all the way to the Lusher place. When we got upon the higher ground the road took us past a large pile of cut-up fire wood that was covered with two feet of snow. Looking it over I decided that I would climb to the top and slide off. A good idea maybe, but I should have given the bucket of milk to Mildred. I climbed on top, but when I slid down, the slope was too steep for me and I fell down right on top of the bucket of milk. Not only was my leg wet from the milk, but we didn't have any milk to take home. Back to Gibersons' house we went. Wib straightened the bucket out so the lid would go back on and Mollie gave us a new bucket of milk.

## WE BUILD A NEW ICE HOUSE

One Saturday Dad said, "Let's go to the timber behind the lake and cut some small poles and build a new ice house." There was an old ice house below the dam at the lake, but it was in very bad shape. It was nearly filled with sawdust. Dad cut down several trees around five inches in diameter and cut them up into eight foot lengths for framework. We tore down the old ice house and built the new one next to the pile of sawdust. Dad made a frame about eight feet by eight feet. Then we took the boards from the old ice house and nailed them on the outside of the framework. During the following week Dad put a roof on the shed and covered the inside walls with one-inch-thick edged slabs. (When sawing lumber, the first piece cut from the side of the log is called a "slab." A short piece is cut from each side of the slab to form a piece of lumber, flat on one side, and rounded on the other side, which still has the bark.)

Dad filled the cavity in the walls with sawdust for insulation. There was still a lot of sawdust left so we leveled the floor with about four inches of it. He built a new door on the side facing the dam. We made a temporary ramp that ran from the lake to the ice house.

When the ice on the lake was around sixteen inches thick we sawed several lines sixteen inches apart and twelve feet long. We then took a big pointed bar and stuck the ice to break it into 16" cubes. Then we slid the ice blocks down the ramp and into the ice house, placing the ice blocks all around the floor leaving two inches between them. When the floor was filled, we covered the blocks with the sawdust filling the spaces between the blocks of ice and adding about four inches on top. Then we laid another layer of ice blocks on the sawdust. In all we had four layers of ice blocks. We covered the top layer with several inches of sawdust. We had enough sawdust for the first year, but we would have to get some more sawdust during the summer. We used aged sawdust because new sawdust from green timber would mold, get hot, and possibly burn. We had all the ice we could use or sell during the next summer.

Several of the kids came over from town and helped clean the snow off the ice so we could have an ice skating party. After a couple of hours of skating we went into the house where Mom had cake and homemade ice cream. This turned out to be something we did many times during the winter.

When the ice became cut up and rough from ice skating or from melting snow we cut several holes in the ice and put a two by four board in the outlet headgate. This raised the water in the lake so water would boil out of the holes in the ice and soon cover the area we had cleaned off. As soon as the lake was covered with water we would remove the board to stop the water from coming out on the ice. We did this when it was clear and cold, and after only one cold night we would have mirror slick ice to skate on.

I spent a lot of my free time trapping snowshoe rabbits, which I sold to Frank and Annie Ruth for twenty five cents each. Mrs. Olson also bought rabbits from time to time. We sold the furs to Sears and Roebuck Co.

I split wood for Nettie Bailey, Hattie Lund, and Miss Badger for extra money.

Around the first week of March bluebirds would arrive. By the middle of April robins were singing their evening song. Many camp robbers (gray or Canada Jays) stayed all winter. They nested in the high mountains in snowbanks during February and early March. As soon as the ice and snow melted around the creek and beaver dams the blackbirds showed up. We loved to hear the spring song of the many birds after a winter of silence.

## CHAMBERLAINS OPEN FRISCO CAFE' IN SPRING, 1937

Ken Chamberlain remodeled the west side of the garage to accommodate a café. They opened the café for business in the spring of 1937.

Johnnie Nix was hired as a cook. Dade Ritter also worked as a cook when he and Billy Shoemaker weren't prospecting for gold.

Up to now, the only places in town where people could gather and visit were the Frisco Post Office or the Frisco Spring, but you had to stand up while you talked. At the café, you could sit down and talk over a cup of coffee and possibly a piece of pie or maybe a Saturday evening dinner. It was a big boost for the community. They were soon able to get the Rio Grande Trailways bus stop.

Not long after the Chamberlains opened the café, Mildred started working there as a waitress. She worked as much as she could during the years she was going to high school and several years afterwards.

One winter Ben Staley, using his team and sled, hauled ore for Dade Ritter and Billy Shoemaker from the Roe mine. He dumped it where they had built an ore bin on the edge of the Forest Service Road going up Meadow Creek where the trail takes off the road to Lily Pond. In the spring, the Chamberlains took their dump truck to the bin and hauled the ore to Leadville. Chuck said, "Boy, that sure was a lot of hard work, I must have shoveled at least a million tons of ore."

When spring came we bought two milk cows from Mr. Pruitt, a friend who lived in Palisade on the western slope. One cow was mine; I had made enough money through the fall and winter ($85.00) to pay for my cow. We named Dad's cow Aunt Clari. I couldn't think of a swell name to call my cow so she always went by the name of The Heifer.

They both had their calves shortly after they arrived. Dad had a welder make us two branding irons. The brand was "J R," Dad's initials. Shortly after we received the irons we discovered that they were built with the "J" reversed. It was easier to change the register at Breckenridge than to have them remade.

It was then necessary to do a little work in the barn and build a corral around it. Two owls took up quarters in the top of our barn. There was a platform we stood on when using a pulley to haul hay to the loft. This was a perfect place for a nest. One thing I couldn't figure out was why one owl would sit up in the barn at dusk and call out to her mate, "Who, who, who?" The mate would answer back, "Who, who, who?" Almost every night during the spring and fall they would converse. I doubt that they ever found an answer to their questions, but I loved to listen to them. Many times I would sit on the front porch and listen to them long after dark.

We spaded the ground on the southwest side of the barn and put in a garden. The garden was large enough for us to have all the vegetables we could use with some to sell in Frisco.

## AUNT CLARI CHEADLE

Aunt Clari was my Mother's double cousin. Mom insisted that we call her "Aunt" because she was Mom's age. Aunt Clari was a spinster school teacher. She taught school at Alma, Colorado. She loved music and always started an orchestra among the students as soon as she arrived at a school. At the end of each school year, she would arrive at our home for a visit and time to relax and rest. When we moved to our mountain ranch she continued to come and visit for a couple of weeks.

She colored her hair orange and sometimes the coloring would give her neck an orange cast. She did something to her eye lashes that made them look long and black. This might have worked on a younger lady, but was not very attractive on her. She was very kind to us, but was always reminding us that we shouldn't do this or that, or she knew a better way to do whatever we were doing. Even though our way had already proven to be a good way of handling the chore, we still had to try it her way.

She was a bit bossy, but then maybe we needed this special guidance when she came to visit.

She enjoyed our pranks and humor. Sometimes she would see through a prank and manage to turn it around so it would backfire on us, yet we looked forward to the time each year when she came to visit.

Some years later a friend of mine, Keith Lawrence, and I were talking. Since I knew he had gone to school in Alma, Colorado, for several years, I asked him if he remembered Aunt Clari Cheadle.

"Do I know her," he roared, "she taught me for two years and I spent more time sitting on a stool in the corner looking at the wall than I did at my desk."

When Aunt Clari would arrive at our house, Mom and Aunt Clari would tune everyone else out and it would take at least two long days for them to catch up all the news from each side. Aunt Clari didn't want to milk the cows, but she was always doing part of our other chores to give us more time to show her the sights. She went on many hikes with us. She didn't fish, but she went along and would cheer when we caught one. It seemed like a game with her to pull some prank on me, and I sure did my best to pull a prank on her every time she came to visit.

***Aunt Clari on a trip to Lily Pond***

## NEWLYWED HOSPITALITY

***Howard and Lura Belle Giberson in front of the Wib Giberson home.***

Howard Giberson courted a gal named Lura Belle who came with her folks to Ophir Lodge for a summer vacation from Michigan. In time they were married and moved to the Lusher Place. One evening after they were settled they invited us four kids over for cherry pie and homemade ice cream. This was great. We visited for a short time when Lura Bell dished us a generous piece of pie and a scoop of ice cream. It was delicious.

Howard was cutting up with Dean calling him Sy for fun when he noticed that Dean was having a problem cutting the pie crust so he asked, "Do you need a sharp knife?" Howard was trying to help Dean and at the same time not draw attention to a possibly tough pie crust when Dean, a smart-aleck nine-year-old, answered, "I don't think a knife will work; where do you keep the ax?" I think this could possibly hold a place in the Guinness Book of Records as the most embarrassing moment for Howard, Lura Belle and probably Mildred and me. Howard, after a long moment of silence, said, "Sy, pick it up with your fingers." I didn't know what to say and I felt sorry for Howard and Lura Belle after their neighborly kindness.

## BUILDING A GRAIN BOX

One evening as we sat down to do the milking Dad said, "Harold, the grain sacks have holes in them, and the grain is spilling out on the floor."

"I know," I said, "I've seen chipmunks and mice in the sacks almost every time I open the bags to get some grain."

Dad said, "After we're through milking, I'll show you how to build a grain box. I think maybe squirrels are also helping themselves to the grain, but with a grain box we can keep them all out."

After the milking, Dad showed me how to build a great big box. It would be big enough for us to put in five or six one hundred pound sacks of grain for the stock. I was excited; I always loved having a project to work on.

I got up early the next morning and right after breakfast I went to work on the grain box. Dad had me draw a picture of the box, showing the measurements. We didn't have electricity, and for that matter, we didn't have an electric saw, so I had to cut all my boards with a hand saw. My box turned out to be two feet six inches from front to back, three feet six inches high on the back side, three feet high on the front side, and eight feet long. I hauled all my lumber down to the barn before I started cutting up the boards. Two hours went by in about ten minutes.

Mom came down to the barn to see how I was doing. After she left I was sure I had her approval for my project. The only thing that bothered me was the fact that she wanted Dad to build the top, which would consist of three doors that would hinge in the back and lift up to get into the box. I wanted to build the total box all by myself.

I hardly had time for lunch, but when Dad came home from work in the evening, the box was done except for the top. I had it in place in the barn where we were enclosing an area to make a harness and grain room. Dad looked at my project before we sat down to do the evening milking.

Looking over the box Dad said, "Looks like a good job. I was thinking of something a little smaller but I am sure we will need all the room."

"Dad, I almost cut two feet off the end of it, but when I laid a board across where I was going to cut it, it looked too small."

"It is just the size we need; in the morning I will show you how to build the doors."

When I finished milking my cow I took another look at the box before I went to the milk house with the milk. Dad followed right after me.

Mom asked, "Russell, how does the box look?"

"Just what I wanted, Minnie. Harold did a good job building it."

After supper Dad and I went to the barn and put two sacks of bran and one sack of oats in the box. "This will be a lot better now, we won't have to worry about the stock getting into the grain or the little animals eating holes in the sacks," Dad said.

When we put the sacks of grain into the box, there was a

couple of chipmunks in one sack of grain. They left in a big hurry.

"Dad," I said, "I think we should get a cat."

"It sure wouldn't hurt anything," Dad replied, as we headed towards the house.

Dad helped me, or I helped Dad. Anyway, we got some nice doors built and installed on the top.

"Now, nothing can get inside the box."

## UNCLE LYNN RIDES THE NARROW GAUGE TRAIN

Right after school was out Uncle Lynn sent us a letter stating that he would be arriving at Bill's Ranch on Wednesday to visit us. He rode the narrow gauge railroad from Denver to Bill's corral where the train stopped and let him off. We were there waiting when the train came. This was exciting! When Uncle Lynn went back to Nebraska, we went with him to Bill's corral and waited for the train to come from the west. It wasn't long till the train appeared about a quarter of a mile away. The engineer gave a short whistle and Uncle Lynn waved his arm at him. The train gave a long whistle when it came to a stop where we were. Uncle Lynn climbed aboard and with a couple of short whistles the train took off. Uncle Lynn purchased a ticket at the next station which was at Dillon.

## OUR BOBCAT "TIM"

One day when us kids were down at Gibersons' Mrs. Giberson said, "Sue, why don't you show the kids the little kittens out in the barn?" Sue took us to the barn and there were four or five kittens about six weeks old. We picked them up and petted them. I told Sue that Dad had said that it wouldn't be a bad idea for us to get a cat. Sue liked the idea.

"Which one do you want?" she asked. I liked the gray and brown kitten with a short tail, but the girls wanted a white cat.

"Whoever heard of a white cat to keep in the barn?" I asked; but we finally settled on a white kitten which was a little larger than the rest. Also, he was the only one that had a long tail.

"What happened to the tails on the other kittens?" I asked.

"I don't know," Sue replied, "but they sure are cute. As soon as the kittens get a little larger you kids can take the white kitten home."

We rushed home to tell Mom we had a kitten we could bring home as soon as he got to be a little larger. Mom didn't seem to be too excited about the cat, but she said we should have one around the ranch.

Finally the kitten was old enough to take home. We fixed him a nice place to sleep in the barn and Mom gave us a dish for him to eat out of.

We came up with at least a million names for the cat, but "Tim" seemed to be right for him.

One evening in the early fall a mouse ventured out to have a look at the animal that had taken up quarters in the new grain room. The way Tim looked at him, I was afraid we would have to teach him how to catch a mouse. He just sat there licking milk off his paws. The mouse, thinking that he had the go-ahead, moved out a little closer, where he could get a better look at the cat. He stood on his hind legs and blinked his eyes as he looked right into the face of Tim. I thought that he was getting ready to speak, when all of a sudden Tim nailed him. Tim carried him to the middle of the barn and turned him loose. The mouse, not realizing what Tim had in mind, ran around in a circle and then right under Tim. Tim jumped in the air and came down beside the mouse. He grabbed him with one paw and played soccer ball with him tossing him back and forth between his paws and going right across the barn floor at a very fast pace. When he reached the wall at the far end of the barn, he tossed the mouse in the air and caught him as he came down, then he proceeded to play soccer ball with him going back across the barn. Then he let the mouse have his turn.

By this time, the mouse had decided that the cat was playing too rough for him and that at his first opportunity he would run away. Tim put him down and then turned and looked at the wall, as if to say, "I'll count to three while you are hiding and then I will look for you." The mouse started to run, hoping to make it to the back side of the grain box, but almost before he got his feet in motion Tim reached out with one paw and brought the mouse back in front of him. I walked over to where Tim was playing and, boy, did Tim get angry. He grabbed the mouse and let out a great big growl and headed for the barn door. Once outside he disappeared.

As fall approached, Tim seemed to grow into a big cat overnight. He was a good mouser and hadn't lived with us very long when the mice around the barn all seemed to disappear. Tim would chase a squirrel from time to time as if to say, "You had better stay out of my way."

Tim spent most of his nights in the barn, however, on a cold night or a real wet night we would let him sleep in the house.

During Tim's first winter he spent quite a little time in the house at night.

Tim was a very odd cat. When we fed him, he would drink his milk and eat certain things out of his dish, but when it came to meat he would take the meat outdoors and disappear to eat it.

He would eat leftover pancakes for his breakfast. Dad would give him about a fourth of a large pancake and he would take it behind the wood box, or possibly under the cook table to eat it. After his breakfast any leftover pieces were broken up and put on the back porch for camp robbers. As soon as the pancakes arrived on the porch Tim would want outside. He would lie down by the pancakes, keeping the birds from eating the pieces. We finally had to put him in the barn or refuse to let him outside till after the birds had hauled away the pancakes. Sometimes I am sure he just wanted to terrify the birds. After the food was all gone he would want back into the house. Every once in awhile he would catch a camp robber and we would spank him for it. He soon learned to defend himself; if you slapped him for doing something he would growl and sometimes scratch at you. He had a mind of his own and wasn't going to be intimidated by anyone.

One time when I was headed home from Frisco, I met Tim headed towards town. I stopped and petted him and picked him up and took him back home. We kept him in the house for awhile and then he wanted out. I took him to the barn and locked him in. Next thing I knew Tim was going out of sight down the road towards town. I called him and then chased him, never catching up to him. I went to the barn to try and see where he got out. I didn't find out till some time later when I put him in the barn and within two or three minutes he had climbed up into the loft and gone out the loft door and down the side of the log barn to the ground. Then off he went. I think he had a heavy date and wasn't going to be late. All spring he dined and entertained the lady cats of Frisco.

I can just picture him going to the back of a house where there was a lady cat and "meow" saying, "I'm out here, come out and we can play for awhile."

We also found some other strange things about him. When the summer days came, us kids played hide and seek in the yard. During that time Tim had to be kept in the house because he, for some reason, would not let us run in the yard. Whenever we would start to run he would run after us and jump on our backs, scratching and biting.

During the summer he would be gone on a safari for several days at a time. We wouldn't know for sure if he went hunting on the mountain, or if he was over at town courting his girlfriends. One time I did see him on the south side of Frisco up by Rainbow Lake. This was a long way from home. We lived a mile north of Frisco and Rainbow Lake was around two miles south.

The second year that Tim lived with us, several cats in Frisco turned up with bob-tailed kittens. By this time he was a lot larger than any house cat.

## SUMMERTIME

Dad bought a cream separator we had to crank by hand. This was usually the girls' job. After we got the separator we sold cream and butter in Frisco. Even though Frisco was small in size there was always room for one more person to sell their products.

There was lots of work to do around the ranch, but I found time to build a raft. I cut down four dead trees eight to ten inches in diameter; then I cut them into eight foot lengths. I spaced them a little over a foot apart and nailed a two by six board on each end. I nailed one inch boards across the logs between the two by six ends. This made a nice raft. I made a pole out of a green tree about ten feet long and about two inches in diameter. This was to propel the raft in the water as there was no current in the lake.

Dad helped us put the raft in the water. It would hold all four of us kids at one time without sitting too deep in the water. We played on the raft all summer and in the fall we pulled it out of the water and set it on some pieces of wood to keep it off the ground during the winter. It also made a good platform to fish off of.

Our irrigation water came from North Ten Mile River through a ditch that emptied into Meadow Creek, where the Forest Service road went up the mountain. We could then take the water out of Meadow Creek to irrigate with. There were over two miles of ditch to maintain, removing any debris which might keep the water from running during the summer. We also had to open up the old ditches on the meadows and make several new ones. We needed a new ditch that would carry the water to a high spot on our lower meadow. Dad surveyed for a new ditch lateral off the main ditch through the timber to the highest spot on our lower meadow. He fastened his two foot level to a tripod using C clamps. When it was level he looked across the top to a distance that he could clearly see and had me move a pencil up and down on a tree trunk to the spot he was looking at and pound a nail at the mark. Then he would move the tripod to the new spot and repeat

***The diving board and raft on our lake.***

this procedure till we were through the timber and on the highest area of the meadow. When we were finished we knew just where to dig the ditch.

Dad borrowed a team of horses from Gibersons and plowed the ditch around to the high spot. It seemed great when we opened the ditch at the upper end and watched the water flow for several hundred yards to the dry area of the meadow.

We called our meadows the lower meadow, the lake meadow (at the house), and the second meadow, which served as a good pasture for our milk cows. One year we planted our potatoes in one corner of the second meadow. We put a fence around the patch to keep the cows out. The potatoes needed a longer growing season than many summers provided so we covered the potatoes with grass during the night in the spring and in the fall to protect them from the frost. It was a chore to rake the grass off of the potatoes each morning and cover them up at night, but we were able to grow all the potatoes we needed.

During the summer we cut up enough wood to last us all winter. This was my main job. I would drag in dead wood from all around the place and pile it up near the wood shed. I cut some nearly every day, but in the fall we had to finish cutting the winter's supply.

Since the ranch hadn't been occupied for many years, the fences were nearly all down around the place. Dad brought home several rolls of barbed wire from Pete Lege's store in Dillon. Some places we built a four-wire fence. Other places only needed repair to the existing wire. We built the fences inside the ranch out of wood bucks and wood rails or poles.

In June, 1937, Bill and Nellie's mother Jane Thomas died and was buried in Frisco. Her passing left a vacancy in the mountain town. The following year Nellie married Dan Mogee.

***Nellie and Bill Thomas and their mother, Jane***

## THE TRAINS STOP RUNNING

On October 7, 1937, the trains stopped running. I hated to see this happen, but it cost the railroad too much money to operate after the mines shut down and the logging operations nearly stopped. A short time later the rails were removed.

From then on, the mail had to come to Frisco from Kremmling. A pickup hauled the mail to Dillon, Breckenridge, Frisco, Kokomo, and Robinson; and then back to Frisco, Dillon, and Kremmling. It was reported that a letter from Frisco to Kokomo would take five days for the eighteen mile trip.

## A DIVING BOARD FOR THE LAKE

Many times during the summer Tommy Giberson, Neil Westlake, Glen and Millet MacMasters, and other kids came to the ranch for an afternoon swim. We needed a diving board. I found a plank twelve feet long, twelve inches wide and almost three inches thick at the back side of the wood shed. I dragged it to the lake and made us a diving board. This worked fine for some time.

One morning I went to the garden by the lake and discovered our diving board was missing. I couldn't imagine what could have happened to it. I looked everywhere but it was nowhere to be found. When Dad came home I told him about the missing diving board.

Dad said, "I have an idea what happened to it. After supper we'll go look for it. I'm betting that a beaver spotted the board and hauled it off for some reinforcing in a dam."

After dinner we all walked around the lake where we could go without getting our feet wet. Dad went to the upper end of the lake that was hidden from view by willow bushes. Close to where Meadow Creek ran into the lake Dad spotted the plank. It was floating in deep water about twenty feet from shore. There were willow bushes growing in the shallow water along the bank making it hard to see and harder to retrieve. Mildred went to the barn for a rope while Dad and I tried to use a long dead tree to reach out to the plank. By the time we were able to get the end of the tree out to the plank it was too heavy to hold up. Using the rope and a long pole, we were able to guide the plank to shore. When I found time to reset the plank in its earlier setting, I took some bridge nails and nailed the back end to some stakes three inches in diameter that I drove into the ground. I also took some bailing wire and wired the back end to several galvanized pipes driven into the ground. My prevention of beaver stealing worked pretty good. However, about a year later, I was down at the lake and discovered the beaver had gnawed the diving board nearly in two. He didn't take it, but gave me notice that he would take the board if he wanted to. It was at this point that I seriously thought about going into beaver trapping.

## CHICKENS AND RABBITS

Dad bought one hundred baby chicks and then in about a month he ordered another hundred. The chicken house became the east one fourth of a long shed that faced the southeast. When the chickens grew up we kept a dozen hens and a couple of roosters for eggs and an alarm clock.

We also bought six New Zealand White rabbits and built hutches in a column next to the chickens. The hutches backed up to each other with a common wall between them. Later we bought White and Steel Flemish Giant rabbits. The Flemish were big rabbits, weighing up to as much as twenty pounds. These rabbits were raised to sell for breeding stock, but occasionally we sold some for meat. We sold registered rabbits to people in several different states, including a couple of young boys in Rhode Island.

The rest of the shed was a calf shed. The shed was ten feet high in front, seven feet high in the back, and sat three feet into the side of a hill with a grass roof. Every fall we took a hayrack load of slough grass and covered the roof another six inches. We cut the slough grass with a scythe in open spots along the creek. By spring the six inches packed down to two inches. Cutting the grass with a scythe was a lot of work but the ground was too soft and muddy to use a horse drawn mower, even if we had been able to get the mower around the willows.

## DAISIES FOR A WEDDING

In July and August the edges of the meadow by the house were lined with white daisies. There were daisies blooming everywhere you looked. Mr. Wildhack came to the house and asked if he could pick enough daisies for his daughter Mattie's wedding. We all helped him pick all the flowers he wanted. Mattie was marrying Alex England at Ophir Lodge on July 5th. Mom rounded up a bushel basket and we filled it to almost overflowing. Mr. Wildhack at first thought he could carry them loose back to Frisco, but when we picked them he could barely reach around them. I took one side of the basket and Mr. Wildhack took the other side and we carried the flowers to Frisco. Our allergies sure got bad as we walked along the dusty road with a bushel basket of daisies!

In the late summer we had chickens and rabbits, also onions, radishes, carrots, turnips, beets, and head lettuce ready to sell in Frisco. We took vegetables to Frisco twice a week and took orders for rabbits, chicken fryers, cream, butter, and block ice.

We used Bill Thomas's price of ten cents per quart of milk, but when the government put regulations on the milk we raised our price to twelve cents per quart. "Big Mae" Nickelson, who had a ranch on the Blue River below Dillon, said, "I quit selling milk when the 'giverment' required toothbrushes and mirrors in each stall for the milk cows."

In the fall, Mr. Pruitt came by from Palisade and left several bushels of peaches on his way to Denver. He took several crates of our head lettuce with him to sell in Denver.

Dad said, "I want to buy several milk cows. Do you know anyone who has some for sale?"

Mr. Pruitt replied, "I do. I have one cow left that I want to sell. She is a good one, a Holstein and Guernsey mix. She's a very good milk producer and will be fresh (have a calf) in the early spring. Also, my neighbor is selling all his cattle. There are several good milk cows plus some Herefords in his herd."

Dad bought Mr. Pruitt's cow plus two of his neighbor's cows. They were all to come fresh in the spring.

# *PART V*
# *EIGHTH GRADE*

# That Little Log School House

I am dreaming tonight of a school house of logs
Set deep in the Rockies, out west,
Where nobody thought of wearing swell togs,
And each guy was as good as the best.

Where are those youngsters I used to know
Tommy, and Neil and Bill?
I can still see their names all carved in a row,
And in dreams hear their feet on the sill.

It was Mildred I loved, sweet, blonde, and tall
Then Helen so helpful and kind;
But I'm sure it was Thelma I loved most of all
Though I don't think I once crossed her mind.

One teacher stands out in my mem'ry the best,
He was lean, and bronzed, and young.
He always took part in the games with the rest,
And led all the songs that we sung.

The old square piano he played real keen,
When we sang every morning at nine,
With Harold, and Larry, Millet and Dean,
Always one out of tune - or line.

Those brown seats and desks just numbered a score,
Most of them ink stained and worn,
(Up in the attic were stored many more)
Where they looked like my heart feels, forlorn.

On white walls the presidents all were arranged,
Through the doorway our flag was unfurled,
But Oh! how our loves and our lives have changed,
Yes, changed like the map of the world.

Children no longer rush out through the door,
And the bell is silent at morn,
The Clock on the wall doesn't tick any more,
It's hands, like my own, are worn.

Yes, I'm dreaming tonight of a school house of logs,
Nestling deep in the Rockies out west,
And I'd rather be there with my youth and old togs,
Than be President Roosevelt's guest.

Lillian MacMasters, Used by permission.

In the fall of 1937 school again was started with another new teacher, Rose Mary New. Some of the kids from town were over to our ranch to swim and said the new teacher had arrived. I got on my bike and rode to town to see what she looked like. She was standing in front of the school talking to a school board member, Charlie Turner. I rode right on by, but I got a pretty good look. I went about a block on up the street, turned around and came back by. There was a slow grade downhill so I didn't have to pedal. My second look was the same as my first look. She was tall, old, red headed, and skinny as a rail fence. She wore a beautiful red dress which of course clashed with her hair.

School started with 20 students with one or more kids in the first through the tenth grades. What a task to teach (or attempt to teach) this many grades with only one teacher.

Work had started on building Green Mountain Reservoir. Climax was expanding the Molybdenum Mine and this brought several new families to Frisco. Also road work from Frisco to the Vail Pass turnoff was in progress.

The first day, Rose Mary New introduced herself and had each student stand and give their name and address. Most of the kids gave the address, just Frisco. I was glad I could say Meadow Creek Ranch. There were four of us starting the eighth grade: Shirley Hockley, Neil Westlake, Betty Garner, and myself. Mrs. New reassigned our seats so classmates would be close to one another. This was understandable.

The next thing on the schedule was to get our books which were furnished by the school. I think Bill Thomas used the same books I was using thirty five years later. In my class there were not enough books for each of us to have our own book in several subjects.

Mrs. New said, "Harold, you and the dark-haired girl will have to share some of the books. When one of you finishes the lesson, pass the book to the other one." Later I found out the dark-headed girl was Betty Garner.

She continued, "Whenever a class has completed a lesson, one of you hold up your hand and I will listen to you recite. I don't care what subject you study first, just so you study each subject."

I could see some real problems with this arrangement but I didn't say anything.

She continued, "I want all of you to check your ink wells and be sure you have ink. If you don't, raise your hand and I will come to your desk and fill your ink well. All tests will be written

***Frisco School House***

in ink so there will be no changing your answer when you look at your neighbor's paper."

One midmorning, Shirley held up her hand without consulting the rest of the eighth grade, and Mrs. New went to her desk and asked, "What subject do you want to recite in this morning?"

Shirley responded, "English," which was a subject I had not even looked at!

I spoke up and said, "Teacher, I am not ready to recite in English."

Mrs. New said, "Call me Mrs. New and you can stay in during recess and get your lesson." I hoped this was not a picture of the rest of the year.

Mrs. New asked Shirley a couple of questions and went back to her desk. Betty gave me her English book along with a paper with the questions Mrs. New had asked and the answers Shirley had given.

At recess, I held up my hand and Mrs. New said, "I will listen to you recite after recess is over." I sat there wondering what excitement, if any, was going on outside.

When recess was over, I again held up my hand and said, "I'm ready with the English lesson."

Mrs. New came to my desk and asked, "Did you read the lesson?"

"Yes, I did, and I also read the next chapter."

"It is a good thing you did, or I would have to give you an F," she said as she walked back to her desk.

I thought to myself, "How does she know if I really read the lessons?"

Shirley had not understood that we would all recite as a class. Neil and Betty got off easy since neither of them had studied the English lesson. At noon, the four of us got together and decided that, in the future, we would all try to study the same lesson so we could recite together. Later, however, the girls told Mrs. New that they wanted to move along faster in some subjects and requested that we all be allowed to recite separately.

"Won't do no hurt a-tall, a-tall," she said as she walked back to her desk. This left me free to work on the subjects I enjoyed: arithmetic, algebra, geometry, music, art, and caricatures. Caricature models were in abundance in that one room school. My favorite model was the one behind the desk up front. This provided me with many hours of intense concentration.

## SCHOOL BELL SURPRISE

As the school dismissed for the afternoon recess period, I couldn't believe how all the fun and excitement of summer vacation had ended and everyone seemed to be bored — even half sleepy! Not one kid wanted to get a game going. I went into the building and found the teacher so engrossed in a book that she didn't realize recess period should have ended nearly an hour earlier.

I went back outside to try again to energize the kids. One friend told me there would be no fun or excitement until Halloween. I looked up at the school bell and a terrific idea came to my mind.

More than once I had witnessed the teacher pulling the rope so hard the bell would swing back and forth a time or two and stop wrong side up. It would take a hard pull on the rope to get the bell to turn back over. I smiled as I imagined what would happen if I could fill the bell with water.

I went inside the back room and up the stairs to the front of the attic, where the bell rope came down to the lower room. I looked over the project that was now about to be born. The hole in the ceiling for the rope was smaller than I had hoped for. However, with a little work, I built a temporary wall around the hole to hold most of the water for a short time, using some short pieces of wood and several rags that were lying around in the attic.

Having accomplished the first phase of this project I went downstairs and outside using the back door. Several kids were throwing rocks at a can behind the school. Getting their attention, I said, "You may want to be here around eight thirty in the morning when the teacher rings the bell!"

Just then, the teacher came alive and called us in from our recess period one hour and thirty minutes late.

When school ended for the day, did I get the questions!

"What's going to happen?"

"Who told you?"

"I don't believe it!"

At least I had generated a lot of excitement.

"Just be at school at 8:30 and you will find out," I said as I crossed the river bridge and headed home.

After supper, I took a water bucket and some rope and returned to school. I leaned the school ladder against the roof. I filled the bucket about half full of water from the school pump and tied the rope to the bucket. I took the other end of the rope and climbed up the ladder. It took a little work to get to the belfry, but I finally made it. I turned the bell upside down and balanced it, then pulled the bucket of water up and poured it into the bell. It took another trip to the pump to get enough water.

I hurried home and spent a sleepless night anticipating the coming event.

I was early for school, as were about half of the students. About 8:40 a.m., being late as usual, the teacher left her desk and hurried to the back to ring the 8:30 bell.

She broke the silence by saying, "That's strange, the rope on the bell is shorter than usual this morning. She managed to reach high enough to grab the end of the rope and give it a hard tug.

It was even more exciting than I had expected. The water seemed to have grown since the night before. The teacher was drowned! Her curly, red-dyed hair was hanging straight, her dress was soaked and water was dripping from the hem. She looked a mess! Needless to say, she went home to change clothes and redo her hair before returning.

Just eight days later, half the students arrived again before 8:30 which was very unusual, and, again, the rope was shorter than usual.

Now, what would you have done, had you been in her place? Even as a youngster, I thought I would have suggested that one of the students pull the rope while I stood back out of the way! But, no, she walked right over, stretched to reach the rope, and gave it a yank. Nothing happened.

"Sometimes the bell is hard to start," she said, and gave it another yank, and, oh, my, it happened again. The teacher was all covered with water, and water was all over the floor. Again the teacher went home for a much needed change of clothes. Several girls mopped up the water before the teacher came back.

When Mrs. New got back, she said, "If any of you kids know where the water came from, come to my desk and tell me."

My heart sank when one kid said, "You might have left the bell turned upside down and a driving rain from the west probably filled the bell with water." She didn't pursue the questioning and no one suggested that I might know something about it.

For a while I put out a bi-monthly, one-page newspaper, circulation three copies, called "The Foo Town News." I put in ads, the latest gossip, coming attractions, and the rest of the sheet was filled with my cartoon characters. Oftentimes, I would include a caricature of some individual (usually Mrs. New!). The cartoons were sometimes issued in color created with my set of eight crayons. Occasionally, one copy would come up missing and I would have to produce a replacement.

Once in awhile, when I was studying civics, a sudden inspiration for a cartoon would come to mind. Not having paper available at that instant, I would use the margin of the book. Betty and I shared this particular book and more than once Betty laughed out loud when she came across one of the cartoons. That assured me that the picture was worth reproducing.

Neither of us could recite from that book as, on one occasion, I handed Mrs. New the book (to recite) before I remembered my artwork in the margins! When she saw one cartoon, she quickly leafed through several pages and found more cartoons, at least one of which had her name under it.

She gasped, "Fan me before I fall through the floor." Up jumped Chuck Chamberlain, only too happy to oblige her, grabbed a book and fanned her! This cost me at least a week of lost recess time and caused me to get an "F" in Deportment. During recess periods I had to erase all my art work from the book.

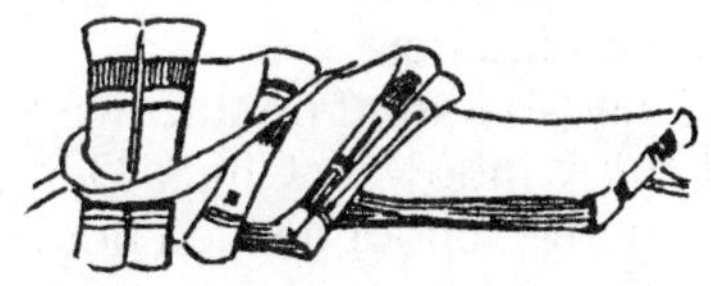

## SKUNK? OH, YES!

One day when I had my face buried in my Civics book, drawing my artwork under the pretense of reading, I smelled a skunk — not something Mrs. New was up to, but a real skunk. It not only seemed like it was in the school, but it was so bad that the smell could have suffocated the skunk. I looked around and everyone in the school was looking up.

Mrs. New came alive and went to the window and said, "I think there's a skunk around here."

Everyone agreed, and in a short minute every kid in the school was looking out of the windows. Chick Deming appeared on main street walking by the school headed home. About an hour after he passed the school the smell seemed to weaken. When Chick's nephew, Neil Westlake, went home he found out what caused the smell.

Chick had caught a skunk in a trap up by the Frisco Depot. After he was nicely perfumed by the skunk, he killed him and put him in his backpack and took him home hoping for a couple dollars for the pelt. When he got home there was a welcoming committee, but not the committee that he had hoped for. His clothes were removed and buried in the yard a long distance from the house. He took several baths and when the smell persisted he bathed himself in his sisters perfume, to no avail. Chick now became the resident of their bunkhouse. Food and water were handed in the door and he wasn't allowed even to breathe on the generous person who so kindly delivered his food to him. Six weeks later he was allowed in the house after a sniffing committee examined him and pronounced him odorless. I never heard what Chick did with the skunk or the pelt.

## THREE MICE IN THE TEACHER'S DESK

Early one morning I was awakened by Dad and Mom moving around in the kitchen. I didn't want to get out of bed till the house was warm.

I had just about gone back to sleep when Dad yelled, "Time to get up, boys." I dressed in the living room beside a cold heating stove. I went to the kitchen and filled the wash pan with lukewarm water from the reservoir on the back of the kitchen stove. After washing up I went to the barn ahead of Dad and put grain in the boxes in the stalls for the milk cows. This was like candy to the cows and it worked like a charm to get each cow to go into her stall as soon as we opened the stanchions. When each cow was in place, I closed the stanchions. This locked their heads in place so they couldn't back out while we were milking.

When I filled a coffee can with grain from an extra sack in the grain room, I saw a mouse in the sack. On a little closer observation I could see there had been more than one mouse in the sack. After the milking was done I looked around for a mouse trap. Not one could be found. I couldn't help wondering why Tim didn't get the mice. Then it occurred to me that I could kill two birds with one stone. I went to the house and found an empty kitchen match box. Just what I needed for a little school project. After breakfast I took the box and went to the barn. It didn't take very long for me to catch three mice that were trying to hide in the sack of grain. I put them in the match box and put the box in my things to take to school. I put our cat Tim in the barn and opened the grain room door wide enough for the cat to go in and out. I was sure if he didn't catch any mice that were left, he would terrorize them till they died of fright.

It had been less than a week since I had told Mrs. New I had seen signs of mice in the back room at the school. She said, "Harold, there are no mice back there and I doubt that there ever were any, you just want to get out of studying."

I gave up on the job, but someone needed to remove all the books from their shelves and boxes and clean the place. The mice had shredded several books. There needed to be a few more shelves built and then all the books on shelves replaced, throwing away all the damaged books and boxes. Of course this would have to be done during school hours.

When I got to school I waited till Mrs. New went to the back of the one room school to ring the nine o'clock bell. This worked out fine, I opened the box and let the mice out in her top desk drawer. Then I took my seat as usual. I studied hard, but I kept an eye open every time the teacher opened the center drawer to her desk. The day went by and not a sign of the mice. I was sure the teacher opened the drawer at least five times.

Another day went by and not a sign of the mice. I was afraid they would soon leave to look for food and water, but my only hope was that they might find the teacher's lunch. She usually put it in the drawer that had now become the home of three mice.

It was winter time, but the cold and snow didn't stop most of the kids from going outside during recess period and at noon time. I suddenly felt that I just couldn't take part in the outside activities. I sure wanted to see the excitement if it ever took place.

I wanted to tell all the kids what I knew, but if I did I knew some one would let the cat out of the bag and I would get another F in deportment.

Another day was ushered in and still no sign of the mice. I had about decided that I would have to do this job over again when there was a terrifying scream. I looked up and Mrs. New was on top of her desk in a sitting position. I can't imagine how she got up there so fast and without moving a muscle. It had been only a moment ago that I had looked up as I turned a page in my civics book. At that time she was sitting there engrossed in her reading. I followed a couple of kids to the front of the room to help her.

After stuttering a little and gasping for air she finally said, "There's a mouse in my desk drawer." To add misery to the event the mouse was in her little package of cookies.

When Darrel opened the drawer a little wider the mouse decided that it was best to leave the area. Not giving any regard to the distance to the floor, he jumped out of the drawer and hit the floor running. A fast survey of the area told him there was room to go under the door to the back room which he executed without any delay.

I helped Darrel take the drawer outside to get rid of the rest of the mice, if any. We found one mouse hiding under a pile of papers. We let him go his own way in the snow. I don't know what happened to the third mouse.

When we went back into the school room Darrel put the desk drawer back in the desk minus the pile of papers. Mrs. New was now standing up on her desk.

She said in a very frigid tone, "Harold, go to the back room and get a chair for me to get off the desk."

I rushed to the back room to get a chair. I looked and looked for a chair with a broken leg, but I finally had to settle for a sound one.

Darrel and I helped her down and when she looked into the drawer she said, "What happened to the papers that I had in my desk and where is my bag of cookies?"

Darrel, noting that I was not in a position to talk for fear of laughing said, "There were mouse droppings in the cookies and we had to throw most of the papers out because the mice had shredded them." The real reason was some of the papers had pictures I had drawn of the teacher. I thought the pictures looked just like her, but on another occasion I lost my recess periods for a couple of days because she didn't think my drawings resembled her. It was hard to be a cartoon artist in a school that had a teacher who confiscated your art work.

A member of the school board, Charlie Turner, brought up a couple mouse traps for the teacher to rid the place of the mice. Her scream had frightened the living mice around the school so bad that at least a month passed before a mouse ventured back into the building and was promptly executed in a trap.

## SOME OF TIM'S SHENANIGANS

One evening our family was all gathered in the living room for a family get together and entertainment. Entertainment was usually playing music, reading, and maybe playing a card game together. Tim wasn't usually invited to this affair.

We borrowed sheet music from Sue Giberson. Sue would buy the sheet music and after she had played it for awhile she lent it to Mildred and me. We went to Gibersons' and picked up the music. After we were through with it we took it back and traded it for more.

When the evening's entertainment was over and everyone was headed to bed, Dad called from the back bedroom, the folks bedroom, and said, "Harold, don't forget to remove the seat in the rocker before you blow the lights out."

I took the seat out of the rocker and leaned it against the wall. It was a cold winter night and Tim was spending the night in the house. Dad had removed the screws from the seat on the rocker so we could take the seat out when we went to bed. This would keep Tim from sleeping on the rocker seat, leaving hair on it. I went to bed. Presently I heard Tim in the living room. I looked out of my bedroom door just in time to see Tim jump up into the chair, or so he thought. Up he jumped and went right through the seat area and landed on the floor. He just stood there a minute under the chair growling and growling. He didn't try to see what had happened, he turned around and headed back to the kitchen where he had a nice bed all fixed up. I would love to know what he said, but then if I knew, I would have wanted to wash out his mouth with soap and water and that might have been very hard to do.

When the snow got deep, we had to use skis or snowshoes to go to Frisco. We usually would use our skis, even if the trail was packed enough for us to walk without them. On several occasions in the evening I would be heading to Frisco on my skis and find Tim on the trail. He would almost always refuse to jump out of the trail to let me go by. One time he jumped on one of my skis as I slid by him on the trail. I am sure it was the only place for him to go unless he got off the trail into the deep snow. I nearly fell when I suddenly had this heavy weight on my ski. He must have weighed around twenty pounds. He didn't jump right off as I expected him to. We traveled quite a little distance before he decided to abandon ship.

This opened a new thrill that we could give him. I would grab him and hold him on a ski and slide down the hill behind the house. He soon seemed to like it or at the least decided that he would humor me. Several times that winter he jumped on my ski when I was skiing on the trail towards town. Whenever I could, I would pick him up and park him on my ski. I might have thought he was too scared to move anticipating what was ahead, but knowing Tim and his attitude and temper, he would do just what he wanted in any situation.

One evening I came home from school and decided I would do a little ski-jumping, on the jump I had built behind the house, before it was time to do the milking. I fastened on my skis and stepped out on the packed snow in the yard. Here came Tim. A thought entered my mind. I picked him up and headed to the back of the house. I got all set and ready to go down the hill. Instead of going alongside of my jump I decided it would be a thrill for Tim if I took him over the jump. I set him on my ski right in front of my foot and held him there as we started down the hill. He tried to abort his part of the trip right after we started down, but I held him there till I had to make my jump. Over the jump we went, Tim growling all the way down the hill. I landed and I was barely able to keep from falling. Tim was on his own. As I made my jump he made a better and longer jump than I did.

When he landed in the snow I couldn't see him for a minute. He worked his way back to the packed snow, and back up the hill to the house he went.

When I got back to the house, Tim was nowhere to be found. He came in late for his dinner and growled at me when I tried to pet him. I wanted him to go to the barn for his night's sleep as I didn't want him lurking around the house, nursing a grudge, while I was asleep, but he stayed in.

## I THREW THE CLOCK

It was one of those long dreary days at school. Buffalo and Peak One were obscured from view, proclaiming the approaching snowstorm. The lamps had to be lighted before noon. It seemed like the day would never end. Shirley asked Betty if we could find a subject that we could recite in and that would help use up part of the day. Betty and I discussed the situation at hand and decided to bypass the recitation for the day. It soon would be time for the afternoon recess and that would be a welcome break.

Glen MacMasters, whose seat was in the back of the room, entertained several of the kids around his desk by trying to pull his own head off. I passed a note back to him and suggested that he try screwing his head off. Back came a note saying that he would try but he didn't know which way to turn it.

While this was going on Millet, Dean, and Tommy were having a competition trying to see who could stick the most spit wads to the ceiling with a rubber band.

I went up to the teacher's desk to sharpen my pencil. While I was cranking on the sharpener Glen pointed to the clock making signs to turn the clock around so he could see what time it was. I picked up the clock and threatened to throw it at him. He cradled his hands together as if he would catch the clock, so I had no alternative but to throw it. It was a perfect throw, but the teacher looked up while the clock was in mid-air. Glen, seeing the situation, quickly dropped his hands behind his desk so the teacher couldn't see he was the designated catcher. The clock sailed on by him and hit the wall at the back of the room with a great big crash. This alerted everyone in the room that something was in the making or had been made and failed. The glass front on the clock popped off and shattered all over the floor. One hand departed in one direction and one leg took off in the other direction.

Mrs. New jumped to her feet and rushed to the back of the room. She stood there looking at the floor and shaking her head. She said, "Fan me before I fall through the floor."

Up jumped Chuck and again did his best to fulfill her request. By this time I realized I was in a very bad situation. The only thing that I could do was to ease back to my desk and hope that she hadn't noticed me as she rushed to the back of the room. Several other kids gathered around her and one kid picked up the clock, or what was left of it, and handed it to her. Another kid retrieved the leg and one hand and gave them to her. She just stood there looking at the remains.

I opened my math book and quickly put a couple of equations on my paper. I looked back to see how things were going and the teacher was still standing there with the clock in her hand.

"I just can't figure out how this could have happened," she said.

Someone yelled, "It's time for afternoon recess." In the absence of a watch or clock, Mrs. New dismissed the school for recess period. It was just as well, though, as every kid in the school was gathered at the back of the room to see what had happened.

A thought entered my mind. I jumped up and ran to the front of the school room and picked up a dustpan and a broom that was kept there to clean the snow off your feet in case you went outside to the outhouse during school hours. I proceeded to sweep up the broken glass and ignore the many questions that were asked by some of the sleeping pupils that didn't see what was going on. According to my watch, recess turned out to be thirty minutes instead of fifteen.

My reliable time piece was a pocket watch that Dad had given me. Beginning when I was six or seven years old I was the proud recipient of Dad's old pocket watches when they stopped working. I always had several watches around. I would clean them and take parts from one watch and put on another. I always wore a dependable pocket watch which came in handy at this particular time. Dad bought most of his watches for a dollar each.

The hand bell rang, ending recess period. Mrs. New took her place at the front of the schoolroom and demanded, "I want someone to tell me just how the clock got to the back of the room."

Millet, bless his heart (and give him an "A" for effort), said, "I think the clock had been hanging on the wall in the location where it fell and probably the nail that it was hanging on got tired and let go, causing the clock to fall to the floor."

"Fan me before I fall through the floor," exclaimed Mrs. New.

The alert and always ready to help Chuck jumped up and rushed to her side and again fanned her as if he were afraid she really would fall through the floor.

"I'm sure the clock was on my desk at noon and who would put it on the back wall anyway?" she asked, with a lot of ice in the tone of her voice.

Another, not overly bright, kid said, "I looked up from my book just in time to see the clock flying through the air heading towards the back wall." This drastically reduced the chances for an argument that someone had hung the clock on the back wall. Another kid held up his hand and proceeded to tell Mrs. New what he thought he knew about the clock.

"Well, Mrs. New," he drawled out, "I went up to your desk to sharpen my pencil just before noon and the clock was on your desk then."

"Oh, my," I thought, "How am I ever going to get out of this mess, I am sure to get another 'F' in deportment. Someone is sure to tell her what really happened."

Suddenly she looked right at me and said, "Harold, tell me what you know about the clock." I tried and tried to find a reasonable answer that would explain how the clock got to the back wall, but as hard as I tried I couldn't get the right words out.

"Get your pencil out of your mouth and tell me just what happened," she screamed.

I knew then that she knew more than I had hoped she did, so I proceeded to tell her how I thought it had happened.

"I don't believe a word you said," she yelled, "and you had better tell me the truth now, or you can sit at your desk the rest of the entire year during recess periods." What a terrible price to pay for a little incident that really hadn't started out to be anything at all.

"Well Mrs. New," I said, "when I went up to sharpen my pencil Glen motioned for me to turn the clock around so he could see what time it was. I remembered that I promised you yesterday that I would not turn the clock around anymore this year. Keeping my promise to you I decided the only thing to do was to throw the clock to him and he could look for himself. I made a perfect throw, but he didn't try to catch the clock and it hit the wall."

She stood there with her hands on her hips, looking right at me, but didn't say a word.

Finally I said, "I am very sorry for any inconvenience that it has caused," but my apology fell short of suggesting that I would buy another clock.

The day finally ended and there was a big snow storm just starting. To my surprise when school took up the next morning there was a new clock sitting on Mrs. New's desk. I didn't ask where it came from.

## EARLY SPRING CATTLE FEEDING

One morning as we went to the barn to milk, Dad said, "Spring will soon be here. As soon as we have breakfast I'll help you take several forks of hay and spread it in the deep snow just beyond the shed where the cattle are feeding. The cattle will go into the deep snow to eat the hay and trample the snow down. Tomorrow we can do the same thing again, only we want to extend the hay another hundred feet or more. It won't take long till the cattle will have trampled down the snow making a good trail to the creek bank on the lower meadow."

Dad continued, "I'll start burning some willows along the creek bank and the ashes will make the snow melt a lot faster. We can also use the ashes we saved from the stoves and dust the snow in the willows down by the creek."

Dad burned several willow bushes along the creek bank. He cut a hole in the ice on the creek for the cattle to drink from. The creek banks were covered with slough grass and some timothy grass where the water didn't stand. Large patches of grass were exposed as soon as the cattle started to feed along the creek. Then they nearly quit eating dry hay in the corral.

When the snow melted off the meadows we let the cattle feed on the lower meadow till there was new grass in the pastures, then we took them off the meadows. In the spring time we kept the milk cows in the pasture close to the corral and moved our other cattle to a pasture farther away. When the grass was green on the range we moved our beef cattle there.

## WE TAKE OVER BILL'S MILK CUSTOMERS

The snow on the peaks was melting rapidly. Rivers and streams were running near their peak capacity. Mrs. New gave in to the pleas of us kids for a morning hike to look for mayflowers. We hiked up the highway to the Ten Mile River bridge. There were a lot of birds singing their spring songs. It was warm and the air smelled so fresh. It was hard to go back into the school house after a beautiful morning hike, but we did. Every kid was looking for a mayflower, but none was to be found. The next morning Neil came to school sporting the quarter that Miss Badger had promised for the first mayflower of the season. He had found one in their yard and immediately took it to her.

Mrs. New asked me if I knew where she could get some wood for home. I asked, "Are you out of wood?"

"No," she said, "but I need the wood chopped and my son isn't coming up for a couple of weeks."

"If you have an ax I will split you some wood before I go home from school today," I said. She said there was an ax beside the wood pile so as soon as school was out the rest of the kids headed home and I split wood for about an hour. I didn't plan on charging her. She thanked me and didn't mention anything about money. Apparently her son didn't come up, or he didn't split any wood, so I split quite a pile and cut up some kindling for her, later on. I was sure she had plenty to last her till after school was out.

Bill Thomas came over to our ranch and after talking awhile finally said, "Russell would you be able to take over my milk customers? I can sell all the milk I have on the ranch to Ophir Lodge and the cabin folks."

Dad said, "We probably can work this out, after I know how much milk you deliver in a week."

Bill scratched his head and put another dip of snuff in his lip to add to the two dips that he had already put in during the last five minutes and said, "Right now I deliver about three gallons on Tuesday and about four gallons on Friday, but it is hard to say because some people don't take the same amount of milk all the time."

"I just had a cow come fresh and I have another one coming fresh soon. I can handle it nicely," Dad replied, "but when do you want me to take over?"

Bill pushed his foot around in the mud for a couple minutes and finally asked, "Could you start in a couple of days?"

"I wouldn't be able to start that soon," Dad said, "I'll have to buy some bottles and then we should talk to your customers and be sure it's all right with them."

"You won't need any bottles," Bill said. "I have been delivering milk off and on for years and I have never furnished any bottles. Besides you never get your bottles back."

Dad looked at the ground for a minute and then he said, "If everything works out I'll be ready to start a week from Monday."

The next day Dad and Bill went around and talked to Bill's customers. Dad went to Pete Lege's store in Dillon and purchased four dozen quart bottles and two dozen pint bottles plus the bottle caps. We had been delivering milk to Mrs. Olson, Staleys, Mumfords, and Chamberlains ever since we got our first cows, but now we had to add several other people to our list.

Demings were on that list. One Saturday morning when I took the milk to the Deming home someone yelled out, "It ain't locked, come on in." I opened the door and set the milk on the kitchen table. They took two quarts on Tuesday and three quarts on Saturday.

Mrs. Deming said, "We are having breakfast, would you like a pancake with us?"

"I ate just before I came to town with the milk," I said, as I stepped out of the kitchen into the dining room. Mrs. Deming took a plate of pancakes off the warming oven door and set them on the side of the dining room table. A couple of pancakes disappeared before she got her hand away from the plate.

Paul, sitting down to the table, rubbed his eyes, put on his glasses and said, "Toss me one of those pancakes." I could see that this must have been the second plate of pancakes as several people had some partially eaten pancakes on their plates. Chick stuck his fork into the large half of a well syruped pancake from his plate and tossed it to Paul. It bounced off Paul's cup of coffee knocking it over, and continued to the back side of Paul's plate where it turned upside down and fell into his lap. Paul shoved his chair back and stood up. The pancake slid to the floor where it joined a puddle of coffee. Mona, Neil's mother, handed Paul a damp rag from the kitchen to wipe the coffee off the table and the floor. Paul wiped the table and then tossed the rag on the floor where he used his foot to wipe up the floor, then he threw it at Chick. Chick ducked and the rag continued on into the kitchen. I had to move a little to keep from being in the line of fire.

Paul reached across the table and removed a big pancake from the stack and put it on his plate and poured a double helping of syrup on it. He looked at his empty coffee cup and eased around the table to the kitchen door where he met Mrs. Deming with the coffee pot. She filled his cup while she asked Paul a couple of questions.

While this was going on Ray came out of the living room rubbing his eyes and said he had a terrible headache.

Mona responded, "If you had come home before four in the morning, you probably wouldn't be feeling like you had a hangover, which is probably what ails you."

Ray didn't answer, he took Paul's plate and sat down beside Neil. Neil handed him a platter of fried eggs and sausage of which he took his fair share. Then he ordered a cup of coffee.

Bob finished his pancake and eggs without saying a word. He stood up and took Paul's cup of coffee from his hand and gave it to Ray besides getting his own cup refilled.

Mrs. Deming handed Paul another cup of coffee and said, "Paul you had better eat your breakfast." When Paul went back to the table he at first didn't see what had happened to his plate, but when he did he reached across the table and took it back. Ray protested, but let Paul have it till he saw there were no pancakes left on the table, then he reached across the table and took the pancake, or what was left of it, and put it on a clean plate. Paul hadn't seen the fresh stack of pancakes on the way to the table, but Ray did and tossed the piece of pancake back to Paul. The pancake spread a little syrup on Paul's face before it landed on the table in front of him. When the new pancakes arrived Ray stood up and grabbed the top pancake.

Paul hollered, "Here, you can have this cake," as he threw it back at Ray and grabbed a new pancake. It missed Ray and hit Chick in the arm and dropped to the floor. There was not much more than three or four bites held together by syrup. Ray, with a spooky look on his face, sat down and poured syrup on the pancake he had just taken from the new pile. He put his fork in the pancake and raised his arm to throw. Chick grabbed Ray's arm and with a quick throw hit Paul in the face. The cake fell to the floor upside down near the wall. Bob stood up and headed to the kitchen. On his way away from the table he emptied the last little bit of his coffee in Chick's plate. Mona seeing what had happened grabbed her cup of warm coffee and headed to the living room.

***Left to Right, Neil Westlake and some of the Demings: Paul, Bob (holding Ray's son Bobby), and Chick.***

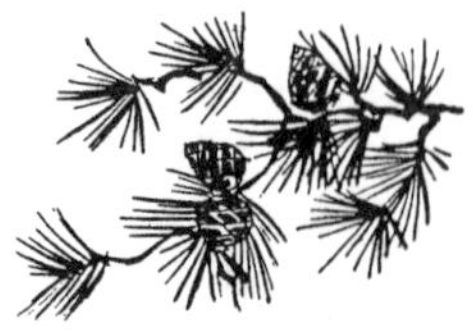

Mrs. Deming had finally placed her feet under the table and had picked up a pancake. She said, "Not again," as she headed back to the kitchen with her plate. While Chick and Ray were having a discussion over the last pancake Paul got up and picked up part of the pancake and threw it at Chick. He wasn't throwing very well as he missed Chick and hit Bob as he came back into the dining room. I looked at Neil just in time to see him reach over the table and pour salt in Paul's coffee while he was getting the pancake off the floor.

Mrs. Deming called out, "Harold, you had better come in here before things get any more sticky in there." I went to the kitchen and on outside to continue my milk delivery. When I got to Deming's front gate I discovered I hadn't picked up the return bottles. I headed back to get them. They hadn't set them outside in the milk box, so I stepped inside where Mrs. Deming picked up several bottles and gave then to me.

While I was stacking the bottles in my milk carrier I heard someone in the back of the house yell out, "What time is it?"

"About eight thirty," was the instant reply.

Just after I got outside the door, a body flew by me so fast I couldn't tell who it was. He jumped into a car in the driveway and roared out of the yard into the street kicking up gravel on the way out.

I stuck my head back into the door and asked, "What was that?"

Laughing, Mrs. Deming said, "Paul has to be in Dillon at nine for an appointment. It's only five after eight so I think he has plenty of time."

From what I discovered the pancake throwing happened quite often in the Deming home. If they were having a friendly pancake war when you entered the house, you were lucky if you didn't get hit in the face with a syrupy pancake.

We delivered milk every day except Sunday, but we staggered the customers so we had about the same amount of milk to deliver each day.

## BETTY GARNER'S MOST EMBARRASSING MOMENT

By spring the number of students in the Frisco school started to dwindle. The Hockleys had moved to Climax before school was out. The MacMasters went to Colorado Springs for part of the winter. Some of the other kids had moved. The Garners stayed till after school was out when they moved to Climax.

It was the spring of 1938. I didn't think I would ever get to graduate from the eighth grade, but the time had finally arrived. Betty Garner and I were the only ones left to graduate in the class. For the graduation exercise I got the job of giving an opening address. I wrote it out and practically memorized it. To add something a little humorous I said, "I tore the seat out of my new pants, but I have other pants at home."

There was no school on graduation day. I didn't feel very good, but I took my bath to get ready for the great event. While I was bathing I noticed there were little red spots all over my body. I picked up a hand mirror and looked at my face and it was covered with little red welts.

"Mom," I yelled, "come in here and see what is the matter with me." Mom came in and looked me over.

"Do you feel sick?" she asked.

"I have a little headache, but that's all." Mom pulled me into the kitchen and said, "Russell, Harold has the measles. He doesn't feel too bad, but we can't let him go to the graduation." After a brief discussion, I was put to bed and the rest of the family went to the graduation. I felt bad that I didn't get to go, but then Mom said it wouldn't stop me from graduating, which sounded good to me.

***Betty Garner and Harold Rutherford. The Whole Class of '38***

When the family came home they were laughing about the story I had written. Mrs. New asked Betty to read it for the opening exercise. She didn't have time to read it before she read it at the exercise.

She read, "I tore the seat out of my pants, but I have more pants at home." Suddenly she realized what she had just read. Her face turned red, she stuttered and stammered and finally reread the sentence. It still said the same thing. She continued and finished reading the address. It ended with my thanking Mrs. New for teaching us for the year and my apology for the little things I did in school, especially my art work.

Soon as I got over the measles I had a lot of work to do around the ranch, but it all seemed like fun to me.

# PART VI
# LIFE ON THE RANCH

***Peak One, Victoria and Royal Mountains reflected in the lake on the Rutherford Ranch***

Ken Chamberlain came to the ranch with a saddle horse named Ribbon. He said, "Russell, you need a saddle horse and I'm afraid of that black horse of Dan Mogee's that you ride all the time. I brought this horse and a new saddle and all I want is to ride the horse once in awhile, probably on Sunday mornings. You will have to take care of her feed, that's all I'm asking." Talk about being neighborly!

Ribbon was a high spirited horse and we needed to ride her almost every day so she wouldn't forget who was boss! She filled in a somewhat vacant spot in our overall life on the ranch. She was easy to ride and one of us kids rode her nearly every day. I taught her to be a good cutting horse. It didn't take but a few times to let her know what she was supposed to do when driving cattle and she caught on. More than once, she left me on the ground as she darted after an independent calf who was trying to take off on his own. If I knew a day or two ahead when Ken wanted to ride her we would have her in the corral and ready to ride.

One morning Dad said, "Harold, I want you to build a bridge across the creek where we go to the Big Spring. We need the bridge, but it doesn't have to be very wide, just wide enough to walk across." He continued, "Cut a couple logs around five inches in diameter and run them at least two feet beyond the creek banks on each side. There is plenty of two by six inch plank around here to use for a decking. Try to get it done before the end of the week."

Previously we had used a twelve inch plank laid across the creek to walk on, but Dad and I were the only ones who used it. When the creek was low in the late summer and fall, us kids usually jumped from one rock to the next across the creek where we had a cattle crossing. I went to the trees west of the creek and found two trees the right size and cut them down. By evening I had a footbridge completed.

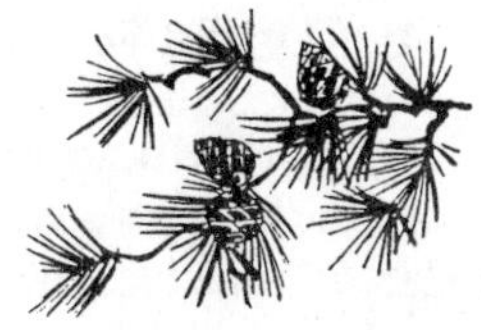

## TRAGEDY IN THE GOAT PASTURE

One day when Dad was working in Dillon, Albert Scheers stopped him and asked, "Russell, do you have any brush, weeds, or small willows that you need cleaned up? I'm looking for a place to put my goats for about six weeks." He continued, "In about six weeks I'm moving on the hill and I'll have all the pasture I need to take care of the goats. Right now I need a place to put them."

After listening to him Dad said, "I have quite a few acres that might be just the spot for them. What are your thoughts and what kind of a deal do you want to work out?" They discussed the situation at hand and worked out a plan. Scheers would bring the goats to the ranch after dinner the next evening. There were six old goats and five of them had twin kids. The other goat would have her kids any day. There was plenty of goat milk left after the baby goats had their fill and we were to be paid twenty dollars for six weeks plus any expenses that we might incur. Plus we could use the extra milk.

Scheers arrived right on time with the goats. He had chains to use to stake them out and collars for all of them. Dad was working in Dillon at the time and Sheers picked him up and brought him home with him. As soon as the goats were unloaded we put them in the end of the shed till we made better arrangements. Dad and Albert went to the buck brush by the Big Spring.

Albert said, "This is a perfect place for them. They will get fat here and you will have all the brush removed without any effort." Three days later the last goat to come fresh had three kids. Some of our milk customers wanted some goat milk, so we didn't have any problem getting rid of the milk.

Several weeks went by and we were getting used to the goats. We staked out two of them on twenty five foot chains. The rest of the goats plus the kids would stay close by. One evening Mildred and I went to get the goats for the evening milking. The goats were in an uproar. One goat was hanging by her chain just off the ground. Her chain was caught near the top of a bent over aspen tree. The only thing we could think of was she must have run and pulled the chain across the aspen tree getting the chain tangled in the top. When it swung back up it lifted her front feet off the ground.

The other chained goat had pulled her stake up and wasn't in sight. One kid was lying down. There was a cut about two inches wide that started by her head and went down her back to the tail, exposing the back bone. One front leg was bleeding. One other kid had a similar cut across the back, but not as long. The rest of the goats were scattered all around in the willows and buck brush west of the spring. They were calling each other and the kids were calling their moms and the moms were calling the kids. It was obvious the goats were badly frightened. It took a few minutes to try to come up with an answer.

All of a sudden the scent of a bear became real strong. Now Mildred and I were about to panic. My first thought was to run like mad to the house, but then the bear would take at least one goat with him. He also might have thought he had found all the goats and we were trying to steal them from him. Either way it wasn't the best for us. After a short conversation we decided to try and take the goats to the barn.

We arrived at the right moment or the bear might have killed several goats. Also the goat hanging in the tree was able to get on her feet a few minutes after I released the chain. A minute or two later and she would have choked to death. Mildred took one goat with a chain and I took the other and we headed towards the barn. Most of the goats came out of the willows when I called them. We stopped when we got to the bridge across Meadow Creek and I went back and drove several more out of the willows. I was afraid to go deep into the bushes as I didn't know just where the bear was. When I went along the edges I yelled and yelled, hoping to scare the bear away.

I drove the goats to the creek where we took count. All were accounted for. The kid with the worst tear could hardly make it. He kept falling down and became the last one going to the barn. I had to help him along.

Dad arrived shortly after we got the goats in the barn. He took one look and said, "We'll have to get rid of the goats tonight or first thing in the morning. The bear'll come back and kill all of them if they're back where we had them." Dean and I did the milking while Dad went to Frisco to call Scheers and talk to him about the goats. Mr. Scheers arrived right after Dad got back from Frisco. We were lucky that we had only lost two kids who had died from their injuries.

Albert said, "The bear will be looking for the goats till he finds them. If you think they'll be safe in the barn tonight, I'll come over in the morning and take them away. I'll have to find a place tonight to take them."

Dad said, "I think the goats will be safe in the barn tonight. I would keep them indefinitely, but I know the bear will be looking for them."

We didn't hear a sound from the bear during the night.

## TIM GOES ON A SAFARI

One day, Tim came to the house from the barn for his usual breakfast of pancakes, milk, and possibly a piece of meat. After breakfast he left the house and headed towards the pasture. This was not his usual routine. He would usually go outside and harass the birds that had gathered on the back porch for a handout, or possibly he would chase a squirrel up a tree in the front yard, and after this he would have a morning nap. In the evening when I went to the pasture to bring the cows in for milking, I saw Tim at the upper end of the pasture eating on a freshly killed rabbit.

"What's the matter, Tim?" I asked, "Didn't you get enough meat at home without going out in the wilds and catching a rabbit?" He answered with a great big growl and headed into the willows, carrying the rabbit with him. I didn't try to follow him. I had learned long ago that when Tim wanted to be by himself it was impossible to find him or know where he went. He would just disappear.

Mom said, "I think Tim has gone on another safari. He left in a hurry this morning and he wasn't here for his evening meal." I told the family about seeing him up by our west fence and he was eating on a rabbit. Mildred chipped in, "He must be going on a hunting trip, instead of going to town to see his girlfriends." She continued, "Last time we saw him heading to the foothills, he was gone for over two weeks."

Just as we thought, two weeks passed and no sign of Tim around the ranch. Whenever he went to town he was seldom gone over two days.

Some company arrived from eastern Colorado and they wanted to go to Lily Pond to take some pictures. We told them it was a little early in the spring to get pictures of water lilies, but I would be glad to escort them to the lakes. The next morning we went to Lily Pond.

While the gang were taking pictures, I decided to follow the inlet to some beaver ponds on the hill above Lily Pond to see if there were any fish there. Sometimes the ponds freeze to the bottom or the inlet freezes up in the winter, killing all the fish. It was a steep climb for a short distance, then a quarter mile walk through very heavy undergrowth. The willows were thick and grew very high. On each side of the narrow drainage were clumps of alder trees dotted with an occasional balsam tree. It was swampy underfoot and slough grass grew to a height of three feet by autumn. I had to stay on the trail till I got to the dams. I watched the water in the dams for a short time when I saw several fish feeding on top of the water. Some of them made big splashes jumping after flies. I wished I had brought my fishing pole with me, but then I could come back later.

All of a sudden my attention was turned to a movement on the hillside across the ponds. There Tim was, sneaking up the hillside trying to get out of sight. I called to him. He never looked back, just kept on running and vanished into the heavy timber. I was satisfied that the fish in the ponds had not winter killed, but I couldn't help wondering about Tim up here in the wilds. I wasn't sure he would ever find his way back to the ranch, but then, he probably knew the area better than I did.

I hurried back to Lily Pond, where the friends were ready to go back to the ranch.

Another week passed and no sign of Tim. Dad thought that he would not return till winter because he had never been gone this long before. One morning while we were eating breakfast, Tim arrived at the door asking to come in. Mom let him in and he hurried to where his dish used to be, but Mom had removed it. He gave a couple loud meows and Mom gave him his usual milk. He acted like he hadn't had a drink since he had left nearly a month earlier. After he drank all the milk he wanted, he ate a big piece of pancake and headed outside. He laid down on the back porch as if he had never been gone and continued his harassment of camp robbers that had collected in the trees waiting for Mom to put pieces of pancakes on the porch.

I stopped at Demings' to see their parrot Polly. She was supposed to say several cuss words plus "cracker," "Polly," "hello," and "goodbye." On another time when I was there she sure did say several unprintable words. She must have been owned by a sailor who didn't know how to talk without cussing. Neil put her on a record on their phonograph and started it running. He held a pencil against the side of the record to slow it down. Polly held on for three or four revolutions before she was thrown off. I think she thought she was singing, but to me it was a lot of squawking.

Neil picked her up and let her have another ride. This time Neil put the pickup head down on the record. It was about three inches from the arm to the record. This was enough room for her to ride around under the arm. She rode around a couple of times and when she came to the arm Neil held her down so she wouldn't hit the arm. She seemed to catch on. When she came to the arm she would duck down. Of course the record was barely going around. Neil speeded it up a little and when she came around to the arm she didn't duck in time and rode right into the arm knocking her off. After a couple more times she seemed to catch on, but when she banged into the arm she said, "Aw, s—!"

After a short rest she got another ride. As soon as she could see the arm she had her choice words to say. She would ride around and rise up just in time to get hit. And again her choice words. Neil took her off the record and set her on the floor. She staggered all over the place. She again repeated a few of her favorite words to describe her predicament, none of which I will repeat.

One morning when I was at the Demings, Polly was sitting on her perch by the cage squawking at the cat Butch. Butch hated Polly and Polly hated Butch. On several occasions they tangled and both of them seemed to come out of the scuffle fairly well if you ignore feathers all over the kitchen floor and the pointed part of the cat's ear rounded off.

Polly hopped down on a chair and squawked again at Butch. When Butch didn't acknowledge the greeting, Polly hopped down on the floor a couple of feet from Butch who was pretending to be asleep on a rug in front of the kitchen stove. I watched this little escapade.

Polly stepped over sideways a couple steps and called Butch a name or two. Butch kept on sleeping. Polly sidestepped over a couple more steps and called Butch all of her choice names. No response. Then Polly screamed and screeched at Butch. Still no response. Polly thought Butch must be deaf so she took several more side steps and screeched again. A slow grin appeared on Butch's face. Polly saw this movement and side-stepped back a couple of steps. She again started hopping sideways closer and closer to Butch. Butch didn't move. Polly hopped around in front of Butch and again side-stepped right up to his face.

Suddenly Butch jumped up and in the same motion reached out and grabbed Polly. Polly did a lot of squawking and grabbed Butch by the ear and held on. Butch tried to pull her off and then he tried to take a bite of her side. Polly let loose of the ear and grabbed Butch somewhere in the mouth area and held on. Feathers and fur flew. After a couple of rolls Butch was growling and crying louder than Polly was squawking. Butch finally thought of his hind feet and brought them around to where he could kick Polly away when she let loose and jumped and flew to the chair seat and then with another jump and wings flapping she made it to the back of the chair. Butch ran under the table and then crept around to the dining room and disappeared. Polly limped for a short time and had lost a lot of feathers. Butch lost a lot of hair and all the whiskers on one side, and he had a cut in one ear about a half inch long plus a sore face!

Demings kept Polly for many years, but finally Mrs. Deming said she had had all of that parrot she could take so she gave her to a neighbor explaining that the parrot's language was so bad she didn't want her around any more.

About two weeks went by when the neighbor returned the parrot. The neighbor said, "We had dinner guests last evening and all Polly would do was cuss. I finally covered the cage with a blanket thinking she would keep quiet, but no! You wouldn't believe what she called me." I don't know what the Demings finally did with her.

## POND IN THE WOODS

One morning after Dad and I had finished the milking Dad said, "It looks like there is plenty of new grass in the pasture for the cattle; I think it's time to move them off the meadows."

"Where do you want to put them?" I asked, as we carried the last of the morning milk to the milk house.

"It's a nice warm morning so go to the rental property and walk around the fence to be sure it is all up in good condition. Then we can move them over there tomorrow. I don't want to leave them there very long, but it will give a little more time for the grass on the range to grow."

After breakfast I took a hammer, pliers, fence stretcher, a twenty foot long roll of barbed wire, and, of course, a pocket full of fence staples. Mom made me a sandwich to take along.

I left immediately and went over past our upper meadow. The creek was overflowing its banks and covering a small portion of the meadow. Some frogs had already claimed squatters' rights to this little lake. They were singing a loud but beautiful refrain as I approached. I crept closer and closer and suddenly all was quiet. I think the choir director must have spotted me coming and stopped the music all at once. I waited a few minutes to see if they would start again. Shortly one very deep bass started and then the rest joined in. I listened for a minute or two and then I headed on to the corner of the rental property.

I walked nearly all the distance around the fence before I found a break in the wire. Two top wires were broken and the two bottom wires needed to be tightened. I twisted the bottom wires till I had them tight and used the fence stretcher on the two top wires bringing the broken ends together. Using bailing wire

I was able to fasten the wires together and make a nice repair job. I continued on around the fence till I got back to the place I had started nearly four hours earlier.

As I started home I decided to go over by Pond of the Woods, a stagnant pond covering about an acre in the timber south of our ranch. Every spring when the snow melted it drained into a low spot creating a beautiful pond for the summer. It had alder trees and willow bushes growing around the sides and a number of large bushes growing on the upper end. Slough grass grew all around the pond. It was nearly hidden from view back in the pine trees, but it could be seen from a spot on the Forest Service road that went from Frisco up Meadow Creek.

I sat down on the bank to eat my lunch and watch some canaries that were flitting from willow bush to willow bush. There were several kinds of little birds that nested in the willows around the pond. Every spring a family of ducks built their nest on the pond, but I didn't see any today. Perhaps a hen was sitting on her nest hidden in last year's slough grass back under the willows that overhang the water. The drake probably was out looking for a good dining spot.

A muskrat crawled out of the water and was sitting on a rock on the opposite side of the pond from me. I didn't know that muskrats lived here. However it was a natural for them with all of the grass, willows, and alder trees growing in and around the pond. Last year I put some frogs in the pond and they were also singing their love songs.

Suddenly there was an increased chirping of the small birds down in the willows. I got to my feet to see if I could see what was going on. Sitting near the top of a large pine tree was a belted kingfisher. I bet I watched him for a full minute before he gave his call and dove down to the water. He didn't dive into the water so whatever he saw didn't interest him after he got a closeup look.

As I headed for home I saw a car stop on the road at a spot where you can see the edge of the pond. I watched to see what was going on. A man crawled out of his car and opened the trunk, taking out his fishing pole and tackle box and headed towards the pond. My first thought was to tell him that it was a stagnant pond and trout couldn't live in it, but then I decided to let him find out for himself.

I headed on home and, after putting my tools and supplies back in place, I decided to have a little fun. I painted up a "NO FISHING" sign and headed back to the pond. To my dismay there were two cars there when I got back and four or five people down at the pond fishing. I didn't dare make a sound nailing my sign on a tree, so I looked around and found some wire by our south fence, which was close by. I fastened the sign on a tree by the road so it could be plainly seen from the two cars parked on the road. I went back home laughing to myself as I wondered what would go through their minds when they gave up and went back to their cars. That evening after all the chores were done and our evening meal finished I went back over to the pond to see if anything had transpired that I ought to know about. The cars were gone and my "No Fishing" sign was still up.

Saturday is a time when many people go fishing, especially if they have to drive a distance. When Saturday evening came I went back to the pond. When I got there I could hear some talking down at the pond, but there wasn't a car in sight. I sneaked down to the pond and hid in the willows and watched for a short time. Two men were fishing. Due to the alders, willows, and pine trees growing right up to the water's edge it was a very hard place to get your line in the water. One man had his line caught in a branch of a pine tree about ten feet above his head. He sure was upset about it. It was too high to reach and it extended out over the edge of the water too far to get hold of. As I watched, he jerked hard on the line and broke it. He said, "Bill, let's get out of here before we get caught."

Bill, not wanting to quit fishing said, "I saw a good mess of 12 inch trout that another guy caught here last week. A little while ago I saw a couple of four or five pounders go swimming by and they were headed over towards that rock where the willows are hanging over the water." (He must have been hallucinating!) "Why don't you fix up your line and see if you can cast over there and hook one of them?" he asked. He kept right on talking, "Since fishing isn't allowed in the lake I am sure there are a lot of big fish in here. You know how it is, some days the fish are biting and some days they aren't."

I sneaked away before they saw me, then I made a few circles to see where they had left their car or whether they had walked in from Frisco. I found the car down the road a piece, pulled off into the timber behind some bushes. I didn't recognize the car and the license tags were not from Summit County. It wasn't the one that was there earlier.

I went back home thinking I won't bother them in their endeavor to catch a mess of fish. I didn't get back for over a week and when I did my sign was taken down and thrown into some bushes. I went home, got a hammer and some nails and went back and installed my "No Fishing" sign on the same tree but a little higher up.

I made several trips back to the pond before I finally found someone fishing. The man fishing was so nervous that I doubted that he could have caught a fish if there were any to catch. He would cast, look all around, lay his pole down and go to where he could see the road through the willows, where a well-worn trail went to the water's edge, fish a few minutes and repeat this same procedure.

Another time I was by the pond and a man and his wife were fishing. I guess that it was his wife. I heard him say to her, "I just saw a big one swim by." I wondered what he could have seen or what brand he had been drinking. Two months had gone by since I first put up my sign and the water still looked as fresh as in the spring. The vegetation in the water and around the water's edge gave it that fishy look. The now packed down trail to the edge of the pond and around the edges made it look like a great fishing hole.

Occasionally one could see a muskrat go swimming around or crawl up on a downed tree in the water. A mallard duck had a nice family, and if you stayed out of sight in the evenings you were apt to see them out for a swim. Usually the little ones were hidden and the old folks gone when the fisherman occupied the banks.

Tadpoles showed up around two sides of the pond causing a big disturbance when anyone would walk by. All this sure did get one's fishing spirit going. It was even hard for me to believe that there were no fish in the pond.

Someone was always taking down the "No Fishing" sign, but I always found time to fix the old one or make a new one.

One time I took several little brook trout from Meadow Creek and turned them loose in the pond. I never saw any signs of them after I turned them loose. It is possible they were caught by some fisherman, or maybe a kingfisher flew over and saw them and took them home to a waiting family.

Anyway, it was a great place to go and enjoy fishing. Even if there weren't any fish in the pond, the fishing was fabulous! I hope the fishermen enjoyed the fishing as much as I enjoyed watching them.

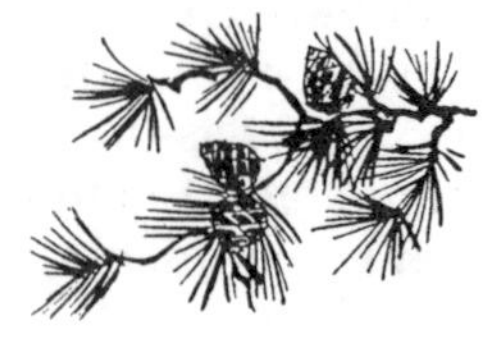

## GET THIS COW OFF ME

My cousin, Deane Devars, from Orleans, Nebraska, made his appearance at our ranch to stay for the summer. We hadn't seen him for a year. I had many things to tell him, and many things to teach him about life on a mountain ranch.

The first evening came and went before we had said half the things we wanted to. Evening means time to do the evening chores. As Deane and I headed towards the barn Deane said, "Harold, I'll help you do the milking, then your Dad won't have to go to the barn tonight."

I was surprised that he knew how to milk so I asked, "When did you learn how to milk?"

He replied, "I have never milked a cow in my life, but I am sure there isn't much to it."

We dumped a small amount of hay from the loft into each manger and gave each cow a coffee can of oats mixed with bran and then opened the barn door. All the cows hurried into the barn and into their stalls to eat their oats. This is like giving a kid his favorite candy.

I locked each stanchion and then we washed each cow's bag and prepared them for milking. Helen arrived with several milk buckets and then we were ready to milk.

I said, "Helen, tell Dad Deane is helping me with the milking so he won't have to come to the barn tonight."

Deane asked, "Which cow do you want me to milk first?"

"Take this black cow, she is very gentle and easy to milk," I said.

"I don't want to milk her," he said, "I want to milk the meanest cow you have."

***Too bad Dean tried to milk Aunt Sara (right) instead of the black cow (to her left).***

"Well, here's Aunt Sara, she had a calf last week and she sure has a bad disposition. She will kick you at least ten times during each milking. Before you milk her let me tell you a little about her.

"We named her Aunt Clari because she looked so much like our Aunt Clari. They both have the same color of orange hair and many other similar qualities, but I won't mention them at this time.

"After accidentally calling the cow Aunt Clari in front of our Aunt Clari a few times Mom made it apparent that something had to be done. The tone of her voice quickly made us understand that there was no room for negotiation. After a lot of discussion and debate we finally arrived on the name of Aunt Sara instead of Aunt Clari. This pleased Mom as she was the one who spearheaded the change."

The cow was a Jersey and Guernsey mixture with a light orange color. Her legs were white and she sported a white spot on her face and had long black eye lashes. Her horns were supposed to have been removed. However, while one side was missing, the other side had about a four-inch-long horn that curled along the front of her face. It seemed rather strange that whenever she wanted to butt anyone she knew which side to use.

She sure was contrary. No matter where you wanted her to go or what you wanted her to do she would try to do the opposite. Sometimes she would be standing in the corral, chewing her cud with a smile on her face, and if you walked along side of her, her foot would automatically kick at you. She would go on chewing her cud as if nothing had happened. She would kick you when you were washing her bag getting ready to milk and then look around to see what you thought of the situation. I think she guaranteed her kicking and if you weren't satisfied with it she would only be too happy to do it over.

Before we owned her, I have an idea she stepped on a can, cutting her left rear foot which never healed properly. Most of the time the foot never bothered her. She didn't limp with it, but if you tried to hurry her, or do anything she didn't want to do she would limp badly.

We had a gate that opened to let the cows go to a second meadow to feed. We used this meadow primarily so they would be easy to find in the mornings. Sometimes, however, we would put them in the meadow during the day.

We opened the gate by lowering poles on one side to the ground. The gate consisted of five horizontal poles spaced about a foot apart and built so we could move the poles to the right or left. By sliding the poles a foot on one end the poles would drop to the ground, still leaving the opposite ends in place in the fence. This made it easy to open.

Normally we would let the poles down only on one side and the cows would walk across the poles and go into the second meadow. Not Aunt Sara, she would stand at the gate and refuse to cross the poles. If she was the last cow to cross, it would work fine, but usually she would be in the middle of the bunch and none of the cows behind her could go through till she did. We would have to drop the poles on both sides in order for her to cross. If you accidentally left the poles down on one end and she happened by and saw the gate was open, she had no problem crossing. But then you would have to let the other side down to get her back into the pasture.

Many times when you went to the pasture to bring the cows in for milking she would be missing. This of course caused one of us to be out looking for her. Some cows do this when they are about ready to have their calf, but she practiced it most of the time.

Dad came home one evening with a larger than standard size cow bell. We immediately put it around her neck.

"This will end her leaving the rest of the cows and forcing us to hunt her," Dad said, "Now it will be easy to find her."

However, we soon realized she must have had a college degree in walking while wearing a bell around her neck. She was the only cow I ever saw that could walk a mile through willows and cross the creek, and not ring the bell once.

She also had the ability to swing her tail around and pull it back, snapping the end of her tail with perfect accuracy. This was fine for a fly sitting on her back, but it was hard on the guy who was trying to milk her. Also you could clean and wash her tail and two hours later it would be a dirty mess.

If she wasn't practicing snapping her tail on you, she would hold her tail right next to your head or face when you sat down to milk her. I think she kept it dirty just to harass the one who had to milk her.

After I had given Deane her brief history with all of its ramifications, Deane grinned and said, "This is the cow for me, I'll show her a thing or two. Where is the milk stool?"

"There is one hanging up at the end of the barn, next to the grain room door," I said.

Looking at the milk stools hanging on the wall Deane asked, "Is there only one leg on a milk stool?"

"Sure," I replied, "Look at what I am sitting on. It is easier to get out of the way when a cow kicks at you with a one legged stool."

Aunt Sara kicked Deane several times while he was washing her bag and getting her cleaned up ready to milk. I showed Deane how to sit down on the stool, put the milk bucket between his legs, put his head against her side, and squeeze and squirt the milk into the bucket. "Squeeze with one hand and then with the other. This way you get a rhythm going and you can soon get the cow milked," I said.

"Boy, this is no problem," Deane said, but I noticed instead of facing the side of the cow directly he had partially turned himself around looking towards the rear of the cow to watch her leg and ward off a blow from the foot when and if it did happen.

This wasn't the best idea because it would leave his face vulnerable to her tail. I had forgotten to tell him that she would hold her tail around in his face most of the time while he was milking her. She also would swing her tail around into your face and then rapidly jerk it back to make a good whip-lashing effect which would terminate somewhere on your face.

Five minutes and a pint of milk later and there were no major problems. Then it happened! Aunt Sara kicked, spilling the bucket of milk. The blow knocked Deane to the floor nearly under the cow that was standing behind him. The milk stool landed in the middle of the barn at least ten feet behind Aunt Sara.

Deane got up, washed off his hands, got a clean wash rag and tried to clean his leg that had slid along the floor, now wet and slick from spilled milk. He stepped over to the corner of the barn, where we had a table to put milk buckets ready to use. He picked up a clean milk bucket and started all over again muttering to himself as he seated himself on a now wet and messy stool on a slick floor.

Aunt Sara gave him a small kick, almost small enough to be called a love pat. Deane said, "I think I have her under control now and she knows who is boss."

Just then she let go with a nice pile of you-know-what and, as if that were not enough, she emptied her bladder at the same time.

I went to Deane's aid, helping to clean up the mess. If it wasn't slick earlier it sure was slick now. To paint a more clear picture of the barn, it had a sloping floor that emptied into a gutter at the back of the cows. When we washed the floor it would drain into the gutter. We could wash out the gutter and it would drain outside the barn.

Once again Deane sat down to milk. By this time I had finished one cow and was starting on another. Helen was on hand to carry milk up to the milk house and bring back clean buckets. In a minute or two Aunt Sara kicked him again. He was able to move the milk bucket and himself just enough to save the milk bucket from getting kicked. Then, "Crash!" the bucket turned over and skidded towards the middle of the barn along with the one-legged stool. Aunt Sara's foot had also dented the side of the bucket and Deane was left sitting on the floor. A mad scramble got him out of the way just in time to keep him from being kicked again by Aunt Sara.

Once more Deane had to get a rag and clean off his stool, arms, and leg, wash his hands again, and start over.

Deane, also being a relative of Aunt Clari and knowing her very well said, "Boy, she is about as contrary and determined as Aunt Clari." Deane continued, "I'll show her! I'll tie her feet together, then we will see if she can kick or not."

I figured Deane had never heard of "kickers," so I got up from my milking and got him a set and helped him put them on Aunt Sara.

Kickers are two metal clamps shaped to fit the cows legs with an adjustable chain fastening them together. The clamps fasten on each leg of the cow and hold her back feet close together. If she tries to kick, her foot is held to the other foot by the chain and she can't get it up high enough to get it in the bucket, or to kick you in the leg. If the cow puts all her strength into a vicious kick with one foot it will pull the other foot along with the first foot and then there has to be a real act of balancing or else the back half of the cow will fall down. While the cow is trying to keep from falling down you had better grab your bucket and stool and get out of the way.

I fastened the kickers so she had about ten inches between her legs. That wouldn't give her enough swing with her foot to kick you very hard. I stepped back out of the way so Deane could get seated on his stool and ready, once again, to milk the cow.

With another clean bucket and strong determination, Deane said, as he once again sat down to milk Aunt Sara, "I will milk her this time or she will really be in trouble."

Without any warning, once again, Aunt Sara tried to kick him! What an awful commotion! Aunt Sara must have realized she had to kick with both feet at once, otherwise she wouldn't be able to kick at all. With all the effort she could muster, she kicked with both feet at once, landing with one foot in the bucket and the other foot held just outside and near the top of the bucket with the kicker. The chain that was holding her feet together mashed the side of the milk bucket. By this time the floor was slick from all the milk that had been spilled, and the time the bladder decided that it could help her a little by dumping some water on the floor, not to mention the mess her bowels had contributed to the project.

I leaned around my cow to examine the mess Aunt Sara was in. I had to laugh seeing Aunt Sara standing there with one foot in the bucket and the other foot held close to the top of the bucket by the kicker chain, her tail swung around and held firmly against Deane's face. Every once in awhile she would raise her tail up a few inches and then push it down again, then swing it around to her other side and give it a full swing back around on the front side of Deane's head quickly pulling it back, causing the end of the tail to snap and burn in his face. Deane was still sitting on the stool, his legs tightly holding the bucket. The stool was leaning so far to one side that I thought any minute the leg would skid out from under him. He wasn't milking but he had a death grip on the cows teats.

I stood up for a minute to see if I could see Aunt Sara's head and try to see what she had in mind and what method she planned on using to get out of this mess. She was eating on her hay and acted like she didn't know anything was wrong. Unbelievable!

I looked back at Deane's shoulder, which looked like you had taken his shirt and scrubbed the floor with it. His pants on one side and his seat looked like he had been standing too close to the back side of Aunt Sara and she had failed to notify him that her bowels and bladder were about to relieve her of at least ten pounds. His hat was red when he entered the barn, but now was sporting a medium brown color. There was a brown smear across the side of his face that ran from his ear across his cheek, missing his mouth by a narrow margin, and on to his chin where it terminated with a big red welt.

I looked over the situation: Deane was trying to move his feet enough to be able to stand up, but nothing matched up very well. The bucket with Aunt Sara's foot in it had been pushed to the rear and a little bit to the outside where Deane sat pondering his next move. If I had been Deane, I would have made a break for it while everything was calm, as Aunt Sara had demonstrated this wouldn't last very long.

"See what a mess you got yourself into," Deane growled. Just then she tried again to kick, not with one foot but with both feet at once.

I bet she was planning this jump and kept on eating hay when I looked around my cow to see what she was trying to do, or I should say, what she was planning on doing. It didn't work. Down she went on the floor with Deane under her. Aunt Sara had a surprised look on her face. I don't think she thought it would happen like it did.

The bucket served very well in this mess by holding part of Aunt Sara's weight off of Deane. He had one leg on each side of the bucket. Aunt Sara's feet were still close together and the back portion of her body was resting on Deane's legs and the now mashed up bucket. Her feet were extended out towards his chest, still fastened together with the kickers.

Sara tried to get up by kicking both feet at once. As I looked at the problem ahead, my first thought was to stop her feet from moving, or move them in another direction. One little shift could position her feet next to Deane's face. I handed my two-thirds full bucket of milk to Mildred, and rushed to Deane's aid, laughing as I put my foot on Aunt Sara's leg to stop her from kicking.

"Are you hurt anywhere?" I asked.

"I can't tell," Deane cried, "just get this cow off me before she kills me."

Deane wasn't hurt, but he couldn't move. By this time Helen had gone for help.

When our dads and Dean arrived, Dad unlocked the stanchion and, with a lot of work, we slid Aunt Sara off of Deane and unhooked the kickers. She got back on her feet by herself. It took a can of oats in her box to persuade her to go back into the stanchion.

Deane headed towards the house for a bath and clean clothes, still grumbling about what he was going to do to Aunt Sara.

When I delivered milk to Wortmans at the Frisco Hotel, Mrs. Wortman opened the door and said, "Harold, come in, I want to pay you." I went into the kitchen and waited.

Mrs. Wortman picked up her purse and after a quick look at the bill said, "I'll have to go to the bedroom and get some money." She laid her purse down and scooped up a fresh pancake from off the grill and put it on a plate at the table. She then took a couple of meat patties and placed them on the cake. Then she poured a cup of coffee as Anthony, her son entered the room.

Mrs. Wortman said, "Anthony here is your breakfast, you had better eat it before it gets cold." Anthony nodded as he sat down to the table. Mrs. Wortman disappeared into the living room and before she got out of sight Anthony got up and followed her.

They had a great big dog that was sitting by the kitchen stove sort of licking his chops. I didn't know whether he was thinking of me for breakfast or something off the table. I am not sure of what manufacturer's brand of dog he was, but I think someone told me he was a Doberman. He stood up and took a quick look at me, causing me to consider a quick exit, when he headed to the table and ate the meat and pancake with about two bites. When he heard someone coming he headed back to the kitchen stove where he was sitting when Anthony left. Anthony sat down, took a couple of swallows of coffee, picked up the bottle of syrup, and looked at his plate. After the third or fourth time he looked at the plate and glanced away he went to the stove, opened the warming oven and removed two hotcakes. At the table he poured syrup on the meat and cakes and took a big bite.

I couldn't decide whether to tell him what I had seen or to keep quiet. I looked over at the dog and the dog was looking right at me so I quickly decided I wouldn't tell on him if he wouldn't tell on me: On Halloween he had seen me with a gang of kids when someone in the bunch had poured white syrup on Wortman's outhouse seat. Anthony struck up a conversation with me until Mrs. Wortman returned with the money.

## POPCORN SERENADE

Uncle Lynn and Aunt Helen came to visit and since we already had a house full of company they decided to go to Bill's Ranch. My mother's cousin, Guy Devars, had purchased a cabin from Bill called Little Chief. This would be the abode of Uncle Lynn and Aunt Helen for the next seven days. Each day they came to our ranch to fish and to fellowship. They ate most of their meals with us but they had several breakfasts and one or two dinners at Ophir Lodge.

Uncle Lynn and Aunt Helen were very outgoing, so they got to know several people who were taking vacations at the lodge from various places in the U.S.

On one of their daily trips to our ranch, Bill Thomas came over with them. Bill mentioned while talking to Dad that he had seen mountain lion tracks behind his corral by the railroad grade.

Dad said, "We've seen some fresh tracks around here too, and yesterday I heard a lion scream in the distance when I went out to do the evening milking."

Dad continued, "One time Pete Prestrud told us how every once in awhile a lion would take her cubs and go on a safari between Buffalo Mountain and Dickey Mountain. Her trip would take her through your place and past our ranch to Chief and Buffalo Mountains.

"Oftentimes we see lion tracks around the Frisco Depot and around the Buffalo flume on Chief Mountain and up North Ten Mile Creek. North Ten Mile Canyon is a regular habitat for lions."

***Fun with the family.***

"I don't want the lion to scare my cows and cause them to give less milk," Bill said. "I'm selling all the milk the cows give now. Mrs. Mix (at Ophir Lodge) would take more milk if I had it."

Bill continued with a twinkle in his eye, "I think I'll put a couple of bells on the cows and if I hear the bells ringing in the night, I will use my 30-30 rifle on that lion."

Dad grinning said, "I am sure there are lions around most of the time, but they stay out of sight and we wouldn't know they were around here except for the tracks we see."

Dad continued, "Don't go outside after dark and you will be all right." Dad knew there wasn't any toilet inside and all hands would most likely have to go to the outhouse after dark.

Uncle Lynn and Aunt Helen were taking this all in and were getting more alarmed all the time.

The year before when Uncle Lynn and Aunt Helen were visiting us right after their marriage, they wanted to camp out so they borrowed a tent and stayed in our yard for several nights.

One morning Uncle Lynn said, "I heard you kids trying to scare us last night by walking around the tent and kicking a can around. Helen heard that funny little grunting noise you made. I'll tell you what, you didn't scare us a bit."

Mom, listening to the conversation said, "Lynn, I don't think the kids bothered your tent last night." Turning to me she asked, "Did you kids go near the tent last night?"

"No, we didn't," I said, "I'll bet it was a bear."

Off to the tent we went to see if there were any tracks around that would give us a clue as to what they had heard. Sure enough, there were bear tracks in the dry dirt at the side of the tent. When we showed the tracks to Uncle Lynn and Aunt Helen they were scared to death. That ended their sleeping in the tent. It was too bad, as I had plans for a lot of fun with them.

With refreshed memories of that scare Aunt Helen, Uncle Lynn, and Bill Thomas headed back to Bill's Ranch. After dropping Bill off at his house they went to their cabin, Little Chief.

All went fine until just after dark. Uncle Lynn and Aunt Helen were enjoying the evening fire in the heating stove when Uncle Lynn opened the door to go out and get another log for the fire.

He called, "Helen, come to the door. I think I can hear a cow bell ringing in the distance."

Helen agreed, "It definitely is a cow bell ringing." It would stop fr a minute and then ring again.

"I'll run over to Bill's house," Uncle Lynn said.

"You can't leave me here alone and I'm afraid to go out in the dark," Aunt Helen said with a quiver in her voice.

They slammed the door shut and listened for the bell. All they could hear was the soft patter of light rain on the tin roof of the cabin. It had started to rain just before dark. Time moved on. Aunt Helen had just let loose of the grip she had on Uncle Lynn's arm when the quiet of the night was broken with a loud scream that ended with a groan or possibly a growl. It seemed to be right outside of the cabin. Then the cow bell gave several clangs right by the cabin door.

"I'm sure a lion is chasing the cows," whispered Uncle Lynn as he gripped Aunt Helen's hand. It was obvious that the lion was right up by the cabin door.

"What will we do now?" Aunt Helen whispered, as she broke out in goose pimples.

"I don't think a lion could get into the cabin, do you?" she asked, trying not to be too alarmed.

Uncle Lynn rechecked the lock on the door and then moved the big rocker over against the door. Just then they heard a scratching on the corner of the cabin and another blood curdling scream pierced the night.

Now it was time to take drastic measures. "Helen, I think that the lion just clawed the cabin. Maybe if we blow the light out he will leave," whispered Uncle Lynn. Then all was quiet for a while and about the time they decided the lion was gone they heard another terrifying scream right outside their door. Panic gripped them both.

"It's the lion; what can we do?" Helen whispered.

"I don't know," groaned Uncle Lynn. Just then it sounded

like the lion was going to get in the cabin. There was lots of clawing and rubbing on the cabin and the bell gave a couple of clanging tones and the tone ended with a dull thud and another scraping noise on the side of the cabin.

It had seemed a little cool in the cabin, but now Uncle Lynn took his hankie and wiped the sweat from his face. He could picture the lion eating on a cow just outside of the door and maybe he would try to hide what was left of the carcass in the cabin. The very thought almost paralyzed his legs, but he had to do something. He tried to whisper to Aunt Helen, but his voice just seemed to come out in spurts and grunts.

Finally he grabbed Aunt Helen's arm and motioned her to the table. With one frantic push they moved the table over to the middle of the cabin and put a chair on it. Then they got on the table and Uncle Lynn helped Aunt Helen on the chair so she could climb up into the loft. Aunt Helen tipped the scales at well over two hundred pounds dripping wet.

The loft could be used for storage or possibly a bedroom with a four foot ceiling. When Helen got up into the loft Uncle Lynn handed her the poker, a broom from behind the heating stove, several blankets and two pillows from the bed. Then he crawled up into the loft and, taking the broom, he pushed the chair off the table. They hadn't noticed there was a ladder, for this purpose, leaning against the wall beside the living room window.

"Now", Uncle Lynn said, "I don't think the lion could get up here, even if he was able to get into the cabin." Raindrops on the metal roof made it hard for them to hear. About the time they thought the lion had left they would hear the bell ring again and that blood curdling scream.

"No guessing now, I am sure I know what is happening out there," Uncle Lynn said. "We hear the bell and then all is quiet. The lion has killed a cow right outside our door and while he is eating on the cow it makes the bell ring. He must be calling to a cub or two to come and eat their fill." Having settled on what was happening outside they took turns trying to sleep.

"Lynn, I sure would like to go to the bathroom, if there only was one inside the cabin," Helen groaned.

"I'm having a little problem of my own. I hope I can get by till morning," Uncle Lynn whispered. "Can you hold out till morning?"

"It'll be hard, but I'll have to," Helen whispered. Uncle Lynn finally drifted off to sleep.

"Did you hear something, Helen?" Uncle Lynn asked as he sat up.

"I haven't heard anything except the rain on the roof for over an hour. I am sitting up because I don't dare try to lie down till I go to the bathroom," Helen moaned.

Uncle Lynn sat up for a moment, then laid back down pulling a blanket up to his neck.

In the early morning hours the rain stopped and as daylight approached there was promise of another cloudless morning.

Lynn, Lynn," Helen whispered, "It's daylight and I have been awake for a long time. I haven't heard a sound outside for hours."

Uncle Lynn raised up, looked around and asked, "Is it daylight outside? Oh, my back, sleeping on these hard boards has about killed me. I can't wait till I can go to the toilet. Surely someone will come and rescue us soon."

"Don't bump me, Lynn, I sure have to go real bad. How are we going to get out of this loft?" Aunt Helen asked. With a lot of working around Uncle Lynn got down along the side of the cabin wall by a window. He put the chair back on the table and helped Aunt Helen down. They were still afraid to open the door and look outside.

Suddenly there was a call from outside, "Wake up folks, it is a beautiful, fresh morning after the rain last night." Off to the side went the rocker and Uncle Lynn opened the door. Never was anyone so glad to see someone as they were as they stepped outside in the bright sunshine and described the terrifying night they had just gone through.

Bill listened patiently and nodded sympathetically as they told of their last ditch effort to hide in the loft.

Bill said, "I don't see any dead cows around here, so I tell you what, go down to my house and there is a kettle of hot water on the stove and wash up." He continued, "There is a clean towel hanging on a nail by the wash pan. Help yourselves and then go up to the Lodge and have breakfast on me this morning. You will be in time to catch the first call for breakfast."

Breakfast was served on one long table. All guests ate at the same table at the same time.

Uncle Lynn asked, "Do you think we will be safe if we go to your house and then to the Lodge?"

Bill said, "You will be safe; there are a lot of people moving around. I am positive there isn't a lion in the immediate area now."

Bill continued, "I had better go look around and see what happened during the night and I will catch up to you folks later."

We were finishing a late breakfast at our ranch when here came Bill Thomas on foot. He was all out of breath, laughing so hard that it was hard to tell if he ran the two miles from his ranch to our ranch, or was just out of breath from laughing.

Bill said, "A lion kept Lynn and Helen in the loft of the cabin all night." He laughed so hard, he could hardly tell us what had happened. Finally he got out what Uncle Lynn had told him about the terrifying night. Then he proceeded to tell us what had really happened.

"It was really simple," he said, "I put a bell on Popcorn, my donkey, so I could find her when I wanted her. It was raining out last night and I imagine the donkey headed to the cabin to stand under the roof overhang on the front porch so she could keep dry."

Bill went on to say, "I heard her bray several times during the night and I guess she must of had an itch and rubbed it against the corner of the cabin. Anyway, I never thought it would be hard to tell the difference between a donkey singing and a lion's scream." He was still laughing when he asked if one of us could take him back to his ranch before he got caught. I got the job of taking Bill home.

At breakfast, Uncle Lynn had not spared any of the agony and fear they went through during the terrifying night. He had a sympathetic audience and some people expressed fear of going out of doors till something was done with the lion or lions. Unable to see Bill around close at hand Uncle Lynn and Aunt Helen drove over to our ranch and told and retold of the terrifying night.

They stayed for lunch and during lunch someone in our family started to laugh and then everyone laughed and laughed. We then told them Bill had put a bell on his donkey he called Popcorn, and that Popcorn had probably stood under the roof overhang on the cabin to get out of the rain. Every once in awhile she got lonesome and would let out a long, loud bray. She probably got an itch and rubbed the itch on the corner of the cabin. When she would swing her head it would ring the bell. They couldn't believe that it could be a donkey making all that noise. After going over it one more time they decided that they would go over to the cabin and get their sleeping bags and come back and sleep on the living room floor.

I went with them and of course we saw Bill Thomas as we pulled up beside the cabin. He told them that he had told everyone at lunch that they could go on outside as the lion was only his friendly donkey called Popcorn.

Uncle Lynn said he was so embarrassed that he thought they would never go to the Lodge again. However, the guests at the Lodge had invited Uncle Lynn and Aunt Helen to the Lodge for dinner and a time of fellowship that evening. They had a great time, but some people still believed that it was a mountain lion while others weren't sure. Not too many people ventured very far away from the Lodge for several days.

For years my aunt and uncle got picture cards and little donkeys from the many friends they made at Ophir Lodge.

## TIM ATTACKS MR. RUDY

With the coming of summer the authorities on many and various topics and subjects made their appearance. This particular summer, our authority on cats was a gentleman named Mr. Rudy, a school teacher from Denver. Mr. Rudy came over to the ranch for some butter and spied Tim. "That sure is a big cat, where did you get him?"

I told him all that we knew about Tim, and that we thought he was mixed with a bobcat.

"I'll tell you what I think," he said. "There are only two possibilities: One is the cat is mixed with a bobcat, or else he is mixed with a Manx cat. Now those Manx cats get great big and they are bob tailed. He must have gotten that bobtail from his dad and that long white hair from his mother. Of course Manx cats have heavy hair, but it is only of medium length."

Tim was sleeping with one eye open on a throw rug beside the wood box in the kitchen. Mr. Rudy stooped over and reached down to pet him. Tim laid there just like he was going to love the petting, possibly with a grin on his face, but when Mr. Rudy's hand touched him, up he jumped, spitting and growling at him. Tim made a couple swipes at Mr. Rudy's hand, scratching it badly before Mr. Rudy could get his hand out of the way.

Trying to soothe Tim, who by now was eagerly awaiting the opponent's next move, Mr. Rudy said, "I wouldn't hurt you, Tim." Just then Tim decided that he had gotten by with the first attack so he proceeded to grab Mr. Rudy by the leg, scratching and biting. I rushed over to Mr. Rudy and grabbed Tim. Tim held on. The only way I got Tim to release his hold on Mr. Rudy was to squeeze his jaws till he let loose. Mom rushed for her first aid kit as I escorted Tim to the door, where I gave him a good boot with my foot. He growled and spit at me all the way out of the door. He sure was in a bad mood or possibly he was embarrassed over his actions. As if!

Mom fixed up Mr. Rudy's hand and I guess all was forgiven.

"I sure would like to have a cat like that," he said as he gazed down the trail where Tim had disappeared. "Maybe I can get one of his kittens from a litter around town." I told him of a family that had four or five bobtailed kittens that I would guess were Tim's.

After Mr. Rudy went home Mom said, "I don't know what we are going to do with that cat if he doesn't get a little more civilized. His social skills are about zero most of the time."

## HOMEMADE FISH HATCHERY

Early one morning Dad and I went down to the big spring to find a better way to get to the little spring, where we got our drinking water. (We didn't drink the water from the Big Spring because it had a sulfur taste most of the time.) Our path between the springs was on peat moss and water oozed up around your shoes as you walked along.

"Come here, Harold," Dad called, "I've been looking at the baby trout that hatched out this spring. Look at them! There must be thousands!"

I hurried over to where Dad was looking into the lake portion of the spring drainage. The lake started at the spring where the water came out of the ground around two feet wide and grew wider to about one hundred feet wide, where it tapered back down to two feet when it flowed into Meadow Creek. It was about two inches deep at the beginning and gradually deepened to about thirty inches where it entered the creek.

Dad said, "I wish there was a way to keep the fish in one place by themselves till they grow up to five or six inches long." I could almost see the wheels turning in his head. The ground along the side of the spring lake was covered with peat moss and if you stood in one place for a minute water would come up around the sides of your shoes. At the outlet Dad outlined his thoughts.

"I bet we can build a wooden box in the outlet with a screen in it that will keep the hatch in the lake all summer and keep the big fish from coming into the spring and eating up the little wigglers," he said.

With the new path put aside for the time, we headed to the house. At the house we built a box three feet by three feet with vertical two by fours on each side to drop in a wooden frame with a screen on it. By evening we had the box with the screen in it firmly in place in the big spring outlet.

"This will work fine," Dad said, "but there are a lot of problems that will have to be taken care of before we have this all worked out." I took a coffee can of bran and sprinkled it on the water. Those little wigglers sure did boil the water for a few minutes.

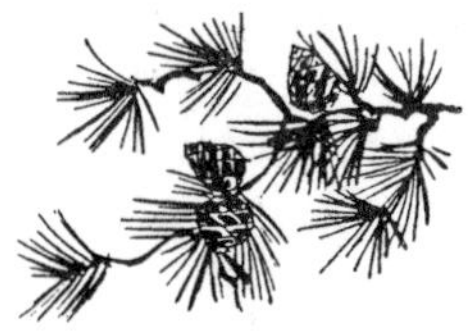

The next morning I made two more framed screens for reserves. Dad scouted the area to see where we could move the little wigglers when we would have to open the screen and let the brook trout back in the spring for their fall spawn.

The big spring emptied into a beaver pond on Meadow Creek. From this pond, there was a small stream of water that went into another pond, then it emptied back into Meadow Creek. Dad decided that the second pond was a natural for us to put the little wigglers in.

It took several weeks for us to find time to work on a good outlet. Dad got a four inch pipe six feet long with an elbow one foot long on one end. We buried the pipe a foot deep in the dam with the elbow turned up out into the water in the pond. The lower end of the pipe was over two feet above the water in Meadow Creek. The stream of water going out of the pipe was not enough for the fish to go up into the pipe and if they did they didn't have enough water spilling into the pipe to allow them to swim out of the pipe. The beaver piled mud and willows on the dam not realizing the outlet was through the pipe extending out into the pond. We put a screened box in the inlet which worked great except eventually, beaver, muskrats, and just trash would plug the screen. Every week we would have to remove the screen and clean it.

The last of August we seined (netted) the little wigglers (brook trout) out of the big spring and put them in the beaver pond. They were from one half inch to one inch long. Then we removed the screen from the big spring outlet. A short time after we removed the screen the brook trout from Meadow Creek came into the Big Spring Lake to spawn.

The next year we turned the little fish from the dam into the creek. Some of the fish we took to several locations on the ranch and one time we took a couple cans of fish to Lily Pond. By this time they were four to five inches long and really fat. It was hard to move them very far because you had to have oxygen in the water for the fish to live. When we moved fish to a new location we planned it so we could stop every twenty or thirty minutes and change the water in the cans.

## CHURCH COMES TO FRISCO

In the early spring of 1938, Rev. Ord Morrow came to Summit County. He worked at the Parker Ranch for a short time and then at Ken Chamberlain's garage in Frisco. He received board and room plus a dollar a day. He started a Bible study which met every Friday evening in the schoolhouse. Frisco finally had a community church!

Rev. Morrow became an itinerant preacher of sorts as Sunday mornings he preached in Climax, Sunday evenings he preached in Dillon, and Tuesday evenings he went to Montezuma if the roads were open.

He purchased two lots and was given one more lot two or three blocks east of the store and built a two-room house. It looked like he was here to stay. The house was covered with imitation brick siding. There was no interior wall covering the first year, but the ceilings were covered with one-half inch Celotex. The floor was concrete. It took a large heating stove and lots of wood to keep it warm in the high country during the winter.

On September 2, 1938, Ord married Opha Morrison at his brother's home in Climax.

Every Friday evening much of Frisco gathered to listen to Ord teach God's word from the Bible. On one of these times he called for all those who wanted to give their lives to Christ to gather up front of the school room for prayer and commitment to Christ. Several of the young people and one or two adults responded to the call. Dean, Helen, and I were among the kids. I hadn't realized before that it was a personal commitment that each individual had to make to Christ. No one could do it for you. (Mildred had made a commitment while we were still living in Eckley.)

This commitment changed my life. For one thing I started going to church at Climax Sunday mornings with the Morrows where I played my mandolin accompanied by the piano. Sunday evenings I went to church in Dillon and once again I was able to play my mandolin while Mildred played the piano for the singing.

Ord and Opha loved to ski but they never tackled the Piston Hill. They often would ski to our ranch and then we would all ski on the hill behind the house till Mom would call us in for cake and ice cream before they headed for home. It sure was fun going down the hill in the dark.

Many times in the winter the Morrows would invite all the kids in town to come over to their house for inside games and refreshments. Those were wonderful winter evenings to remember, full of the glow and warmth of fellowship and friends.

In the late summer of 1940 the Morrows moved to Lincoln, Nebraska, where he went to work for "Back to the Bible" on the radio. His preaching could be heard on the radio for over thirty-five years before he retired.

Before he left Frisco, Ord went to Denver where he contacted Harold Thompson. Harold and his wife Ethel had just finished their Bible training at Prairie Bible Institute at Three Hills, Alberta, Canada. They were ready to go wherever the Lord led them. The Morrows generously gave their property to Harold and his family.

Harold Thompson held services in the same places where Ord had started. Harold, also, was a man of God and believed and lived what he taught.

Oftentimes he was without funds for gas to go to Climax or to Dillon on Sunday. When this would happen he could be found on his knees calling on God to supply the need. He never missed a meeting because he didn't have money to buy what he needed!

Harold and Ethel raised their family in Frisco. In time Harold started a summer camp, and recruited other dedicated people to work in the camp during the summer.

Earl Von Ehrenkrook was one of the first guys to work in Thompsons' summer camp. He had driven his Model T to Frisco from Denver and it had taken him seven hours to make the trip over Loveland Pass! Earl was a man of few words but he stated, "I sure was glad I had someone with me to help push the T over the top."

When Earl left in the fall I bought his Model T for five dollars! He generously threw in several extra tires and one extra battery. Dad showed me how to hook up the magneto and I used it when the battery finally gave out.

As soon as I became the proud owner of the Model T, we converted it to a pickup by removing the top and doors and building a wooden bed on behind. This gave us a pickup to use around the ranch and to deliver milk to Frisco.

The next year Earl got married. He and his wife, Gladys, went to Julesburg to start a church ministry. Earl's brother Bernard spent the following several summers in Frisco teaching Bible school and working in the summer camp, or wherever he was needed most. A lady named Bernice also came to Frisco to work in the camp ministry under Harold Thompson. A couple years later Bernard and Bernice were married.

***Part of the Rutherford Clan: Harold, Helen, Mildred, Mickey, Margie, Toddy, Dean, Beulah, and Juanita.***

## I DUMPED THE GIRLS OUT OF THE MODEL T

One weekend during the summer nearly all of Uncle Sam's girls and the Haislett family came to the ranch. Sunday afternoon I took all of the gang that could hang on for a ride up to the foot of Chief Mountain in my Model T. I had never heard so much yapping since they got me to ride down the stairs in that metal bath tub when I was a little kid in Eckley. They kept telling me how to drive. As we were traveling along a thought occurred to me.

I said, as I unscrewed the wheel and passed it back, "If you don't like the way I drive, you can all drive the way you like." This brought screams of not less than five million decibels! Talk about excitement! Then I had a hard time getting the wheel back soon enough to make a curve, but I made it just in time!

Later, having a lot of confidence in my driving skills, I was turning around and talking to the girls and failed to see another curve coming up fast. We hit a tree going full blast at maybe ten miles per hour! Several of the girls fell out, or as they told my folks, were thrown out. Mildred's glasses were hanging on a branch of a tree just a little higher than I could reach. Not always knowing when to keep my mouth shut I said, "Mildred, you must have put your glasses up there, so you probably know how to get them down." The silence that greeted my feeble attempt at humor was deafening. Well at least no one was hurt but the Model T.

All the girls had to walk about a mile to the ranch which they did with a noticeable absence of smiles and a lot of mumbling under their breath. With much difficulty I managed to get the Model T home. The fan had cut a nice piece out of the radiator and the radius rod was badly bent. Henry Ashlock took a torch and straightened it out and Ken Chamberlain repaired the radiator. The Model T was once again ready for use!

As soon as I got the Model T running I continued to use it to deliver milk in Frisco.

One noontime I picked up Glen and Millet to take them home with me. We went up Main Street to the café where I turned north to the River Bridge. Glen and Millet were sitting in the back with their feet hanging out. I think they were having a political discussion about the price of putty in Peru. Glen hit Millet on the shoulder with his fist and Millet tried to push Glen out of the back end of the pickup.

There was a bump in the road where we crossed Galena Street so once again here was a golden opportunity staring me in the face! As I crossed over the culvert I speeded up a mite as we hit the bump. Glen and Millet landed on the street. I looked back and there they were still sitting on the street carrying on their political discussion.

Glen was a master at tying flies. I watched him tie little #18 flies using tweezers instead of his fingers. I usually had about a dozen of his best kinds in my fishing box. When I ran low of a certain fly he would tie up a handful for me. He made many kinds that he named himself. These usually were the best flies for the particular season.

## KEN CHAMBERLAIN BRINGS HORSES TO THE RANCH

One evening Ken and Betty Chamberlain came over to the ranch for a visit.

During the conversation Ken said, "Russell, you need some work horses."

Dad said, "I'll get a pair as soon as I can, but I use Giberson's and Dan Mogee's. I have one of Dan's horses that I have kept for a year or more. Last year we had a team from early spring till after our haying season."

"I'll buy you a new wagon, harness, and a couple of work horses, besides the saddle horse I brought over here last year,"

Ken said. "All I want is for you to let me use them once in a while. Of course, you will have to feed and take care of them the year 'round!"

They discussed it for awhile and then Dad decided it would be a fine opportunity for us. About a week later Ken arrived at the ranch with a team of black horses. They were work horses and not broken to ride. After we got acquainted with them, us kids decided to ride them. We started with a horse blanket on their backs and led them around the corral. After a few trips and a few days later we led them around with a gunny sack filled with dried grass. Then we threw a saddle on and continued to lead them around. They were happy that they were not pulling a wagon or mower.

Finally we cinched the saddle and led them around. One horse acted like he wanted to buck, but hardly got his front feet off the ground. One morning I put the saddle on one horse and climbed on. I thought he was going to buck, but, instead, he backed up all around the corral! After I did this several times I took him for a ride to Frisco and back with no problem. He didn't understand how to follow neck-reining, but he understood a slight tug on the rein. The other horse soon fell in line so we rode them around quite a lot, usually bareback.

## A SUPER TRUCK BRIDGE

While we were milking Dad said, "Harold, I made a little circle on the island and there is a winter's supply of dead wood in standing trees. If you cut a lot of them down and pile them up I have an idea how to get them to the shed without taking a lot of time. I bought the running gears from a truck Ken Chamberlain was tearing up. We can buy a pair of tires and tubes and then we will have a two-wheel trailer."

Dad finished milking his cow and started another cow and continued, "We can take the pickup bed off the Model T while we are hauling wood. I can build a bolster on the back to haul the trees to the wood shed. When we get enough trees hauled, we can get someone with a power saw to cut the trees up into stove lengths. We can put one end of the trees on the bolster and the other end on the running gears and chain the logs to the bolster and the running gears. We won't have to haul heavy loads, but we can haul several times the amount you can on the Model T truck and it will be a lot easier than using the Model A."

"This sounds exciting to me," I said. "I can push over a lot of the little trees and cut down the ones that won't push over. I can start tomorrow and put the trees in big piles."

Dad said, "While we're waiting for tires we need to build a bridge. The Model T won't have enough power to cross the creek where the cows cross. We can build a bridge below the cow crossing where the creek is narrow."

Dean helped me with the two-man saw and we cut down several trees. We spent several days piling up small trees. I also cut down a number of larger dead trees.

All was quiet on the ranch as I was too busy for any extra undertakings.

I cut down four green trees around eight inches in diameter for the stringers for the bridge and skidded them to the creek with a horse. They were very heavy, but I managed to get them in place. I put two logs side by side and took number nine wire and fastened them together. Then I spaced the tracks so each pair would match the wheels on the Model T. I pounded heavy stakes in the ground on each side of each pair of logs so they couldn't move. I also put #9 wire from one pair of treads to the other pair so they couldn't spread in the middle. I decided I could cross the creek with the Model T this way till I got time to cut poles to make a deck. I went across the creek this way for a week or more hauling small amounts of wood to the creek bank.

Enabled by my crude but stable bridge I was able to take a load of trees to the wood pile by the wood shed. The following days the girls helped Dean and me load and haul the rest of the wood to the shed. The running gears worked perfectly. The Model T had no problem moving a pile at a time. We wanted to haul as much wood as we could in one day to surprise Dad. We hauled eight or nine loads during the day and, boy, were we ever tired out. I left the last load on the running gears and the Model T so Dad could see how we hauled the trees.

Dad was amazed when he saw how much wood we had hauled. "I can hardly believe my eyes," he said. "I didn't realize that the bridge was ready to use. You kids have done a great job.

"When I get done with the job I'm on, I'll take a day or two and help you finish getting the wood in. Then we can get someone to power saw it up," Dad said.

The next week we hauled about all the trees I had piled up. It was a lot of fun getting the wood in, even though it was a lot of hard work. My bridge worked so well I didn't try to build a deck on it. With no margin of error to work with I had to have the running gears directly behind me and once in a while I had to back up a time or two to get lined up. We hauled so much wood that Dad did other things rather than help haul wood.

One evening Ed Riggs came over and wanted to buy four logs nine feet long and eight inches in diameter for corners on his cabin. He wasn't going to "log cabin" the corners. (When you log cabin a corner it is like lacing the ends of your fingers together. Every other log goes over the top of the previous log that is running at an angle. Using an ax the logs have to be fitted together. They protrude beyond the walls of the cabin usually one to two feet.)

The easier way, but maybe not the best, is to stand a two-inch by eight-inch piece of lumber in the corner and nail it to the ends of the logs. Then you stand an eight inch log, similar to the one that Ed was buying, in the corners to fill them out.

Dad said, "Ed, come over when you have some time and I will take you to the island. You can pick out the logs you want and we will cut them down and haul them to your place."

On Saturday when Ed came over Dad said, "Let's go over and mark the trees. I'll cut them down and haul them to your place today."

Ed, Dad, and I headed to the island. As we got to the bridge Dad stopped and stood there looking at the bridge. Finally he said, "Did you cross the creek on those logs?"

I replied rather nervously, "I hauled all the wood across the bridge and didn't have any trouble."

Dad, sort of growling said, "That is very dangerous. I am surprised you would try it without finishing the bridge." After a little discussion we continued to the island. In a few minutes Ed found the trees he wanted. Ed and Dad cut them down and cut them the proper length. I cleaned the branches off of the leftover tops.

Ed asked, "Do you think Harold can chance one more time crossing the creek to get the logs? I sure would like to get them to Frisco today."

Dad rubbed his face a couple times and finally said, "Harold go get the Model T and the running gears and meet us at the bridge." I drove the Model T to the bridge and got there just as Ed and Dad arrived. They watched as I drove across.

"I see no problem, Russell," Ed said, "but I'd be afraid to drive across myself." They got in the T with me and we drove onto the bridge. The logs sure were heavy, but with a little work and using a couple poles for leverage we got them on the T and the running gears. Dad and Ed rode back to the bridge and got off there. Dad watched the back wheels while I drove across. This had been Mildred's job when we were hauling the wood.

Dad said, "Harold, it works a lot better than I could imagine, but don't haul any more wood across the bridge till we get the top on. If you ever had a wheel go off the logs, or if the logs spread, you could turn the T over in the creek and get hurt."

The following week us kids covered the bridge with four inch poles. Dad brought home some good used two-inch by eight-inch plank for treads. We laid two plank side by side for each tread. This made a good bridge, but the cows still chose to cross the creek at the cattle crossing.

## A BEAR GOT GLEN MAC WHILE SNIPE HUNTING

One summer day when I delivered Mrs. Olson's milk she said, "I want to have a party for all of the kids in town. Do you think we could get them all here tomorrow evening?"

"What will we do and how many kids will be able to come?" I asked.

"I talked to several people when I went for the mail and I guess there could be around fifteen kids. I want to have the party as soon as possible as I heard another family is going to leave in a couple of weeks. The Martz family is also here for the summer and there are three kids there," she replied.

"I'll deliver my milk and go home and see if I can get the girls to help spread the word," I said. I knew it would be no problem for my sisters. I rushed around with the milk deliveries and went home. Mildred and Helen went to Frisco with me and we talked to every one of the kids in town including the two new families that had moved to town after school was out. I left word at the post office for Darrel Bailey.

Mrs. Olson planned on having popcorn, a taffy pull, and ice cream and cookies. We were to take our ice cream freezer along with one the MacMasters had. Mrs. Olson also had a small freezer that could be used if it was needed. The games that were planned consisted of monopoly, Chinese checkers, card games, and dominos. I figured we could go with those for awhile as I tried to conjure up something a little more lively.

We milked a little early and arrived at Mrs. Olson's shortly after five thirty. By six there were seventeen kids assembled and the ice cream freezers were cranking. The outside games were nicely in progress when somehow the conversation came around to snipes.

"What is a snipe?" Jean Martz asked.

"Well, it's a game bird a little smaller than a teal duck," I replied as if I were one of those summertime visiting authorities. Different kids kept talking about it and it seemed to me most of the kids had never heard of going snipe hunting. "You got to be kidding me! You've lived this long in the mountains and have never been snipe hunting?" I asked.

Not to be outdone, Darrel Bailey volunteered that he and his brother had gone snipe hunting a couple of weeks earlier and got several birds.

This was too much for Glen MacMasters. "Did you use a shotgun to hunt them?" he asked.

Darrel realized this was an opportunity to play a trick on Glen by giving him details on the art of hunting snipes. "Oh, you don't hunt them with a gun. You must hunt after dark. You take a big sack and a flashlight and quietly go out into the woods along a stream. You also take a couple of small sticks to prop the sack open and then take the flashlight and shine it into the bag. You should have a couple of other people to walk around in the brush and spook the snipes. When you scare them they will fly up and away. They will only fly about a hundred feet when they will light again, but if they see the bag with a light shining into it they will, for some reason, head to the light. As soon as they are in the bag the person holding the bag has to snap the bag closed or the snipe will get out. As soon as you get one snipe you need to set up another bag and continue the operation."

Glen turned to me and said, "It's hard for me to believe that there are any snipes in this area. Have you ever seen a snipe around here?"

"This is one of the best areas for snipes," I said. "You don't hear much about snipe hunting because they are about the size of a pigeon and it would take several of them to make a meal for a family. I'm sure you have seen them along the banks of the river. It's usually best to hunt close to a stream because when they are scared they will fly low over the water." I was thinking about the road along Ten Mile River.

Glen, showing a lot of excitement, asked, "What would you think if some of us went above the bridge on the Ten Mile River and hunted for a few minutes this evening? I think I may have seen a snipe several times when I was fishing along the stream."

George put in, "I'd like to go just as soon as it gets dark. I went several times last year and we had luck of some kind every time we went out." He failed to say what kind of luck they had.

Glen disappeared into the house and asked Mrs. Olson if we could borrow two or three burlap sacks and leave the party for a few minutes. She went into the wood shed and got us several sacks and handed Glen a flashlight.

Barely able to keep from laughing she said, "I think you'll need the flashlight, if you're going to hunt snipes."

We all went to work freezing the ice cream and some of the kids started popping popcorn. The party was in high swing! Mrs. Olson had a batch of taffy candy cooking. She had fastened the handle of a hayhook on the door casing near the top of the door and held it in place by turning a wood knob that wedged the handle to the door casing. I think this had been done many times before. She was a pro!

She then took some butter we had brought from the ranch and rubbed it on her hands. Then she took a handful of warm taffy and started molding it in her hands. After rubbing butter on the hook she rolled the taffy till it was about two inches in diameter and about four feet long. She took the taffy by each end and swung it over the hook and pulled it to her till it was about to pull apart, then she made a ball out of it and rolled it again into a long rope and repeated the operation. It was a fascinating thing to watch! She swung the taffy over the hook till it got so stiff it was hard to roll or pull. At this point she put it on the table and formed a roll about two inches in diameter and cut it in several pieces that would fit on a platter. Then she took a knife and cut it into pieces about an inch long.

Asking for volunteers to try their hand on the next plate of taffy, she started with Thelma, who was the first to volunteer.

All of a sudden George noticed it was getting dark. "Hey!" he said, "if we're going to go snipe hunting we'd better get started; I don't want to be gone too long since the taffy is about ready to eat."

We got all set up with the sacks and the flashlight and then George, Eddie, Tommy, Darrel, Glen's brother Millet, Dean, and I headed to the west side of the bridge, escorting a very excited Glen. As we approached the west side, I could see we had to have a better place to hunt snipes. It would be impossible to hunt snipes and sneak around Glen on the way back to the party without his seeing us.

"Hey, guys," I said, "this isn't a very good spot. If we go up the river a short distance, there is a good spot where the road runs along the edge of the water. We can walk up the road and get a snipe and be back to the party before they get the taffy all pulled."

This sounded like a good idea, so up the river we went. In a few minutes we placed Glen, with specific instructions, on a sandy bar alongside of the water. The rest of us went out into the willows and made a lot of racket.

Occasionally someone would yell, "I just flushed a snipe."

Darrel went back to Glen and asked, "Have any snipes come by yet?"

"I haven't cornered any, but a bird flew by and I think it was a snipe. I think you guys are too noisy, and don't yell at me and expect me to answer, 'cause my answering will keep the snipes away."

Now that we had Glen all set, we gathered together and headed back to the party. Some time went by and Glen hadn't come back. A little concerned we returned to where we had left Glen at the sandbar. When we got there, Glen was nowhere to be seen. The sack was still there, however the sticks were out of the sack and it was lying flat on the ground. The flashlight was still on and lay about ten feet away.

"Hey," Darrel said, "what happened to Glen?"

At first I thought Glen had realized the prank and was hiding a few feet away. We called and called but all we could hear was the call of a night hawk and an owl calling to her mate. Suddenly the friendly night took a sinister feeling.

George grabbed the flashlight and looked around on the sand. Suddenly he yelled, "Look, bear tracks. A bear got Glen!" All heads were together looking at the spot where George was shining the flashlight.

I said, "It sure is a bear track, and looks like a pretty good sized one." Dean and Millet took the light and, shining it around, we could see bear tracks coming to the spot where Glen had been. There was a spot where a hole four inches wide and a good two feet long was dug out of the sand. The tracks leaving the spot looked like the bear was dragging something but my mind wouldn't allow me to think it could be Glen. We examined the tracks again and again and called and called. No answer.

A short time ago there had been muffled laughter, snickering, and even a giggle, but now silence fell on the gang of pranksters.

My legs would hardly hold me up. I finally said we had better go to the café and call the sheriff. My heart ached for Glen.

Millet said, "I hope Glen is all right."

"I hope the bear isn't going to eat him," Dean remarked. All this talk didn't help. It was just silence as we walked back to the bridge. I think everyone was praying for Glen.

"We had better tell them at the party what has happened and then go to the café," I said, in a very low voice. It was hard to talk with the horrible lump that had formed in my throat.

Back at Mrs. Olson's gate it was as if we had run into a plate glass door at full speed. The effect couldn't have been much different as we all spied Glen at the same time, inside the house. Here he was, our fallen comrade, having the time of his life enjoying the party while we were outside shaking with fright at the thought of his unknown fate. I wanted to get mad, or kick him or something. "I would like to get mad, but let's face it, we're all tickled to death at seeing him alive," I said.

Inside the house they told us Glen knew all about snipe hunting.

"How did you make the tracks?" I asked.

"It was simple," Glen said. "As soon as you all quit calling, I took off my socks and shoes and walked on the ball of my foot and my toes. I took my hand and scooped out a hole in the sand to look like the bear did it. When I made the tracks heading away, I wiggled my foot around to make deeper tracks in the sand. I knew you guys would think they were made by a bear."

Betty added, "Glen was back to the party before you guys came back the first time. When you came back Glen hid in the other room till you left again."

The party was a big success even though several of us were discomposed for a while. I swore I wouldn't pull another prank for at least two weeks.

## KENNETH CALDWELL ... A NEW BEGINNING

In the fall of 1938 there was a problem between the school teacher and the school board. Most of the kids, including us, didn't return to school, Mrs. New resigned, and Frisco was without a teacher.

And then a miracle happened. Kenneth Caldwell came to Frisco for the weekend. Kenneth was a friend of Bill Schweitzburger, who had a sister and brother-in-law, Jeannie and Johnny Nix, living in Frisco. Kenneth was working as a counselor and teacher at Number 9 Downing Street in Denver.

Johnny Nix had Kenneth talk to Ken Chamberlain about a dishwashing job and after they talked for a short time Ken found out that Mr. Caldwell was a school teacher.

Ken said, "I sure could use you but we desperately need a school teacher, since our teacher just resigned. If you want to teach you can make more money teaching than I can pay you for working in the kitchen."

Mr. Caldwell said, "I'd love to have the job. When can I meet with the school board?"

Ken Chamberlain said, "There's a house warming party tonight for the Allens. The Allens have just finished remodeling the house they bought and moved from the Excelsior Mine. It had been used as an office for the mining company. Go to the party and if none of the members of the school board are there I'll run them down in the morning."

None of the board members was there so Ken Chamberlain made arrangements for Mr. Caldwell to meet with the school board on Sunday. He was immediately hired for the job and was to be paid $100.00 a month. The twelve kids that presented themselves were not as many as the previous year since several families had moved to Climax.

This was the start of a new beginning for Kenneth Caldwell and many other people in Frisco and Summit County.

Kenneth rented a place from Mrs. Frank Olson, who was still the school janitor. He couldn't pay till he got his first month's paycheck. He borrowed $7.50 from me to buy coal and paid it back by early spring.

Kenneth could hardly wait to marry his college sweetheart, Maxine. They were married in January 1939. Maxine was a great addition to Frisco. She had had polio as a kid and was slightly handicapped when it came to skiing and ice skating, but she was very active in music, church, and parties. She had an unusually good voice and often sang in church.

As soon as Kenneth got the school running smoothly, his thoughts turned to music. He had a degree in music and was very talented. He shared this great gift with everyone he came in contact with.

An orchestra was started, although some of the kids had never had an hour's instruction in music. Kenneth patiently taught the kids music in the evenings and on weekends. All of our family played; Mildred on the piano, me on the mandolin, Helen on the guitar, and Dean on a mouth harp.

Dean had expressed an interest in playing a violin so Dad bought a violin from Pete Lege's store for him. Pete had taken the violin as payment on a food bill of less than ten dollars.

(Nobody knew just how valuable the instrument was, but it eventually was appraised at over a thousand dollars! It was a sad day when the fiddle, treasured for both its monetary and sentimental value, was destroyed in a horrific fire years later at Helen's home in Sandpoint, Idaho. Helen acquired the violin for her eldest son after Dean died in 1950 on a Naval rescue mission out of Adak, Alaska.)

Tommy Giberson played the mandolin banjo, Ord Morrow the violin, Opha played the guitar, Leafie Sampson played the clarinet. Chet Sawyer from Dillon played the sax, Mary Wood from Breckenridge a clarinet and her brother John played a trumpet. Millet MacMasters played a violin and Glen played a trumpet. Some other kids played instruments for awhile, then dropped out or moved away. Also there were a number of adults and kids who played part time.

Chick Deming sang and someone said Bing Crobsy couldn't sing any better than Chick could, especially the song, "You Old Indian Summer." I am sure everyone who ever heard him sing agreed to this.

We had sixteen musicians playing for the Christmas program and, when Easter arrived, our orchestra played a recital in the town hall. It was beautiful and certainly a tribute to the Lord! Well, that is, mostly so! Ord Morrow and I were to play a duet with the rest of the orchestra playing softly in the background, but after the first few notes I lost my place and couldn't find it, even though Mr. Caldwell all but yelled the notes to play. I just followed along playing in harmony. Kinda. (Not my proudest moment!)

When the spring recital came around, there were a lot more people who performed. We even went to Alma where, under the direction of Kenneth Caldwell and my Aunt Clari Cheadle, we played in a musical with the Alma musicians. This was quite an undertaking, especially when I considered how many of the kids couldn't read music when school had started the previous fall. Now they were playing a large assortment of instruments and music. Kenneth worked hard to help each kid or adult read music and play their particular instrument. Many people in Summit County took music lessons from him.

Mr. Caldwell also had a drama class and put on a number of plays using many adults in the community. Besides teaching music to kids in the school and many people outside the school, Kenneth had a class called music appreciation. In this class, the school kids were exposed to all kinds of music. He also was very good in teaching academic classes. If a pupil was having a difficult time in a subject he would spend extra time helping that student understand the difficult part and get back on top.

One Saturday afternoon a gang of kids went to the Piston Hill to ski and Kenneth joined the ski party. Kenneth had never had skis on before, but he was game for anything. He went to the steep side of Piston Hill and shoved off down the hill with his dress coat trailing behind him. About a third of the way down the hill he lost his hat and his balance. One ski went up in the air, and then back down on the snow and then the other ski copied the first ski. He squatted down till his seat scraped the snow, then back up he stood, as if someone was taking a picture of him and he was a four star general. He leaned over first to the front and then to the back. One arm would go in the air and then it would reach off to the side and then back to the snow, but not quite. Then the other arm took a turn and reached for the snow that was traveling past him so fast that there was no place to grab, then his arms would reach in the air for something unknown. He came to a place in the snow where there was a small dip. This did it! His arms and legs refused to retrace their many maneuvers and he nose dived into the snow. Someone picked up the ski pole that he had dropped when he shoved off. Even Peter Prestrud, a famous jumper named in the Colorado Hall of Fame, couldn't have put on a display more elegant than this.

Monday morning Mr. Caldwell came to school with a very stiff neck. Different kids took turns massaging his neck and after several days he was back in shape. For several years after that the Piston Hill was avoided by Kenneth.

## BEN STALEY'S DOG, THE CAT KILLER

Ben Staley came over to see if Dad could use him during our haying season. While Dad and Ben were talking, Ben's dog, Spot, came running up and Ben picked him up. He was a little brown and white, short haired dog. He had a fierce bark and was considered to be a cat killer.

Dad said, "I'm glad you picked up your dog because our cat is around here somewhere and he is certain death on dogs."

Ben laughed, "Don't worry about my Spot. He removed nine lives from several cats in town this last summer, but I don't want him to kill your cat." Ben went on to say, "Why don't you get your cat and put him in the house so I can let Spot down?"

"I think Tim will stay out of the way of your dog, but maybe you need a small rope on your dog to keep him with you," Dad said laughing.

Looking at me Dad continued, "Harold, see if you can find Tim and put him into the house till Ben goes home." I looked everywhere, but he wasn't to be found.

Ben finally put Spot down and the dog proceeded to look for Tim on his own. We did our milking while Ben watched and visited. Spot was in and out of the barn constantly so I finally got up and closed the barn door to keep him out. The cows were getting real nervous with his running all over and were taking their wrath out on those who were milking them, with swift kicks. We finished milking and took the milk to the milk house. When I came out of the milk house I saw Tim trotting along headed towards town.

"Hey, Ben, where is your dog?" I asked. Ben whistled, and here came the dog. Spot came up to Ben and then he saw Tim going down the road. Away he went, barking as he went.

Tim heard Spot and stopped and turned around with his back bowed and the hair on his tail standing straight out.

Ben yelled, "Spot, you get back here." Ben whistled and whistled but to no avail. The dog had a job he thought he should do and there was no turning back now.

Spot caught up to Tim and there was a terrible jumping and rolling, barking, and growling. You couldn't tell which tail or foot or paw belonged to whom and the noise was murderous!

All of a sudden here came Spot, headed towards the house as fast as he could with Tim on his back. Spot rolled over several times before he got up to us, but Tim stayed right with him, chasing and jumping on his back, then another roll over. Then Spot was up again still heading in our direction with Tim hanging on. Spot ran to Ben and Ben grabbed for him. He missed the dog and Tim held on as they went by. What a terrifying noise! Spot's barking had turned to a pitiful cry and Tim was making enough noise for at least six fighting cats. Back down the road they went, rolling over. Then off they would run for a little way, and then another roll. Each time they rolled Tim's feet would remove a little more hair off Spot's back.

Ben took off after Spot on a run! It was quite evident that the dog would get to Frisco before Ben would get to our gate.

"Harold," Dad yelled, "take the pickup and follow after them, and if you can, try to get the dog into the back of the pickup."

I headed down the road and picked up Ben. By this time we couldn't hear Tim, just a wailing noise in the distance that I took to be the dog. I headed towards Frisco with Ben. Just as we got to the River Bridge, here came Spot out of the willows running as fast as he could. Ben yelled at him, but Spot didn't hear him; or maybe he thought that since he had his feet in motion he wouldn't stop and take a chance on that cat catching him.

I took Ben over to his house and let him out. Spot was sitting at the front door pleading for some one to let him in. He was shaking all over. Ben got out of the truck and ran over and petted the dog. His back looked like it needed a hair transplant, his neck and both front legs were covered with blood. He held up one leg that had a sizable cut running from the shoulder to the end of his paw.

"Ben," I said, "I think you should take your dog to the vet in Breckenridge."

Ben replied, "He'll be all right, but I'll bet he killed your cat along the way somewhere."

Just then Mrs. Staley, his wife, opened the door and tossed out an old quilt on the porch floor and said, "Ben, I told you that someday Spot and that big black dog at the hotel were going to clash. What chance would Spot have with a dog three times as large as he is." Ben didn't answer. He helped Spot onto the quilt.

Ben said, "You'd better get me some warm water and I'll see how bad he's hurt. You may have to call the vet and see what we need to get to put on all his cuts."

Mrs. Staley was standing by the door and, looking over the situation, she said, "It looks like a mountain lion has gotten hold of him, look at all those slices on his back."

Looking at me, she said, "Thanks for bringing Spot and Ben home." Then she turned to Ben and said, "I'd better hurry over to the store and call the vet."

I wished them well and hurried out to the pickup. I don't know if Ben ever told her what had really happened, but when

Ben came over to work in the hay fields, he never again brought Spot with him. It was probably by mutual agreement.

We didn't see Tim for a couple of days and when he came home there didn't seem to be a mark on him, however, when he jumped off of a chair to the floor, he raised up his paw and growled at it. Then he sat down and gave it a good washing. I don't know whether he had a cat vet in the high country that he went to, or if he wasn't hurt that bad, but whatever it was, he was not much worse for wear. I am sure that after the fight, he had to get well-groomed before he could go out on the town to spend the evening with one of his many girl friends.

Back when the mining boom was on, the Excelsior Mine had installed a generator on North Ten Mile River at the bottom of the canyon. A wooden pipe ran from the lake at the Square Deal Mine carrying water down to the generator; furnishing electricity for Frisco as well as the mine. However, after the Excelsior Mine closed the generator was removed and Frisco was left with no electric power in February, 1913.

In July 1940, after 27 years, electricity finally came back to Frisco.

## THEY MISSED THE TROPHY BUCK

Every fall some of our friends came to visit us during deer and elk season. Fall in Frisco with all the beautiful gold and red leaves of the aspen trees was quite a contrast to the brown sand hills of Yuma County. I loved this time of year. I loved to hunt and fish, especially with our friends. I got out of school for a few days during hunting season to help Dad with the chores, and I also got a chance to do some hunting.

In 1938 the hunting party consisted of Eldred Haislet and his dad Frank, Ross Twedell, and Tip Murheid from Yuma County, and two brothers, Joe and Mike McLean from Colorado Springs, besides Dad and myself. Ross and Eldred's wives, Nancy and Mabel, came along to help Mom with all the extra work. We had to borrow extra horses to have enough to accomplish what we wanted to do for hunting.

Dad planned to go with the Yuma County hunters up Salt Lick Gulch to where it meets Buffalo Mountain and hunt in that area the first day. I was to take Joe and Mike up to the ridge above Lily Pond so they could hunt in that area. Dad made arrangements for someone in Frisco to come over and help with the milking and delivering the milk during the week of deer hunting.

At three A.M. Dad yelled, "Harold, it's time to get up and get the horses in the barn and get ready for breakfast." I had been awake off and on during the night anticipating the coming hunt, but now I was very sleepy. I crawled out of bed, dressed, and headed to the corral. I put the horses in the barn and gave them their grain. Then I put on their saddles and fastened a scabbard and a rope to each saddle.

I headed back to the house to see who was up for breakfast, but when I got there, there was a line a mile long waiting to use the wash basin. I grabbed a towel and some soap and headed to the irrigation ditch below the house. The water was about as cold as it can get and not turn to ice. When I finished I gave the soap and towel to one of the other hunters who had washed here with me on other occasions.

We had bacon, eggs, hot cakes, and of course coffee for breakfast. I didn't like coffee so I had hot chocolate. For each hunter, Mom made a lunch of sandwiches, apple, cookies, and coffee in a jar, all done up in a bag.

After breakfast I went to the barn for our horses. I tightened the cinches and tied them at the gate that went into the back pasture. Joe and Mike were going to ride up over the foothills to the base of Buffalo Mountain and then on to an area above and north of Lily Pond where they would leave the horses in a small grassy meadow. I was to go back home and in the late afternoon I would go back to where the horses were and guide the hunters back home.

Dad was to ride to the top of the ridge above Salt Lick Gulch and spook out big bucks for the hunters, who were scattered along the drainage on stands. Well, hopefully so. (A stand is a place which we have previously determined to be a likely place for elk and deer to cross or feed. A hunter will stay at the stand for several hours or even all day.)

I put my rifle in my scabbard, tied my backpack with my lunch in it to the back of my saddle, and checked Mike and Joe to be sure they were ready to ride.

It was just breaking daylight when we rode along our north fence line to the northwest corner, where we had a gate. Once through the gate I again tightened the cinches on the horses and headed up towards the foothills. I took the lead, with Mike and Joe following in single file.

After we made the first little hill, I stopped to let the horses get their wind and to point out a few landmarks that they should know. We rode a little farther when a doe jumped from behind some willow bushes and took off on a run. We watched her disappear into the aspen trees below. This got the hunters excited! They started talking and I thought that the sun would come up before they were ready to travel again.

I heard them tell several stories of previous hunting experiences and the hundreds of deer they had shot. I nudged my horse forward and they followed, ending the stories for the moment.

When we arrived at the Buffalo Ditch, I had them dismount and lead the horses across. The banks were steep where we climbed out. Besides helping the horses, I wasn't sure the riders and horses would make the crossing with the riders still in the saddles. After leaving the ditch we headed across an open area where sagebrush stretched several hundred yards in all directions.

All of a sudden I noticed the horses were sniffing the air and looking ahead up the hill. I stopped and pointed to the horse's ears and then I put my finger over my mouth indicating not to talk. We sat there a minute or two looking over the foothills. I couldn't see anything, but I felt sure we were close to something. It could be some stray range cattle but they were all supposed to be off the range by now.

After a couple of minutes we rode on up the trail. It brought us to the top of one of many ridges. We stopped to scan the hills and especially check out the edges of little meadows where the aspen trees grew in abundance across the ridge in front of us. The hunters rode up side by side and it seemed like what one did the other one did. They both took their field glasses and leaned forward in the saddle to scan the area. I didn't need my glasses. The horses looked forward again.

I studied a little clump of trees and some tall willows for a sign of deer. Suddenly I was rewarded with deer horns extending above the sage brush. My heart beat fast! I slid off my horse just as a big buck stood up. I whispered low to the hunters and finally I had to run around to one of them to get their attention. They sat in their saddles taking their time while they looked the buck over using their field glasses.

Joe remarked, "That is about the size of the buck I got a couple of years ago." Mike just sat there and looked at the buck! The buck was not over two hundred yards from us.

"Tie your reins together and run your arm through the loop or the horses might try to run when you shoot," I whispered. I couldn't believe all this was taking place and the buck was still there. They slowly got off their horses and knelt down beside the horses on one knee. They both, at the same time, levered a shell into their rifles. I sure was getting nervous. "That buck must be blind and deaf," I thought. They both aimed, and aimed, and aimed. I was about to get my rifle when they shot at the same time. The noise was deafening.

Suddenly the buck came alive! I think he was still asleep when the blast broke the silence, bringing him back to reality. He must have been dreaming of something great, but now, where did all that noise come from!?! I could almost see a big question mark over his head. He didn't run, just stood there looking around. The hunters, just like a pair of highly trained militia men, stood up together and ejected their spent cartridges. Each levered another shell into the chamber, then they knelt down, and again they aimed, and aimed, and finally shot again. They missed the buck with the first shots and it was apparent that they had hit the buck in the same place again.

In all the excitement, I failed to notice that neither one of the hunters had done as I told them about holding on to the reins. Both horses tolerated the first shots, but when they shot again Mike's horse took off on a dead run to parts unknown. I made a quick pass to get the reins, but he was too fast for me. I grabbed the reins of Joe's horse and held him with my horse.

Once again they stood up, ejected the spent cartridges and levered in more shells. Then they knelt down together and aimed again. The silence was again broken with a terrific roar. I was watching the buck who, by this time, stood there laughing so hard that he forgot to head for cover.

On the third shots, one of the hunters hit the ground under the buck. The buck finally came to his senses and put his legs into gear and headed towards the timber on a run. Once again the experts went to work, as slow as before, and fired again, just as the buck made it to the timber. One hunter said he had hit the buck on the last shot, but I was sure he hadn't. I gave Joe his horse and Mike got on my horse and we went to the aspen trees where the buck had disappeared. I looked around for a short time and decided the last shots had gone in the general direction of the first shots. Mike asked, "What are we going to do now?"

Joe said, "I'll ride after the buck and Mike can wait here while Harold goes and finds Mike's horse."

"Joe," I said, "I'll bet that buck is at least a couple of miles from here by now." Giving it some thought, I suggested, "I'll take you to the place where we had planned on leaving the horses. Then I can walk back and find Mike's horse." With this worked out Mike got on my horse and immediately my horse took a dislike to him. He bucked very slightly a couple of times and then he proceeded to dump Mike right there in front of everybody. Mike wasn't hurt, but he sure was afraid of the horse. I held the horse while Mike got back on.

We didn't travel over a hundred yards when my horse walked close to a tree, nearly dragging Mike off his back. We stopped and I had a heart to heart talk with the horse. I reinforced my talk by picking up a stick about three feet long. All went fine till I came to a dry ditch about eight feet wide and four feet deep. Joe rode down into the ditch and back out without any trouble, but my horse refused to cross the ditch. I took the reins and tried to lead him to no avail. I handed the reins to Mike and stepped around to the back of the horse to use my enforcer. The horse, noticing what I was about to do, looked at me with a smirky smile and tried to jump across the ditch. He could have done it without a rider on his back, but now he landed short of the mark by at least a half-width of the ditch. Mike landed in the ditch and the horse was standing against the edge of the bank looking around acting like he didn't know what happened to his rider. I was glad the horse didn't decide to go looking for the other horse. Mike got up and said he wasn't going to get on that outlaw again. We traded horses. Joe got on my horse and Mike got on Joe's horse. Joe said, "I won't have any trouble with this horse."

With the rifles exchanged we headed on towards our goal. All went well until we rode right into a three point buck and several does. I was in such a hurry I grabbed both horses reins and let the hunters do their thing. Mike, thinking that this horse was easy to get along with didn't take time to get off the horse and fired his gun right over the top of the horse's head. For the third time this morning he found himself on the ground.

Right after he shot, Joe, who at least remembered to dismount, squeezed off a shot in the general direction of the deer. I looked all over the area where the deer was when he shot, but I couldn't find a speck of blood anywhere.

Undaunted by all their poor shooting, we continued towards the area we had planned for them to hunt. I decided I should leave both horses with the hunters and go back to the ranch on foot.

When we arrived at the little meadow, I staked out one horse and turned the other horse loose. He wouldn't go very far from the other one, unless the hunters decided to target practice where they were tied up. I didn't think my horse had mellowed any in his opinion of Mike.

I gave them all the directions I could, put on my backpack, took my rifle, and headed back toward the ranch. There had been so much excitement that my stomach demanded some nourishment to keep me going, so I ate one sandwich and left the rest of my lunch with Mike.

I was wishing I wouldn't have to come back up to bring them out, but then, if they got lost, or if they got a buck, it would be best to be out of the area before dark. I doubted the second option based on their morning's performance.

I went down to the "notch" in the fence on the north corner of the Lusher meadow feeling sure I would find Mike's horse around that area or by a gate in the notch. When I arrived at the gate there stood the horse. She had a grin on her face and insisted that I let her in on the Lusher meadow. I gave in and opened the gate. I rode her across the Lusher meadow to our ranch.

About three in the afternoon I took the horse and headed back to where I had left the hunters. It was an uneventful trip; however, I saw several deer when I crossed the trail to Lily Pond. I would have killed a buck if I could have gotten a good shot. They were in the aspens and I didn't see them till I was right on them. By the time I got off the horse the buck had disappeared in the trees. Several does seemingly thought I wasn't interested in them and grabbed a few more bites before they left.

I soon found the horses where I had left them. After the horses gave each other a little greeting, I tied Mike's horse up and made a small circle in hopes of finding a trophy buck. I returned in about an hour.

Joe had arrived ahead of me and when I arrived he told me he had seen several deer and saw a cow and calf elk during the day, but he didn't get to shoot again. He hadn't seen Mike since early afternoon. He said Mike shot shortly after they got there, but after looking around for awhile they couldn't find any blood so they decided he had missed.

While we were talking we saw a weasel jumping along so I threw a stick at him. He stopped and looked at us and then ran up a tree. He was nearly all white. (For some free information, weasels are brown in the summer, but in the winter they turn white with black tips on their tails. In the winter they burrow under the snow and every twenty feet or more they will surface, look around and go back under the snow. They eat squirrels and rabbits and other small animals of the forest.)

Mike finally made it back to the meadow. I was sure glad to see him. I didn't want to be in this area after dark.

When we were all saddled up and ready to travel, I decided to go back to the ranch the way I had come back up that afternoon. We rode south over to Meadow Creek drainage and found a trail that led to a Forest Service road that would take us back down to the ranch. The trip back went like clock work. We arrived at the ranch about dark. I took care of the horses and with a quick wash-up I was ready for supper.

Dad arrived shortly before we got back. They had one large five point buck that Eldred had shot in the middle of the morning. They had seen several does during the day, but only got the one big buck.

All the hunters wanted to get a trophy buck and had decided to not shoot a doe or a small buck till the last day of the season, when they would go for meat only. Dad wanted to bring half of the buck back in the evening, but his horse had different plans.

Dad said his horse Hazel had carried out game many times, but while they were dressing out the buck, Hazel suddenly got lame standing there watching them! They hung the buck on a tree branch about four feet off the ground. When Dad tried to take Hazel back up the ridge, she could hardly walk. Dad left her in an open area and made a little jaunt to the top of the ridge on foot. Dad laughed as he told how Hazel could hardly walk as he led her back off the ridge towards the ranch, but when she realized he was headed towards home, suddenly she was healed. She walked right along and her foot didn't hurt anymore.

A good hot supper prepared by the cooks helped the aching backs and sore feet. After dinner Mom chased all the hunters out of the kitchen to the living room where they could make plans for the next day's hunt. You could feel the excitement and enthusiasm as they told and retold of their day's hunt. Two more days passed and Mike and Joe remained unsuccessful.

It was another beautiful morning. I took Joe and Mike to the top of the ridge north of our ranch, where a trail goes to Salt Lick Gulch. Dad had shot a deer the day before and two of our hunters had gotten their deer the last couple of days, but no trophy bucks.

Dad thought the hunters might do better if they stayed on a stand all day and didn't walk around. Deer were traveling back and forth across the ridge. I found a nice grassy spot and left my horse to graze. I took my rifle and walked down a trail that goes along the top of the ridge. Suddenly the silence was broken by a shot in front of me. I ran a short distance from the trail I was on and got down on my knee and watched in hopes some deer would come down the trail. My heart was pounding so hard it was difficult to listen. I took a deep breath and watched. All I could hear was a little juno bird in the trees. I finally left my place and headed down the hill to where I knew there was a pothole or a small slough in the timber. When I got there, two hunters were sitting on a log. One told me he had fired the shot but he hadn't hit anything.

I went back up the hill and got my horse and led him down toward the Lusher meadow. Just above the meadow I tied the horse to a tree and walked down to a little grove of aspens. I had seen deer there several times during the summer and I hoped there would be a nice buck there. I sneaked along just as if there were one hiding behind the next tree. All of a sudden I saw a movement in the trees. I stopped and watched. Out came several deer. There was a nice three point buck in the rear of the bunch.

Dad only allowed me to have one shell in the gun and one shell rolled up in a hankie in my pocket. When I shot I knew I had killed my first deer! I dressed him out and threw a rope over a heavy branch and used the horse to pull the meat up off the ground. I put a stick in the cavity to hold the sides apart. Then I covered the meat with an old discarded sheet. This way the meat would cool out overnight and not be touched by birds and animals till we got back to take it home. I should have gone back to the ridge, but I was so excited I went home first and told Mom I had my deer.

I went back to the ridge where I found Mike and Joe. They had seen several deer, but they hadn't shot at any. Hiding my excitement, I nonchalantly drawled out that I had my buck hanging up.

I said, "It isn't a big one like we saw a few days ago, but it's the meat that we're after." We went back home and arrived a little later than I had wanted to.

Dad asked, "Well, did any of you get a deer today?"

Proudly I said, "I shot a three-point buck and left him hanging."

Then Dad said, "Good for you! We'll go get your deer first thing in the morning. Did you hang him high enough that weasels and coyotes can't get to him?"

I assured him that the deer was several feet above the ground. Joe and Mike complained that they had not been able to connect.

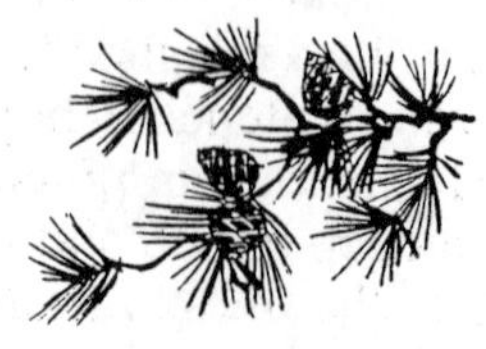

## HALLOWEEN FUN ... DARREL FALLS OFF THE ROOF WITH A BUCKET OF WATER

Halloween arrived before it was time! Most of the kids in town got together to terrorize the peaceful community of Frisco. We started at the upper part of town asking for handouts. Occasionally we "accidentally" upset an outhouse. When we got to the store, Guy Cannam gave us each an apple. Several kids bit into their apples thinking they had something good to eat. Suddenly, it felt as if flames were shooting out from our mouths! Were we ever fooled! The apples had been filled with red peppers. This called for action!

Glen said, "I know what I'll do. I'll put a tooth pick in his doorbell." He ran home and shortly came back with several toothpicks. He stuck one in the button and the bell kept ringing till Guy appeared at the door.

He said, "If you don't like what I gave you, just do it one more time and you'll be really sorry." We wanted to harass him, but common sense (if any of us had any) told us to leave him alone. We moved a car that Ken Chamberlain had stripped down to make a trailer to the front of the store.

Then Darrel climbed up on the roof over the back door of the store with a bucket of water. Glen rang the doorbell and Darrel was to pour the water on Guy when he came out. Guy came out, but Darrel couldn't see him so all was lost. Once more Darrel got on the roof with a bucket of water. Glen rang the doorbell and Guy came out. He couldn't see anyone so he came out a little farther. Darrel leaned out to see Guy and just as he saw Guy, his feet slipped and he fell on top of Guy getting himself and Guy wet.

Guy growled, "What were you doing on my roof with a bucket of water?"

Darrel mumbled and gurgled, rubbed the wet side of his pants and finally said, "I can't remember."

Guy had to laugh at the stupid answer. He said, "You get all the kids to come to the front of the store and I will give each one of you a candy bar if you will take the trailer back to Ken and not bother me for the rest of the night."

I think nearly all the kids were close enough to hear what he said and ran to the store entrance. Guy came out with a box full of candy and every kid got his choice of a candy bar. We took the remains of what was once a car back to Ken's garage, satisfied with the evening.

## CANDLES ON THE CHRISTMAS TREE

Christmas arrived with Kenneth Caldwell leading a Christmas musical program at the Frisco Town Hall. Mildred and several other kids helped decorate the tree. They moved the piano over by the tree and Mildred stood on the piano to put the decorations around the top area. She also put the candles on the high area which was just short of the ceiling. After she finished, the piano was moved back to where the orchestra was to be sitting.

Chick and Paul Deming and Chuck Chamberlain put over one hundred candles on the balance of the tree! While the orchestra played Christmas hymns, they lit the candles and the town hall lights were turned low. It was beautiful! They had several buckets of water in case of a fire, but each candle was removed as it burned low, so the water wasn't needed. Presents were handed out to all the kids in town including preschoolers. What an impressive evening!

## WINTER PARKING: A LONG WAY FROM HOME

Right after New Year's Day we had a big snow- storm which lasted for several days. We could not drive our pickup to the ranch because of the deep snow. One year we had the road plowed to the ranch, but in a few days the wind had blown the road full again.

Dad said, "Harold, when you go to Frisco today stop in at Mrs. Olson's and ask her if we could leave our pickup battery in her house when we leave the pickup at the River Bridge. Tell her we will give her milk and butter for pay."

When I delivered the milk to Mrs. Olson, I knocked on the door and when she opened the door I said, "Mrs. Olson, if it is O.K. we are going to leave our pickup at the River Bridge for the winter. We will give you two quarts of milk a week and two pound of butter a month if we could leave our pickup battery in your house when we are not using the pickup."

She said, "You don't need to give me anything, I will be happy to help you. When you drain the water out of the radiator I will always have a tea kettle of boiling water to put in your pickup when you need it. I have an old tarp that you can put over the engine to help keep it from getting so cold."

"Thanks a lot, but the folks want to give you something anyway."

When school was out in the afternoon, I pulled off the road at the River Bridge and parked the pickup. I drained the water out of the radiator, then I took the battery and set it in a box that Mrs. Olson had provided. I took her tarp and some old rope, covered the hood and tied the tarp down with the rope.

When we needed the pickup I would put the battery in it and try to start it before I put the water in the radiator. If the pickup started I would pour the water in the radiator. If the car wouldn't start I would put the water in the radiator and cover it up. If the hot water didn't get it started, I would drain the radiator so it would not freeze before I asked Dad to help. He would fold up a small rag dipped in kerosene and fasten it on a piece of bailing wire. Then he would light the rag and hold it under the engine, heating the oil in the bottom of the engine. If it was real cold he would use another lighted rag at the same time under the transmission. After a few minutes the oil in the pickup would be heated enough for the engine to turn over. Sometimes we would also jack up one rear wheel which made it easier to start (because there were fewer gears to turn over in cold transmission fluid).

As soon as we were finished with the pickup we would follow the same procedure. This was unhandy, but meant we could use the pickup and not worry about freezing the engine and radiator.

We usually were able to drive the pickup home by the first week in May. It usually required shoveling through some snowdrifts and driving out in the timber around others.

## THE FISH CAME ALIVE

One fine morning I rode down the hill on my skis behind the house to get a bucket of drinking water from the spring. The spring never froze where it came out of the ground. I filled the bucket and headed to the house going across a beaver dam. The ice had melted along the dam exposing several feet of water where I saw a number of fish feeding on top.

I went to the house, set the bucket of water in the usual place in the kitchen, took my fishing pole and a piece of meat, and returned to the open spot at the dam. I had only a small place to cast in. To my surprise a fish grabbed the bait on the first cast. I jerked and the fish was hooked. I went up to the open water and pulled, thinking I would bring up an eight or nine inch trout. The fish went back under the ice and swam around several minutes before I was able to get him to the open water. All of a sudden he came to the surface and when I pulled he actually swam right out into the open water where it was spilling over the dam. I laid the pole down and took off my skis. I got down in the willows by the dam and threw the fish out into the snow where he came off the hook. I took a willow and hit the fish on the head and he quit his flopping. I picked him up and headed to the house. He was twenty-two inches long and very fat.

When I got about halfway up the hill he came to life and started flopping. I finally dropped him in the snow. I didn't have anything to hit him with this time and I didn't want him to flop around in the snow and bury himself. I took off my ski and hit him with it. Just as I swung the ski at him, the ski I was standing on let loose and I went down the hill backwards for twenty or thirty feet before I fell. What a predicament! I finally waded around in the snow to where the fish was. He wasn't moving, so I put my skis back on and tried again to side pat up the hill. Just before I got to the top of the hill the fish came alive again and once again I was forced to take my ski off and hit him on the head.

Mom and some of the family were standing at the top of the hill laughing at me. I don't think they realized that the fish could get lost in the deep snow. When I hit him this time I was headed slightly down the hill. As soon as I swung at the fish my ski again let loose and back down the hill I went. I am not a one-ski expert, but I went away out on the meadow before I fell. One of the spectators above turned a couple of skis loose headed down the hill for my transportation back up the hill. One ski went quite a distance, but the other one stopped about thirty feet beyond me. I managed to get the ski and go back to the fish. My other ski had gone down the hill and had to be retrieved later.

I picked up the fish and side patted a few more feet up the hill when he again started to flop. I pitched him uphill as far as I could and patted up to him. I took off the skis and reached around in the snow, got a good hold on him and threw him again as far as I could, which was by now the top of the hill. I trudged up, picked him up, and took him to the back porch. By this time my hands felt frozen. I still had to go back and retrieve my skis.

If I had been thinking I would have broken a willow and put it through his gill and saved all this trouble. Oh, well, hindsight is better than foresight.

## SKI JUMP ON THE PISTON HILL

One Saturday several of us went to the Piston Hill to ski. The Piston Hill lies south of Frisco between Frisco and Bill's Ranch. We patted down the snow on the north side and made a number of runs down the hill that would take us to the main drag. We would crow hop back up the hill till it got too steep, then we would have to side pat the rest of the way to the top. Alongside of our patted slide area we tramped down the snow for a foot trail to walk back up. Eddie said, "Let's make us a jump on the back side."

"A good idea," I agreed, "but we will need a couple of shovels."

Neil volunteered, "I'll go home and get a couple shovels." Neil and his mother lived with his aunt, uncles, and grandmother.

He went down the front side of the hill and before he got to the main road Eddie said, "I'll go and get a scoop shovel and a long piece of rope. The rope might work to hang onto to get back up the hill."

I slid down the back side in the deep snow. Then I patted sideways back up the hill. By the time I got back up the hill Neil had arrived with the shovels, and Eddie showed up a few minutes later. It was a warm day and the snow was melting. We shoveled the snow and in a short time we had a good jump made. It was around four feet high. It was just the height of Eddie's sister, Janet. I got the privilege of going over the jump the first time. It wasn't a very long hill, but it was fairly steep. I made a good jump and then everyone else tried it out. I think we were jumping around thirty feet or so.

While we were jumping, Chick Deming, Neil's uncle, stopped by on his skis. He was on his way to check his traps up by the Frisco Mine.

Chick said, "When I get back I will show you guys how to jump," and went on his way.

Eddie said, "Let's make the jump a little higher to give Chick a real thrill." We all went to work and built it another two feet higher. Then we all tried it out and thought it wasn't too bad.

Chick was a very good skier and a good jumper so we felt it wasn't a good enough challenge for him.

"Maybe we should build the end higher and dig some snow out of the approach," I suggested.

Neil said, "I probably won't dare go home this evening, but let's see what we can do." After a while we had the jump we wanted. I thought it would be almost impossible to jump off of.

It went downhill and when you got just short of the end it took a nearly vertical angle. We took Eddie's rope and tied a handhold along the side of the jump. I let myself down on the jump and then jumped off the skis to the side. Then, standing next to the jump, I pushed the skis over the top. This made tracks looking like someone had already gone over the jump.

We skied off the front of the Piston Hill till Chick came back. He came up on the front side and went to the back side.

"Looks like you kids added a lot to the jump," he said.

Eddie said, "We added a little snow to make it a bit more fun." Chick was wearing a backpack and it was full of traps. He had a twenty two rifle in his hand.

He squared himself around and started down the hill. Everything went fine till he hit the jump. He went up into the air, I mean *high up into the air* getting tangled into a branch of a tree. He came down not over ten feet in front of the jump and almost on his head. Traps flew out of the backpack and in the scramble he dropped his rifle. He unbuckled his skis and fished around in the snow for his rifle. He picked it up and put it under his arm. He shook the snow out of one glove and picked up his hat and shook the snow out of it. He was standing in at least four feet of snow.

Eddie took one look and said, "Janet, let's go home." With that they headed out.

Neil and I went to the top of the hill. After one more look Neil took off down the hill towards his home. I took one more look to be sure Chick wasn't hurt and, seeing he was O.K., I went down the front of the hill and on towards the ranch.

A couple of days later at school I said, "Neil, what did Chick have to say?"

Neil said, "Aw, he gurgled and growled and gave me all kinds of threats, but that was all. If he gives me any trouble I'll set a mouse trap in his boot."

(In 1999, I talked to Chick for the first time about his famous ski jump. I said, "You really went straight up and came down right in front of the jump."

Chick replied, "I went up so high I got tangled in the branches of the trees; it was terrible frightful.")

## OUR ORCHESTRA WENT TO BRECKENRIDGE IN A BLIZZARD

During the late winter our orchestra went to Breckenridge for a music recital at the annual sports and achievement competition. We were again to play with the Alma orchestra conducted by Aunt Clari and Kenneth Caldwell. Our group wasn't as large as usual, but there still were twelve of us including the adults. Neil drove his Uncle Bob's new Pontiac. Tommy Giberson, Mildred, Helen, Dean, and I rode with him. Gay Loomis from Dillon, plus Kenneth Caldwell and Chet Sawyer also drove. Several people went specifically to hear the music. It was nice in the morning but clouds were sitting on Buffalo Mountain, warning us that a storm might be in the making. The roads were snow packed, but good.

The music program was a big success. Residents of Breckenridge and some of the people from Dillon had prepared a lunch for us after the late morning program.

As we started home around two thirty in the afternoon we were surprised to see about three or four inches of new snow and it was still snowing hard. At times you could see less that ten feet ahead.

Kenneth wanted us to stay close to him because of Neil's age. Mildred assured him we all felt secure with Neil's driving. Neil took the lead and all went well for a short time until we saw a shadow at the side of the car. I got out to see what the shadow was. It turned out to be a railing at the side of a bridge where the road crossed the Blue River. We inched along and after many stops to check where the road was, we arrived in Dillon. After dropping off the Dillon gang we headed to Frisco. It usually took about ten minutes to make the trip to Frisco, but that day it took us just short of an hour.

When us kids got home from Frisco there was over fifteen inches of new snow since we had left the ranch that morning.

*My Champion White Flemish Giant Rabbit on an Orange Crate*

## KID, YOU'RE LEANING AGAINST IT!

We had raised rabbits for some time when Mrs. Dodge from Englewood wanted us to bring several of them to Denver to a Rabbit and Cavy Show. We had bought our start of rabbits from her. The Dodge family came to our ranch several times a year to see how we were doing with our rabbits. The rabbits were supposed to be Dean's and mine and the chickens were to be the girls'. Dad, Dean and I selected one New Zealand White, one Steel Flemish Giant, and one White Flemish Giant for the show. I was to make the trip.

We built boxes with screen doors on top. We put in cans for food (pellets) and water, with grass for bedding and additional food. I made one box for the White Flemish rabbit and one box with a division in it for the other two rabbits. The Steel Flemish was two months old while the other two rabbits were grown.

About ten in the morning I got on my bike that I had purchased from Howard Giberson, and with an overnight bag I headed to Frisco with my rabbits. All went well till I started down the Frisco beaver pond hill. I was nearly half way down the hill when I met a car coming up the hill. There wasn't enough room to pass, especially with me and the boxes of rabbits. I turned off the road towards Ten Mile River through brush, tree branches, rocks, and real rough terrain. I dropped both of my boxes and it took over an hour to catch one rabbit after the screen lid came off. I finally got organized again and headed to Frisco and Harold Thompson's, where I would get my ride to Denver.

When we arrived in Denver, Harold took me to 44th and Federal where I caught a streetcar to downtown Denver. I set the two boxes of rabbits behind the operator's seat. I got off the street car a couple of blocks short of the loop. I walked around a building that I thought was the right building, but the street signs didn't seem to be in the right place.

Getting weary I finally asked a policeman, "Can you give me directions to the Denver Coliseum?"

He looked at me and then looked at my boxes with the rabbits and then he came right up to me and said, "Kid, you must be lost, you are leaning against it." I was so tired I wasn't even embarrassed. He left and (thirty minutes later!) I found the right door to go in.

Once inside I couldn't find my ticket. Through my pockets I looked, and back through again. I finally said, "I guess I will have to purchase another ticket."

The gal in the window looked at me and asked, "Do I see a box with a rabbit in it?"

"Yes, I'm entering three rabbits in the Rabbit and Cavy Show."

"You don't need a ticket, just a free door pass that looks similar to the paper in your hand."

I looked at my hand and there was the red paper I thought was a ticket wrapped around my second finger and sticking out from my hand about three inches. Now I was so embarrassed my face turned close to the color of the pass.

"I'm sorry, I didn't realize what I did with it."

"No problem, wait here for a couple of minutes and I will take you to where you need to go." Boy, was I excited. She was a very pretty girl, but what an impression I had made. She grabbed one box and took me to the place I needed to go to register my rabbits and for two days be rid of them except for feeding them mornings. While I was registering, Mrs. Dodge showed up and asked me if I had any trouble finding the place.

Before I could answer my escort said, "He did fine, he came to the ticket booth and asked for directions and I brought him here per your request."

Not only was I embarrassed, but I was also tongue tied. The next day I finally got up enough courage to ask Mrs. Dodge about the girl.

She said, "The girl is a new friend, Alice. We sold some rabbits to her brother and dad early last spring."

As she walked away she turned around and said, "Pretty nice gal, huh?"

Our White Flemish Giant won first place and the New Zealand White won a second place. The Steel Flemish Rabbit didn't even get honorable mention, but I don't think he cared. When we won a first prize it was music to our ears, moneywise. All winners would be announced in a newsletter to all members of the Rabbit and Cavy Club. This advertisement would always bring a number of sales for pedigreed rabbits.

At the end of the Show Mrs. Dodge invited me to the Rabbit and Cavy Banquet in one of the large hotels. During the dinner their son Stewart was playing around and got the tines of his fork stuck on either side of the bone in his rabbit leg. He tried to cut the bone with a dinner knife. While he was sawing away he pulled the knife too far and the blade dropped off the bone, and on the forward thrust the knife pushed the rabbit leg off his plate and across the table into a very dignified lady. The barbeque sauce colored the front of her very low cut dress and maybe a little of her front where the dress didn't cover. Boy was she upset!

I couldn't hear what she said, but her look was so chilling that I wasn't sure I wanted to know.

Stewart, ignoring her frigid remark said, "Lady, as soon as you get the rabbit off the floor please send him back to me and maybe I'll be able to get a replacement." The party continued.

After the party I went to the Dodge home for the rest of the night or what little was left. I caught a bus to Frisco the following morning.

⁂

Oftentimes in the evenings we would go fishing in the lake by the house. When I threw my fly, or any kind of bait that would stay on top of the water, they would grab it. This was sure a lot of fun and, besides, we had lots of fish to eat. A spring below the lake furnished a good supply of fish.

## THE STRUGGLE TO GRADUATE

Going to Frisco or Dillon was not hard, and most of the time fun, but if you had to go any great distance it could be difficult, winter or summer.

In the fall of 1939 Mildred was unable to go to Breckenridge High School because she had no transportation. Kenneth Caldwell asked Mildred if she would like to assist him with music and other projects. She accepted and was able to earn credit in a couple of subjects at the same time.

In 1940 Mildred went to Alma to finish her senior year of high school. She stayed with Aunt Clari who was teaching there. After a couple of months Mildred discovered she couldn't get the right credits from Alma so she quit and moved back home. She went back to work for Betty Chamberlain in the café.

Mildred never said anything but I am sure she was really disappointed. Well, the Lord moves in mysterious ways we are told, and none more mysterious than good old Chuck Chamberlain. Chuck was making freight deliveries for the Schaefer Truck Line in Breckenridge plus several other towns. He was taking his senior year in Breckenridge High School. Well, wouldn't you know Chuck and Mildred worked it out so she could ride to Breckenridge with Chuck. It made long days for them, but they both graduated in the spring of 1941.

***Aunt Clari, Aunt Mabel, Mom, and Uncle Lynn in front of Frisco town hall.***

# PART VII
# SPRINGTIME
# ANOTHER CYCLE BEGINS

**Frisco, Colorado during the early years**

## ACROSS THE SLOUGH HOLDING THE COW'S TAIL

Every spring a time was set up to brand all the spring calves and any cattle we had purchased. This was done before the cattle were turned out onto the open range for the summer. We didn't have a lot of calves to brand. Our neighbors helped us with our branding and then Dad helped them in return.

Saturday was set for the branding at our ranch. We had about ten or twelve calves to brand and two cows that we had recently purchased. Dan Mogee, Bill Thomas, Ben Staley, and Howard Giberson came to help with the job. We had the calves in the corral and everything that would be needed to do the branding was ready. We wanted to get it done before noon. Oh, yes, I forgot to say that we had one cow that we wanted to dehorn also. Down to the corral we went.

The fire was already hot and in came the first calf to be branded. Two men would throw the calf on her side and one man applied the branding iron. One guy would remove the little buttons that would grow into horns, and if it was a bull calf they would castrate him. Mom said she didn't want Rocky Mountain Oysters so Ben Staley took them home. It was amazing how fast this crew could get the job done.

All went like clockwork till we tried to brand the second cow. Instead of putting her on her side we put her in a loading chute with the front partitioned off. Once she was in the chute a couple of poles were put across behind her so she couldn't back out.

Just about the time Dan was ready to apply the branding iron she decided she wanted no part of that, and it didn't happen! She backed up, breaking one pole and then she managed to turn around in the chute and broke the lower pole in her hasty retreat. Instead of stopping in the corral she headed to the fence and to my utter surprise she jumped the fence breaking the top rail, heading into the pasture.

Dad said, "Harold, take the horse and go get her." I had wanted something to do so I got on the horse and headed to the pasture. I was sure that she would go for the willows on the upper end of the pasture, a distance of a little over a half mile. I didn't see her anywhere, so I went to the west fence. No sign of her there. I rode all over the pasture and still no sign of her so I rode back to the corral.

Dad said, "We've finished the branding. She'll show up and we can brand her some other time. It's a little early for lunch, but Minnie has the lunch ready so we can eat now and get a good start on branding Giberson's cattle at the Lusher Place."

There were at least thirty-five or more calves to brand and several two year old cows that belonged to Gibersons.

Howard and Kenneth Giberson, plus a couple of their friends from town that loved to ride and work on the ranch, had everything ready to go when we arrived to help them. Dan Mogee went home after lunch. Wib Giberson arrived soon after we got started.

The branding was a little different here. They had an oblong shaped corral and a hay meadow to keep the cattle in.

The branding soon got under way. They would drive a few calves into the corral and brand them and turn them loose, then drive a few more in the corral. One rider at a time would have to watch the gate to the meadow to be sure none of the unbranded calves would get back out into the meadow. Whenever this did happen one of the riders would have to go after the escaped calf and bring him back.

A rider would rope a calf, then a couple of men would grab the calf and do the branding. After they were through with the calf they would open the gate and drive him out of the corral and rope another calf. This kept two ropers busy roping the calves and driving them back out of the corral. They also had a loading chute converted into a stall to hold a cow. They had a gate on each end of the stall to let the cow in and out. I was surprised how fast they were moving along.

While the majority of the men were working with one calf, someone else would get a cow in the stall and when they were ready they would brand her. Once the cow was branded they would open the front gate and let her out into the meadow before she tore the fence all down. You can't imagine how fast a cow's mood could change.

One time a cow was in the stall and just as they were ready to brand her she managed to back out of the stall before they got the gate fastened. She turned around, ducked her head and ran after the men who were branding another calf. Boy did they scatter. Up jumped the calf that they were branding. Lucky, maybe, I guess, but the rider still had his rope on the calf. The calf tried to run for open territory. I am sure the calf thought that the devil had gotten him anyway. As he ran, he pulled the rope tight, nearly jerking the unsuspecting rider out of the saddle. He did manage to knock Ben Staley down when the rope tightened between him and the horse.

To add to the excitement, after the cow ran through the branding operation, she turned around, ducked her head, and made another pass at a couple of men who had been trying to get out of her way on the first pass. She ran to the back of the corral, turned around and made the third pass through the branding team on her way to the meadow. At least she didn't pay any attention to the men on her third pass, as she headed out of the gate to the meadow. I am sure everyone was glad that she was gone for the time being.

While the branding team was trying to get organized again, the rider that had the calf on the end of his rope was doing his best to take up slack to where they could grab the calf and continue the branding. Sometimes it was best to have a rider on each side of the calf to prevent a lot of jumping and running.

Dad and I were manning the front and back gates on the stall. They would drive a two year old cow up to the stall and at the right moment I would close the front gate and right behind her Dad would close the back gate. This, then, had the cow locked in the stall. The front gate had a wooden box on it with some grain in it. If they weren't too frightened they would settle down and grab a bite while the men were getting ready to brand. After they branded the cow I would open the front gate and the cow would take off.

Most of the time this would work smoothly, however we had one more problem during the afternoon. Bill Thomas took Dad's place helping me, and Dad went to get some wood we had sawed up for the fire to keep the branding irons hot.

The riders drove in another two year old cow and she tried to miss the stall. She knocked Bill down and ran right past him. Making a quick turn she headed back out of the corral. One rider took after her. He caught up to her and threw his rope. The rope fell a little short of its mark, catching the cow's back leg. The rider and cow headed for the meadow. Dad was just starting back to the corral when he saw the cow and rider coming towards him. He threw down his armload of wood and grabbed the cow by the tail as she went by. Why he grabbed the cow's tail, nobody knows but, by this time the rider had released his rope and the cow headed towards a bog, or maybe you could say a slough. It was about seventy five feet wide and over one hundred and fifty feet long. It had several inches of water in it. Dad had grabbed her tail with one hand and seeing where he was headed he held on with both hands. He had hoped to get ahead or at least up alongside of the cow and turn her around. This was now out of the question.

When they hit the slough, water flew everywhere! Dad held on! The cow pulled him through the slough with his feet held together and sliding like he was on a ski. To make matters worse, the cow told her bowels to unload about five pounds in order to increase her speed. When this happened, Dad was covered from head to foot. It looked like he had been painted brown with a spray gun. Dad let loose of the cow's tail and just in time. The cow was approaching a sage brush rise after crossing the bog.

One rider rode up to Dad, and when he finally stopped laughing he said, "Russell did you enjoy your ride through the bog?" Dad just grinned and continued washing his face and hands in the edge of the slough. He walked back over to the branding operation. The work had stopped and everyone was laughing.

Wib asked, "Russell, are you hurt?"

"No, but I sure am wet, I think I'll walk over home and wash up," he said.

Kenneth laughing said, "Russell, don't you think you should put on some clean clothes? This is a clean operation, you know." Just then a rider rode up with Dad's hat.

"Russell, your hat missed the spray painting. It fell off just before you and the cow hit the water."

Still laughing, Howard said, "Russell, if you want to take another ride like that, I am sure we have another cow that will be glad to accommodate you."

Dad headed for home and in about an hour he came back and said, "I am so clean I think I will boss the job rather than work any more today."

They rounded up the cow with the rope on her foot and led and dragged her back into the stall. After removing the rope they branded her and I opened the gate and let her go.

Next they decided to brand the cow that had chased them around in the corral to start with. They drove her up into the stall. I closed the front gate, but Dad and Bill together were not able to get the back gate locked. She backed out, ducked her head and rammed it right through the gate. With a mighty push she jerked the gate free from the stall. With her head through the gate, she and the gate took off for the meadow. As she ran by one startled rider she ducked her head and almost rammed him and his horse. On out to the meadow she went.

Bill, trying to keep his fresh dip of Copenhagen in his lip, and at the same time cuss the cow, finally remarked, "She made me swallow it."

Wib lighted his pipe, and then lighting it again said, "Russell, I think we've had all that the system can stand for one day, let's knock off and finish up tomorrow." With that remark every one seemed to disappear and Dad and I walked across the meadow to our house.

## DAD WORKS FOR MR. ADAMS AND CHARLIE AND RUBY LOWE

One Saturday afternoon in the early summer a car drove up to our yard. The man got out of his car and said, "Is Russell Rutherford around?"

Mom said, "He's in the barn. I can send one of the girls to get him."

"Oh, no, I'll go to the barn and see him." He met Dad at the barn door and said, "Are you Russell?"

"Yes, what can I do for you.?"

He said, "My name is Mr. Adams and I have a ranch below Dillon where the Blue River and Willow Creek meet. Charlie and Ruby Lowe told me you were a friend of theirs and you were a good carpenter. I need a carpenter for awhile."

Dad took off his hat and scratched his head and finally said, "I guess you want me to go to your ranch and do some work."

"I need a room built onto the house and some remodeling done. I want to add another stall on the side of the barn for a garage and a building near the creek for a bunk house and milk house. I would like to get it all done this year, but if you can't spare that much time we can work in your time frame."

Dad said, "I sure could use the money, but I have a lot of work around here I need to do. What will you pay me?"

He said, "I will pay you the top dollar. I need the work done."

Dad said, "I make seventy-five cents per hour, paid every Friday night. I will come home every Friday evening and go back early on Monday morning. I would like to work ten to twelve hours a day. I may need to take a day or two off now and then to help my family keep the work up around here. I don't have a license on my pickup, but I guess I could get one."

Mr. Adams said, "Russell, I'll make arrangements to bring you home and pick you up. I have a man working for me now, but he isn't a carpenter. I will pay him to haul you back and forth as you need. He can also work with you."

He continued, "I would like for you to start in about a week if that would be all right with you. I can come and pick you up, one week from Monday."

Dad rubbed his chin and said, "I don't know when I ever got hired that quick, but it will be all right with me." They walked up to the house together and I followed. Dad told Mom what the plan was. She seemed to agree and offered to make coffee and serve fresh cinnamon rolls.

They talked for over an hour when Mr. Adams said, "I told Charlie and Ruby that I would be back in time to help with the milking. I guess I had better get going." He raised the hood on his Franklin car and taking a can of gasoline he filled a little cup on the top of the engine by each spark plug. He turned the crank once and it started right off.

Later Dad said, "That car is a Franklin. It is an expensive car. I guess the cups of gas help start the car in cold weather, however today I would think it would start easy enough."

Dad went to work for Mr. Adams the following week. On Friday evenings Frank Bibbe brought Dad home for the weekend. On Monday mornings Frank again showed up before six o'clock to take Dad back to the Adams Ranch. This went on all summer long and Dad didn't have to license the pickup.

## GOOSEBERRY PICKING WITH A BEAR

One morning after the chores were done and the milk delivered we went just above the Buffalo Ditch to pick gooseberries. We always tried to pick the berries while they were green, right around the fourth of July. Kenneth Caldwell went with us.

Mom made us sandwiches, as it was nearly lunchtime by the time we got started. Each one had their own bucket to put the berries in and I carried an extra three gallon milk bucket to empty our individual buckets into. There was a large bush over thirty feet across on the hillside where Mildred started. The bush was just high enough where we couldn't see each other if we picked on opposite sides. Kenneth went a little farther up the hill where he stopped. Helen, Dean, and I picked on the lower side of the bush where Mildred was.

As always the mosquitoes were pretty bad. We wore long sleeves and finally I put my jacket on to help keep the mosquitoes off. Every few minutes we would move from one bush to the other, why, I don't know. I guess we thought the next bush was easier to pick on.

At noon we went to the Buffalo Ditch where it crosses Meadow Creek and ate our lunches. I noticed that the red raspberry bushes were filled with little berries and there were a lot of them around the ditch, but it would be another four or five weeks till they would be ready to pick. After lunch we all emptied our little buckets into the big milk bucket, it was over half full.

***Don't Break The Branches.***

Each one returned to their spot to pick. In a few minutes I decided to take Helen and Dean to a bush out in the sun to try and get away from the mosquitoes.

We moved to a spot just above Mildred where I could keep watch over them and give a sympathetic word whenever they needed it.

Mildred said, "Are you kids all right? Don't break the branches. If you need a fresh spot, come around to where I am."

No one answered and after a time Mildred again said, "Stop breaking the branches, there are lots of berries on this side." Still no one answered.

All of a sudden Mildred, getting disgusted with hearing the grunting and tearing up of the branches, set her bucket down and stomped around the bush hollering, "You kids quit breaking the bushes and - - -" About that time, eye met eye! A black bear took one look and relinquished his picking spot and branch breaking and disappeared into the forest.

The sudden scream almost made me drop my bucket. I whirled around just in time to see a bear leaving for areas unknown. Mildred was up the hill in strides that she never before or after was able to accomplish. Mildred said, "I told him, 'You can have this bush! I'll find me another one.'"

Kenneth also heard the scream and came running to see what happened. Mildred's eyes were as large as saucers or maybe a little larger. She rehearsed the meeting several times while the rest got calmed down.

Kenneth said, "Do you think we should pick any more berries? I have half a bucket since noon."

I looked into Kenneth's bucket and laughing said, "Caldwell, the bottom of the bucket is not yet covered." He did have quite a lot of berries for the time we had been picking after lunch, but not half a bucket. After discussing what to do, we decided since the bear had moved on to a place where people wouldn't holler and scream at him we would stay where we were. We went back to picking berries. I noticed we were all picking on the same bush.

## THE FRISCO STORE AND POST OFFICE

In February 1939, Elmer and Esther Swanson, their son Eddie, and their daughter Janet, moved from Denver to Frisco. The Swansons bought property south of the school. Ben Staley built them a little two-room cabin there. In 1940, Mr. Swanson bought the store and post office from Guy Cannam. Not long after they bought the store Elmer bought a Caterpillar to work in the woods. Mrs. Swanson ran the store while Elmer and Eddie did extensive logging on Peak One and Peak Two, but Elmer was always at the post office for the mail. In due time they built a large home there where they planned to live the quiet life, but December 7, 1941, changed all that. Elmer, who was in the Army Reserves, was called to active duty. With her husband off to war Mrs. Swanson closed the store in the fall of 1942 and moved back to Denver. We were without mail for a short time.

In anticipation of the closing of the post office, Mary and Bill Ruth had remodeled a large shed in their front yard. When Mary received her appointment as postmaster, they moved the mail boxes to the shed and it became our new post office.

Before Mary applied for the postmaster job, she and Bill had moved to Uneva Lake to manage the property where there was a large lake, a home and cabins several miles up the canyon from Frisco. Mr. Tutt, of Colorado Springs, owned the property and used it for himself and his friends for a getaway. As postmaster, Mary came down to their home in Frisco daily to take care of the mail.

In the spring of 1946 Helen and Robert (Bob) Foote bought the Frisco Store and post office from the Swansons. In April, 1947, when Bob Foote was appointed postmaster he moved the post office back to the store which they had reopened earlier.

## JAKE THE HAWK

In the early summer Eddie Swanson was hiking around Royal Mountain when he saw where a large baby bird had fallen out of its nest and had fluttered down the mountain for several hundred feet. It was in a very hard place to get to. I happened to be at the store when Eddie came looking for some help to rescue the bird. I went with him and it wasn't long till we had the bird. We didn't know whether it was an eagle or a hawk. It didn't have any feathers on it to give a clue to what it was. He didn't seem to be hurt. Eddie and I fixed a nice place behind the store, Eddie's home, and put him in it. We went to my house and dug a bunch of worms and took them to him. Eddie held a worm over his head. The bird reached up and grabbed it. It was gone just that fast. I took over a can of grain to see if he would eat it. He would peck at it, but his love was meat of all kinds. During the summer it was a chore to keep enough food for that bird.

Eddie named him, "Jake, the Hawk."

He grew like a weed and after he got feathers, we wondered

if he would know how to fly. We took him out where there were no trees for him to get tangled in and tied a string to one leg. He walked all around and picked at things on the ground. On our third or fourth trip he tried to fly. He stretched out his wings and flapped them violently. I guessed the wing span to be nearly four feet. It raised him off the ground, but he acted like he didn't know what to do next.

One day Eddie said, "I took Jake out to the vacant land west of the store with a string on his foot and left him there for most of the day. When I went to get him he acted like I scared him and he flew ten or fifteen feet before he landed on the ground."

We turned him loose to see what he would do. By this time he looked like he was larger than any hawk we had ever seen. We set him on a stump in the back of Eddie's home. He sat there for a minute, then flew about thirty feet and lit up in a tree. We watched him for a short time as he flew around the back yard. In the evening he flew to the cage that was his home. Early the next day he left and was gone all day, but he came back to the cage at night. This went on for several days until he failed to come back to the cage. Over the next couple of weeks he came back for food, but was staying elsewhere for the night. One morning after his breakfast he took off and Eddie said he flew above the tree tops and soon was out of sight.

This was the last time either of us saw him but, early the next spring, there was a large bird, possibly an eagle, sitting on a branch of a tree in Eddie's back yard.

Was this Jake?

***Jake the Hawk.***

## A BEAR! NO THANKS!

One evening in the early fall when we had just finished supper, we heard a commotion on the back porch. Something fell and made a lot of noise. I had decided that Tim was outside and had knocked over a shovel that I had left out there. Dad looked back at the magazine he was reading when we heard more racket on the porch. Dad laid his magazine down and by the time he stood up, we heard the grunting noise of a bear. Mom came out of the bedroom and informed us that a bear was on the back porch. This was exciting!

Mom said, "I suppose he smells the honey that I hung out on the back porch to cool off." Mom had a half gallon bucket with two or three cups of honey that had turned to sugar in it. She had heated the honey in the bucket and hung it on a nail in the porch to cool. The bear didn't understand what she was up to. He thought it was meant for him.

All of a sudden Tim, who was sleeping somewhere in the living room, came into the kitchen on a run and headed for the door. At the door he gave a loud "Meow," as if to say, "Let me out immediately!" He started to give his second request when the bear grunted and made some more racket. Tim stopped short in his tracks and arched his back, the hair on his tail standing straight out, and stood looking at the door. Dad grabbed the rifle off the wall in case an argument started over the honey. He opened the door a couple of inches. Tim cowered up against the edge of the door, sticking his nose against the crack and gave a couple of growls, then he started backing up, still growling. He backed up two thirds of the way across the kitchen when suddenly he vanished into the living room.

Mom handed me a flashlight and Dad opened the door enough for him to go outside. I followed him out in time to see a long yearling bear disappear into the darkness. We took the honey back into the house but I expect the bear still thought the honey was for him!

All was quiet at the ranch. Then again the bear came back to see if he could get his honey. This time Dad took the rifle out and shot it into the air a couple of times to get the bear's attention. This done we figured he would go on home and forget about the honey. Shortly after we had gone to bed I heard the bear on the front porch. I think he had decided that he had better go inside after his gift as no one was going to set it out for him.

We lit a couple lanterns and set one on the front porch and one on the back porch in hopes the light might keep him away.

The next thing I heard was Dad's call, "Time to get up."

As I was dressing I asked, "Dad, did you hear any more of the bear?"

Dad replied, "He was around in the yard several times during the night, but he didn't come in on the porch."

## A BRUSH WITH DEATH

During the summer Dad asked Frank Bibbe if he would like to go trap marten with him in the high country. Frank was excited about it. He liked to be out in the back country and the thought of going with someone to trap marten was right up his alley, although he had never seen a marten.

Marten are a long slender, short legged, dark brown animal with orange under the neck and under the front legs. They are a little larger than their cousin the mink and live mostly in the trees, but also close to water. They live mainly on squirrels, rabbits and small animals. They are very ferocious and their fur is very valuable.

About the middle of November Frank moved in with us for the duration of the trapping season. They bought some additional traps from Sears and then they set out to establish a trap line. They went across Salt Lick Gulch to South Willow Creek and to Haws' cabin. The cabin was a short distance up South Willow Creek from the trail that runs from South Willow Creek to Middle Willow Creek and up North Willow Creek. The trap lines were established up each of the three creeks. They also trapped for a time on the headwaters of Maryland Creek north of North Willow Creek.

It was a short day's trip from Haws' cabin to go up and back on South Willow Creek and Middle Willow Creek. Sometimes Dad would make both lines in one long day. It took a long day to go up North Willow Creek and get back to Haws' Cabin by dark. Going to Maryland Creek added three hours to the North Willow Creek trip. They caught quite a few marten during the last of November and the first week of December.

The latter part of December the storms were coming about every three days and every storm added from one to two feet of snow in the trapping area. This slowed them down. It took them one extra day's stay at Haws' cabin before coming back to the ranch.

They went to Haws' cabin, their high country headquarters, with the intention of pulling their traps for the season. Frank went to South Willow Creek and Dad went to North Willow Creek and Maryland Creek. Dad planned to pull their traps out on his way back, and Frank was to pull the traps out of the upper end of South Willow Creek, but leave the traps close to Haws' cabin. The next day they planned on going up Middle Willow Creek and if there were no marten they would remove the traps from that area.

Frank made his rounds and got back to Haws' cabin in the middle of the afternoon. Dad went up North Willow Creek and brought down the traps to a junction where he left the traps and went to Maryland Creek. Before noon a big snowstorm came in and by the time Dad got back to the junction in the trail, it had snowed nearly a foot. The wind came up making it hard to stay on the trail. Parts of the trail were marked with willow sticks sticking up in the snow.

Dad was carrying a lot of traps in his pack sack. He decided if he was going to make it out that night he would have to lighten his load. He left his traps at the bottom of a big tree, just off the trail. He hung a big red rag on the branch of the tree so he could find the traps later. This helped a lot, but as he left the tree he stepped on a big stump that was covered in snow and broke one snowshoe. He fastened a stick on the side of the broken shoe, but this dragged his energy down. The snow was over three feet deep. It was impossible for him to travel without the shoe. It was dark and he had nearly three miles to go to the cabin. He grew more tired and oftentimes he had to hunt around to find the willow stakes marking the trail. Finally he found himself falling down time after time.

He thought to himself, "If I'm to make it out of here alive, I'll have to stay here and rest till daylight comes. I may not make it out if I get cold." He felt around in his pockets and realized he had dropped his bottle of matches where he left the traps. He crawled up as close to a tree as he could and taking his good snowshoe he scooped snow on his legs. He drifted off to sleep, but was wakened by the howling wind and the swirling snow. He pulled his stocking cap down over his face. He decided he must stay awake to survive till morning.

Dad wondered what Frank would do. What would the family think when they didn't come home when expected. Would Harold know the trail well enough for someone to come back with him and look for them? He drifted off to sleep again.

By a miracle from God he opened his eyes and thought he saw a light. Then he heard someone calling his name. Where was he? Who was calling? He kicked the snow off his feet and stood up. He pulled his cap away from his ears. His legs were stiff. Once again he heard the distinct call and recognized the voice. For a moment he thought he was dreaming, but then he saw a man covered with snow walking slowly along on the trail.

Dad yelled, "Frank."

The snowman stopped and called again, "Russell."

"Over here," Dad yelled, "I sure am glad to see you."

Frank walked to the tree and laid down all the things he was carrying.

He was breathing heavily. Finally he got his breath and said, "I sure am glad to see you. I couldn't have gone much farther."

He reached in his coat pocket and pulled out a jar of hot coffee and said, "Here, drink this." Dad drank about half of the quart of coffee and Frank drank part of what was left.

Frank said, "I think we are only a mile and a half from the cabin. Do you think you can make it that far?"

Dad said, "I could, only I broke my shoe several hours ago and it's almost impossible to walk on it."

Frank said, "While I was trying to think of everything to bring with me, the snowshoes came to mind so I brought a set of bear paw shoes with me." He kicked the snow around to reveal the snowshoes. This was music to Dad's ears and might have saved both of their lives.

Dad said, "How do you feel, Frank; do you think you can make it back to the cabin?"

"I'm doing real good," Frank said, "But I couldn't have made it much farther and then gone back to the cabin." Frank also had several venison sandwiches, a pint of kerosene to help make a fire if need be, a second flashlight and several extra batteries. The kerosene had leaked out and wet the side of his leg.

They ate the sandwiches and decided they could get back to the cabin with first one and then another taking the lead and breaking the trail. They were both wet from the snow and if they tried to build a fire it was marginal whether they could keep warm enough to wait till morning.

Dad put on the good snowshoes and carried the broken ones, and they headed back to the cabin. Several times they got off the trail and had to hunt around for it to go on. They figured it would take about an hour and a half to get to the cabin, but three hours later they opened the door. They could only thank God their lives were spared.

Early the next morning the storm was still howling. Dad opened the door to look out. Another foot of snow had fallen during the night. They both felt better than they had expected, however Frank had a blister about the size of his hand on his leg from the kerosene. Dad brought three marten from his lines and Frank had two from South Willow Creek.

Dad said, "I think we'd better go home. After the storm blows out we can come back and go up Middle Willow Creek."

Frank said, "I agree with you; it may be slow going home, but we will be in the thick timber all the way till we cross the Lusher meadow. If we go up Middle Willow Creek we will be out in the rocks the last quarter mile and it will be pretty tough in the storm to even find the trail; besides, neither one of us are in top shape for such a trip."

Eight o'clock in the morning found them climbing out of South Willow Creek drainage, headed home. They carried the marten, food, coffee, and the broken shoes.

When I went to the barn to start the evening chores, the snow had let up; and when I looked out across the Lusher meadow I could see Dad and Frank just entering it, walking slowly along. I went back into the house and told everyone Dad and Frank were almost home.

I rushed to the barn and milked the first cow; then I went back to the house to hear what they had to say. They had made it back on time, but we were also experiencing a big storm, the same as they had been. We had been uneasy because we knew the storm in the high country was most likely much more severe than ours. (I might mention there was no forecasting of storms in those days. If there had been, we didn't have a radio to hear it anyway.)

About a week later they went back to Haws' cabin and up to Middle Willow Creek. They were unable to find most of the traps. Usually a colored flag was tied to a tree above where a trap was set. The flag had to be a long strip so it could go around a tree. If it were to move in the wind, marten wouldn't come near; however, a Canadian lynx or bobcat could get inquisitive and get into the trap. The snow was several feet deeper than when they had been up there the last trip.

This ended the high country trapping for the year. They trapped up Meadow Creek and on Salt Lick Gulch for the next few weeks. Frank stayed a short time after the trapping was over; then he went to Laramie, Wyoming, where he had relatives.

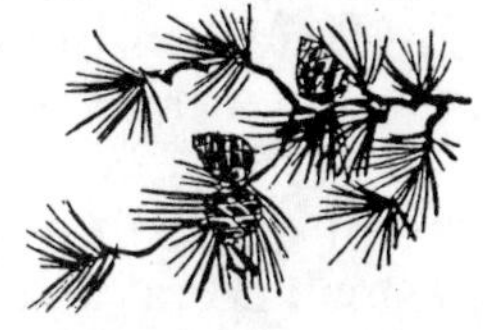

## THE MILK BUSINESS GROWS

Early in the spring we got the opportunity to furnish milk to Climax. We could deliver it door to door or we could deliver it to the commissary outside of the gate. After much deliberation Dad decided that we would take on this extra work. This also required an additional amount of hay during the winter. Dad contacted Mr. Christofferson and arranged to do work for the hay on his ranch called the Dutchman's Place just east of Frisco. We also leased the Bailiff Place, mainly for its hay, from the City of Denver.

Dad and I went to Denver to 2767 West Alameda, an auction corral for buying and selling cattle. This was at the extreme west end of Denver at that time. We purchased 14 milk cows. None of them was fresh at the time, but all were to have their calves during the coming month. We had to enlarge our milkroom. We also got a machine to put caps on the milk bottles, but the girls said they could cap milk faster by hand than with the new capper. We bought another pickup. It was a Model B Ford and served its purpose for a long time.

We delivered milk to Climax door to door and took some milk in bulk to the commissary outside the main gate. Climax was the main world supplier of molybdenum that was desperately needed for the war effort. It was a highly controlled access. During the war several thousand soldiers worked there in the mine and the mill.

It wasn't long till we had calves all over the place. We bucket fed all of the new calves along with the calves that we already had. This sure did add to the amount of work we had to do mornings and evenings. We fed the calves a grain mixture that we added in the milk. We trained them to drink milk by letting them suck on our fingers and then spreading our fingers wide enough to let milk flow between, then sticking our hand into the bucket of milk. The calf would catch on right away that he could "suck" the milk and then graduate to regular drinking. Till they learned, they would bite your fingers, stick their heads in the milk so far they would nearly drown, and if they couldn't get any milk they would take a step back and butt the bucket. If the bucket wasn't fastened down it would turn over and spill the milk and roll away. All this was taking place with your fingers in the calf's mouth. After they were a few days old they would get the idea and then all you needed was a framework to set the bucket of milk in.

We kept the calves in one end of the shed opposite the chickens. There was a small corral that emptied into our larger corral at the barn. Before we milked we would put the calves in the shed or small corral. We tried several methods to feed the calves, but finally settled on a framework that kept the calf buckets from overturning. When all the buckets had their feed and milk mixture in them, we would open the gate to let the calves in. What a stampede! The calves would run to the nearest bucket. There, two or three calves would try to drink out of one bucket. One would then stick his head in and the others would have to find another bucket. Sometimes the first calf would finish his milk by the time the last calf started to drink. Sometimes a calf would stick his head so far into the bucket that when he removed it his ears were covered with milk. This would cause a frenzied rush to his ears!

Feeding time was always a real chore till the calves all had their milk. You can imagine what it was like when they were each six months older and weighing twice as much! You didn't want to be in their path!

## NEVER KICK A PORCUPINE!

One summer morning Dad called out, "Boys, it is time to get up." It was a clear, beautiful morning, not a cloud in the sky. The sun was just making it's appearance in the eastern sky. The air was fresh, but just a little cool. It had rained during the late afternoon and evening the day before. I put my jacket on, as I headed out the door to go to the pasture to bring the milk cows to the barn. When I crossed Meadow Creek I stopped for a minute to see if I could hear a cow bell ring. We put our milk cows in this pasture at night so they could feed in the evening, and be close by in the morning. I couldn't hear a sound but I knew where they were usually bedded down. I headed down a trail that took me along the perimeter of the pasture. A ten minute walk took me to a grassy little meadow alongside a row of beaver ponds. I felt sure I would find them there.

Sure enough, as I approached the meadow, I heard a cow bell ring. I continued over to the meadow, and there they all were. I got them on their feet and to the barn we went. Good old Aunt Sara and I brought up the rear. By the time the first cow got to the barn, Dad and Dean had the stanchions open, grain in the boxes, and a little dry hay from the loft in the mangers. One by one as the cows entered the barn they went into their stanchions and when they were all in place, I locked them.

After washing the cows' bags, Dad, Dean, and I sat down to milk. Mildred soon arrived carrying additional buckets. She took the milk to the milk house while Helen helped Mom both in the kitchen and milk house.

We were about finished milking when we heard a groaning sound coming from outside. Dad jumped up and went outside followed by the rest of us. When we got outside, Billy Shoemaker was standing by the door. Billy was a prospector who lived in the Roe cabin on Chief Mountain.

Dad said, "Howdy, Billy, what brings you around so early this morning?"

Billy didn't have to answer. I looked down at his foot and I couldn't believe what I saw. Bill had several porcupine quills sticking out of the top of his foot and ankle.

Dad said, "Sit down on this old dynamite box." We used the box for me to stand on to put harness on a couple of the large horses.

Dad continued, "Helen, run to the house and get your mother and have her come down here."

Bill's big toe and his ankle were badly swollen and carried a dark cast. Several of the quills were broken off. It looked like he had tried to pull some of the quills out of his toes.

Mom arrived shortly. Bill groaned and said, "Minnie, I sure do feel bad, do you have a bottle of whiskey or something that I can take while you and Russell pull the quills out of my foot?"

Mom replied, " We don't have any whiskey, but I have aspirin, and I can bring a clean pan of hot water to soak your foot in."

Mom went to the house and soon returned with a bucket of hot water and a bottle of aspirin. "This is all that I have in the way of medicine," Mom said.

Billy ran his hand across his face a couple of times and said, "It sure does hurt, Russell; I guess you had better get to work."

"You kids get back out of the way. Dean, you go back to milking. Harold, when you finish your cow you can finish milking the one I was milking."

Mom put a towel on a cardboard box for Billy to put his foot on. She poured some disinfectant on his foot and Dad went to work. He took a pair of pliers and pulled on a quill. It finally came out.

Billy said, "If you cut the ends off of the quills they are supposed to come out easier."

Dad cut the ends off several quills while Mom held Bill's foot. I sure felt sorry for Billy. He moaned and groaned with the pain, but insisted that Dad had to keep pulling them out. Some of the quills came right out, but two of them were almost impossible to remove. One of them broke off out of reach of the pliers.

Mildred and Helen took care of separating the milk and finished getting breakfast ready. I went back to the barn, mostly to see what was happening and of course help where I could.

Finally Dad said, "I have removed every one of the quills that I can, but there still are pieces that will have to come out." Sweat was all over Billy's face.

Mom said, "Billy, I think we'd better take you to the doctor in Breckenridge."

"I'll be all right as soon as it quits hurting," Billy said. He stood up and tried to take a step. He couldn't put any weight on his foot. I wondered how he thought he would be able to get back to his cabin high on the mountain and take care of himself.

Mildred arrived back at the barn with a cup of coffee and a warm plate of pancakes. Billy moved over to a table that we put our buckets of milk on and Dad set up a chair for him to sit on. He sat on the chair and put his foot on the dynamite box and decided that he could eat.

Mom went to the house and presently she returned with a couple of fried eggs and some roast venison that she had canned last fall. Mildred followed with a pot of coffee. The food made Billy feel better. He ate like he hadn't had any food for weeks. He finally agreed to go to the doctor, but wanted us to be sure the doctor was in his office before we went.

Dad said, "Billy, how did you get the porcupine quills in your foot?"

Bill readjusted his foot on the box and said, "You know I have been having a lot of trouble with bobcats running around on the roof of my cabin at night. I shot one the other day and thought that would end all my problems. Well, two or three days ago I was kept awake most of the night with a couple of bobcats on the roof again. I went outside and threw some sticks at them and drove them off, only a day later they were there again.

"Last night I was awakened before midnight. I went outside and shot in the air a couple of times and boy did they ever leave in a hurry. I can't imagine why they would get up on the roof, unless they were trying to get in a squirrels' nest. I went back to bed and somewhere around two thirty or three this morning I was awakened by them again. I got up and opened the door.

"One bobcat, at least I *thought* it was a bobcat, was sitting on the end of my porch. I was surprised that he didn't run. I didn't have my shoes on, but I kicked him as hard as I could and, wow, it wasn't a bobcat, it was a darned porcupine.

"I tried to remove some of the quills, but I only was able to get one out that was on my big toe. My foot started to swell. I poured some cold water on it, hoping that it would stop the swelling, but it didn't help. I got dressed and started to walk down the hill. My foot was cold, but I couldn't see how I could put anything on it. It was hard going downhill in the dark. I picked up a Quaker pole and made myself a couple of canes to help keep some of the weight off my foot. It was throbbing! I knew I had to get some help.

"I usually keep some whiskey but I have been out for quite a spell. I didn't even have any aspirin. It took me about two hours to get to the bottom of the hill, across your irrigation ditch and over here. I had a time trying to cross your ditch. Once I got on the flat ground it was a lot easier to travel. However my foot was hurting so much that I had to stop a lot and rub it."

Mom called and said, "We have loaded the milk in the pickup." She continued, "I found the doctor's home phone number, you can call him and see where he wants you to take Billy."

Billy got in the pickup with Dad and me. We drove to the Frisco Café where Dad had me call the doctor at his home.

When he answered the phone I said, "Doctor, this is Harold Rutherford at Frisco, we have a man that kicked a porcupine by accident and he was barefoot, can I bring him in?"

"What in heck is wrong with him?" he yelled. I told him that we had removed as many quills as we could, but there were some broken off.

The doctor asked, "Is his foot swelling?"

"Yes, it is swelling badly and his big toe is nearly twice as big as his toe on the other foot," I said.

"Are you in Frisco?" the doctor asked.

"Yes," I said, "but we can have him in your office in about thirty-five minutes. I'll unload my milk and then . . ." Before I could finish, he yelled into the phone so loud that Dad could hear him ten feet away. "Forget the milk and get him in here before I have to remove his foot!"

"We'll leave right now," I said. We unloaded all our milk at the café and headed towards Breckenridge. We helped Billy into the waiting room. Dad and I had waited outside for quite a while when the doctor came out and said, "I think I have all the quills out. It will be sore for a few days. If it starts to swell or shows signs of infection bring him back."

Billy came out and got into the truck. "Can we stop and pick up some whiskey in case it gets to hurting?"

Dad said, "We'll get anything you want and when we get to the ranch Harold can take you home in the Model A truck, it can pull the hill." A three speed truck couldn't pull the steep hill up to his cabin.

Several days later we went to the Roe cabin to see how Billy was doing. His foot was sore, but he was working part of each day in the mine.

## LIVE FROG SANDWICH

This year being no exception, we had a letter in the mail announcing that Aunt Clari would be on the bus Friday. We had expected her a few days earlier. The letter explained that her sisters, Aunt Nellie and Aunt Mabel, had been in Denver for a short shopping spree so she had gone to Denver to see them before she came to the ranch.

It was my privilege to go to Frisco and meet the bus. The bus arrived on time and I soon had all Aunt Clari's things in the pickup and ready for the trip to the ranch. I peeked into one box that was quite heavy and sure enough, it was just what I had expected! Fresh vegetables!

"I'm surprised to see you driving by yourself, Harold. Are you sure you can handle the truck?" she inquired as we crossed the Ten Mile River Bridge.

"Sure, I can," I said, "I haul the milk to Frisco every day and deliver it door to door." With this matter settled she sat back in the seat to enjoy the ride to the ranch.

It was just over a mile from Frisco to our house. The trip was made without incident and we arrived at the ranch house without scaring Aunt Clari, intentionally or otherwise. Dad was at work in Dillon, but the rest of the family was there to greet her and, especially, help carry her stuff in.

Time to do the evening chores arrived before we realized how fast the time had gone. Everyone had something special to tell her, but the conversation was pretty much limited to Mom and Aunt Clari. After a few attempts to interrupt, it was apparent that we should listen and not be heard until later.

Mom said, "Harold, get the cows in a little early this evening and do the milking before Dad comes home so we can have a nice, long evening."

I headed for the barn to fill the grain boxes in the manger. I climbed up into the hay loft and put a little hay down in each manger and tossed several forks of hay into the corral for the cows to eat on while we were milking.

Mildred and Helen headed to the pasture to get the cows. Once they were in the corral the gate to the pasture was closed.

We had eleven cows to milk and several more cows were to come fresh any time.

With six of the cows in the stanchions and all the cows washed, I sat down to milk. Dean was doing his share of the milking. Helen was on hand to handle the milk buckets. Dad arrived home a little early but I had already milked three cows when he came to the barn. It wasn't too long till we were finished.

At the milk house we put the amount of milk we needed to bottle in large containers. The rest of the milk was separated. We washed the separator and milk buckets. Nothing else needed to be done in the milk house till morning, but we had a dozen bucket calves to feed plus the chickens and rabbits to take care of.

Mom called out, "Supper is ready." Everyone headed to the kitchen to get washed up. Noting that there were at least three people to wash before my turn came up, I took a bar of soap and a towel and went to the irrigation ditch below the house. With this little job taken care of I went to the kitchen and took my usual place on a bench with Helen at the wall side of the kitchen table.

***Dean and his Brown Trout***

When everyone was seated and grace was said, everybody wanted to talk at once. Mom and Aunt Clari again seemed to dominate the conversation. Dean was trying to tell Aunt

Clari about a turtle he had found, and with the same breath he was trying to tell Dad about the big German brown trout he had caught.

Dad said, "Son, eat your supper and after supper I will look at your fish."

Helen said, "It isn't very big and anyway I helped him get it out of the water."

"You didn't either help me, you just watched me, that's all," Dean yelled.

"Mom, make Dean be quiet," Mildred hollered.

Mom and Aunt Clari kept on talking as if no one else had said a word. Helen and I decided now was the time to start passing the food around. First one dish and then another one added to the movement.

With no one noticing I picked up Mom's plate and passed it on like the other dishes. Dad looked over at me and grinned. I now felt I had a go ahead with this little prank.

All of a sudden Mom looked down and said, "What happened to my plate, Harold?"

"Mom," I said, "you must have forgotten to give yourself a plate when you set the table." Everyone laughed as Dad passed the plate back to Mom, but not before the plate was loaded with food that Mom didn't want to eat.

When dinner was over Mildred and Helen moved the dirty dishes to the work table and prepared healthy dishes of homemade ice cream. Mom got up and produced a nice chocolate cake and passed it to Dad first. Everything would have gone perfectly if Helen hadn't spilled her milk just as we were finishing the cake and ice cream. I couldn't see any reason for it. I had just tipped the bench a little as she started to drink. Too much milk went down at once, I guess, and when she coughed she let loose of the glass to cover her mouth. Mom frowned at me.

Aunt Clari said, "What happened to the dear child?"

Mom said, "Harold tipped the bench just as she started to drink." I don't know how she was able to see what I was doing. I got up, got a rag and helped wipe up the spilled milk, mostly because it was running down on my side of the bench. Helen, of course, had to go to the bedroom and change her dress.

When dinner was finished, the girls washed and dried the dishes. Dad, Mom, and Aunt Clari retreated to the living room. The "Aladdin" lamp that sat on the library table in the middle of the room was lighted and now the room was brightly filled with light. After the girls finished the dishes Dad moved the wall bracket light to a bracket in the living room.

Dad got a stick of wood and put it in the heating stove. "We won't need much heat, but a little fire will keep it warm this evening," he remarked.

I went to the barn and let the cows out of the stanchions and chased them out of the barn into the corral. I opened the gate that let the cows go into the pasture. Within a few minutes I had the barn cleaned out and hay from the hayloft put into the mangers. When the girls finished the dishes they came to the calf shed and helped Dean and me finish feeding the calves. Dean and I fed the rabbits while the girls pulled the cover over the front of the chicken house. I left the barn and hurried to the irrigation ditch and washed my hands.

The evening was filled with lots of chatter and, before we knew it, it was time for bed.

During breakfast Dad said, "Harold, there are several people who would like to make a little trip to Lily Pond. Find out when will be the best time for the others to go and maybe Clari would like to go along." Aunt Clari stopped talking and inquired all about the trip.

"Why, of course I want to go on the hike," she said. "How long will it take and will we have to take a lunch?" she asked excitedly.

Mom said, "Yes, you'll have to take a lunch. I'll put it together and Harold can carry the lunches for everyone in a pack sack."

Mom continued, "John Adams and his wife Bernice plan on being here day after tomorrow for the day. Bernard and his girl friend Bernie can go anytime, that is, if you don't go too early. Bernie told me she likes to sleep in during her vacation, so I wouldn't plan on leaving here before ten or eleven in the morning."

"That'll be O.K. with me and if Bernard and Bernie can be here in the late morning that'll be a good time to leave," I said.

Mildred was going to Frisco to work in the café so she could contact Bernie and tell her of the plans for day after tomorrow.

With plans set in motion Dad left for work at Dillon and I had a big day of getting the irrigation ditch water from North Ten Mile River to Meadow Creek turned on. It was running full of water, but there was a lot of trash in the ditch and in some places it was overflowing the banks. This of course meant I had to walk along the ditch and clean it out. The meadows were getting dry, with no rain in sight. All of our irrigation water came from North Ten Mile River. The ditch ran from North Ten Mile River to Meadow Creek where it dumped the water into Meadow Creek at the foot of the mountain just above our ranch. We could then take it out of Meadow Creek anywhere we needed to.

When I got home in the evening I found out all the plans were made and we would leave the ranch around 10:30 the following morning.

This would be a fun trip. No one but me had ever seen Lily Pond. At the base of Buffalo Mountain there are two lakes. One lake is about two acres of stagnant water. All summer it is covered with water lilies. The other lake covers several acres and has fresh water running into it and has brook and rainbow trout in it. It is a beautiful trip of about two hours up on the side of Buffalo Mountain.

When the morning chores were done and breakfast finished I had about two hours before it would be time to go. I took the shovel and went to our lower meadow to open the ditches that carry the water over the meadow. As I worked, my thoughts turned to the people who were going on the trip. I wanted to do something that would be different and exciting for them. My thoughts finally centered on a little prank for Aunt Clari.

I knew she would be a good sport, and I didn't know how the others might respond if a little prank was pulled on them.

My mind sorted through a number of possibilities, but I kept coming back to the same thing. With this plan in mind I headed to the house and got a small jar. I went to the second meadow where there were a number of frogs practicing their singing for a Sunday morning meeting. I caught one nice frog and put him in the jar. I went to the house, got a nail and hammer and made some holes in the lid. With the lid safely screwed on the jar I put the jar in my backpack. "So far, so good," I thought, but the next phase would be a mite harder.

In the house, everyone was gathered for the trip. Dean didn't want to go. Mom and Helen had all the sandwiches made and some of the special ones had names on them. Hot chocolate and cookies were being served. Helen helped me put the sandwiches in the backpack, while Mom supervised the job. Helen spotted the jar in the backpack.

"What is this for?" she asked.

"I am always needing a jar when I am out like this," I remarked, as I hurriedly put the sandwiches in the backpack to cover the jar.

Bernard carried a gallon jug of water. Each person carried their own drinking cup or glass.

We took the trail that goes through the second meadow, down by the Brandon Hole, and on towards the foot of Chief Mountain. We picked up the Forest Service road at the foot of the mountain.

It was a fairly steep hill for the first mile and then it leveled out somewhat for the next half to three quarters of a mile.

We made it up to the Buffalo Ditch before we had to take a good rest. Several of the gang had cameras so we stopped often to take pictures. Our next large rest point was where the trail leaves the Forest Service road and heads northwest towards the ponds.

As we were resting, Aunt Clari said, "Harold, what was that digging in the side of the hill just above the road?"

"I'm sorry, I forgot to tell what that was!" I exclaimed. "Did everybody see the logs that formed a large horseshoe shaped wooden box at the end of the cutout?"

They all answered, "Yes."

I said, "That is a place where the miners, Billy Shoemaker and Dade Ritter, hired Ben Staley to use his team of horses and sled their ore from the Roe mine to the bin during the early winter. The ore was piled up in and behind the box. In the summer they hired the Chamberlains to use their dump truck and haul the ore to Leadville. Chuck said he had shoveled a thousand tons of ore into the truck. This way they could move ore down the mountain most of the year.

"While I'm telling you a few things I'll tell you about a mountain lion that I saw. I was going to Lily Pond by myself last year and as I approached the creek I saw a mountain lion on the tree that crosses the creek. He was looking down into the water. I just stood still and it seemed like it was a week, but I'm sure it wasn't but a long second when he looked back towards me and with one leap he was across the creek and out of sight.

"Animals usually avoid stopping for more than a quick drink where they can't hear what is going on around them, but something must have caught his attention."

This story brought a lot of questions and excitement. I explained there was nothing to fear and finally, looking at my watch, I suggested that we had better move on up the hill and the next stop would be when we would arrive at Meadow Creek.

Crossing the creek was a little problem. In the late summer it was a little brook flowing gently down the mountain. We could cross by stepping from one rock to another until we were across. But now, with the spring runoff, it was a roaring torrent cascading down the mountain. The roar was deafening making it almost impossible to talk to each other.

With the high water we would have to cross the creek on a tree that had fallen across it below the trail. Even with the water as high as it was the tree was still several feet above the water.

However the tree was wet from the foaming spray. With the spray hitting the tree it could become slick where the bark had come off.

I stopped just short of the creek where we could see the rushing water. I said, "This is a good place for a break and to take pictures. When you have finished taking pictures I'll help each one of you, one at a time, across the water on the downed tree."

Soon everyone was ready for the next phase of our journey. Some faces reflected anxiety, possibly fear, almost terror, as they pondered the crossing. I took the gallon jug of water and walked across the creek on the tree. I took off my pack and laid it with the jug and headed back across.

"Don't look at the fast moving water while you are crossing," I said. "It could make you dizzy."

I hadn't heard anything out of John but puffing all the way up, and once in a while a groan.

He said, "I think one would have to be crazy to cross the creek, but if the rest of you are going to cross on that tree, I guess I will too."

"Who wants to be the first to cross?" I inquired. Aunt Clari crowded to the front of the gang and headed right towards the tree. She climbed up on the tree, grabbed my hand, and we made a fast walk across. Bernie was the next in line to go across and we made the trip without incident. Bernard followed us, and made the crossing without any help.

John decided to go next and he didn't want any help. He sat down and straddled the tree and slowly inched his way across, but not without incident. A year or two ago when Dad and I trimmed the tree to make this bridge I never thought anyone would have to cross by straddling the tree. I had left some little snags on the sides of the tree and when John crossed he snagged his pants. I was sure he cut his leg, but he wouldn't let anyone look. Someone produced a couple pins and his pants were soon repaired. As he crossed, his feet got wet from the water spray.

Next, Helen crossed without any help, then I helped Bernice across. This almost became a serious catastrophe. When we were about halfway across, some bark on the tree gave way and caused Bernice's foot to slide off. I was holding her hand, but then I had to grab both of her hands and try to keep both of us from falling. During the next minute we did a lot of maneuvering trying to keep our balance but we finally got across without any more trouble.

John took Bernice's hand and helped her off the end of the tree and onto solid ground.

Back on solid footing, John asked, "Bernice, weren't you a little scared crossing the water on that log?" I don't know whether she was so scared that she couldn't speak, or if she couldn't hear him standing so close to the roaring torrent, but she didn't answer.

We had a steep climb up out of the gorge that had been formed by many years of water cutting its way down the mountain.

The trail took us up through a large meadow. We stopped often to rest and take pictures of the country below. There was a panoramic view of the mountain range from northeast to almost due south including the valley below. Frisco stood out in our view. Salt Lick Gulch Ridge obscured our view of Dillon. I showed them the peaks where Loveland Pass was and the area where Hoosier Pass was. Also, you could see Dickey Mountain and Ophir Mountain.

We spent quite a little while there and finally I said, "Let's go on up the trail into the timber and find a nice place to eat our lunch." This was the right thing to say. Looking at my watch we had passed the noon mark.

Now the trail was easy to see and just a gentle upward slope. I dropped to the rear as it was easier to go single file up the trail. I stopped in some willow bushes and removed the frog from my backpack and put him in a sandwich, wrapping the wax paper back around him. I put the sandwich back in my backpack and hurried up the trail to the rest of the gang, who now were stopped by a great big root from a fallen tree.

Bernard said, "I would like to give thanks for this beautiful country and the food that will soon be in front of us."

After the prayer I took the pack off my back and proceeded to hand out the sandwiches. Of course Mom had made several extras in case someone needed extra energy.

I handed out most of the sandwiches when Aunt Clari stepped up for her food. I reached in the pack and handed her the sandwich with the frog in it. She took it and sat down by the others who were by this time starting to eat. Helen was the last one to take a sandwich and she sat down by Aunt Clari. Aunt Clari opened her sandwich while she was talking to Bernie, not even looking at it. This could even be better than I thought. The frog decided to stretch out one leg and see if it was possible for him to leave his tight quarters half smothered in Miracle Whip. The leg protruded about three inches out beyond the side of the sandwich, fanning the air trying to grab onto something solid. Aunt Clari, still not taking a bite, just sat there talking, holding the sandwich up in front of her face. About that time there was a horrible look on Jean's face. By now every one saw the frog leg. Bernard quickly opened up his sandwich and put it back together not saying a word.

Suddenly, Aunt Clari stopped talking. Silence reigned for a short minute. She looked at all the gang with a puzzled look on her face. I was sitting by Helen almost facing Aunt Clari. I wanted to laugh, but I didn't dare. She looked down at the sandwich. By this time the frog, realizing that one leg would never get him free from this mess, pushed his other leg out on the opposite side of the sandwich.

She looked at it for a minute and then turned to me saying, "Here, Harold, this has to be your sandwich." I hadn't opened my sandwich, and to my amazement, she turned around, grabbed my sandwich and thrust her sandwich into my hand so fast that it gave me goose pimples. She opened the new sandwich and started eating as she continued on with her story. She didn't even mention the frog.

I don't think anyone was eating now, just sitting there with their mouths hanging open. I laid the sandwich down and if you ever saw a frog depart in a hurry this frog sure did, two big jumps and he was out of sight! I reached in my pack and produced another sandwich for myself.

Now everyone started laughing. After a lot of questions and laughs about the frog someone said, "Clari didn't that frog just about scare you to death?"

"No," she said, "I knew Harold would have a little prank of some kind up his sleeve and I didn't know what it would be or when it would happen, but I was watching." She continued, "I actually could feel the frog wiggling as soon as I received the sandwich. It took all the courage I had not to let on, but I wanted to get the best of Harold."

After lunch was finished, and no one else found a frog in their sandwich, we continued on up the trail to Lily Pond. We arrived at the large lake.

Bernie said, "I was afraid to cross the tree, but I am glad that I did, this is beautiful."

We followed the trail around the right side of the large pond. The fish were jumping.

"I wish I had brought a fishing pole," Aunt Clari said, as she took another picture of the lake.

We had to cross a small rise to the little lake. It was too early in the year to see the lily blossoms in full bloom, but the buds were forming just below the surface of the water. The pads nearly covered the surface of the lake.

Aunt Clari said, "This is truly a beautiful place to go." Another hour passed as we looked at the lakes from different locations. Everyone seemed to hang back, not wishing to go back to the ranch but realizing we must.

Finally I said, "We must leave now, but I have an idea. We can go down over the foothills to the ranch without a trail. It will be a little harder going, but we won't have to cross the creek till we get to the ranch, then we can cross on a foot bridge just below the lake at the house." The only problem that we could encounter would be finding the Lusher meadow covered in irrigation water.

This was music to the ears of everyone but Aunt Clari. She said, "Harold, remember last year when we went on a hike to the top of the ridge north of the ranch, and we had to hurry back downhill to the ranch without a trail. Several of us had blisters on our feet when we got home, however I think we can take our time and still get home by the time you have to milk."

With this idea all approved we hiked downhill below the pad lake. We lost altitude rapidly. Of course we didn't have to stop as often to catch our breath so we made great time. About halfway down the hill we passed by some little lakes that were formed by water from Lily Pond drainage.

These lakes filled with water every spring, but nearly dried up by late fall.

Some beaver, on one of their sight-seeing expeditions, happened across these ponds and immediately claimed the territory. They had cut down aspen trees, as well as lots of willows, and had built a nice summer retreat for the entire family. We stopped for a short time while Bernie and Helen soaked their feet in the water. While we were there two beaver came out to welcome us, but upon discovering that we were not beaver they swatted the water with their tails informing us that we were not invited to their swimming party. Not having an invitation we hurried away. Anyway we needed to keep going.

I think it was easier than I had thought it would be for everyone. We soon arrived at the northwest corner of the Lusher meadow.

Looking over the situation we decided that it would be best to strike right out across the meadow heading straight for the ranch house. We were lucky; there wasn't any water on the meadow, however a smart-aleck horse came running over and terrified some of the party before we got to the fence that ran between our ranch and the Lusher Place.

Back home milk and cookies awaited our arrival. While we were eating Mom said, "Who got the frog in their sandwich?"

Aunt Clari replied with a laugh, "I think it was planned for me, but the frog wound up in Harold's sandwich."

John was talking to Bernard when Aunt Clari interrupted the conversation and asked, "Minnie, how did you know about the frog in the sandwich? After all, you are the one who made the sandwiches."

Mom laughed and said, "You can bet your boots I certainly would not touch a frog, let alone put him in a sandwich." She continued, "I saw Harold put a jar with a frog in it in the backpack along with the sandwiches. I could just imagine the rest!"

## RODNEY THE BULL

One morning during breakfast Dad said, "I want you boys to go over to Bill's Ranch and bring Rodney home." Rodney was a bull we raised from a calf to maturity. When he was little I would grab him by the horns and throw him down. He soon grew too large to practice my bulldogging and roping on. My sisters thought this kind of "training" was the reason that he was so mean. I, however, think he was born mean and ornery.

"Don't take the horse," Dad said. "He'll try to hook the horse with his horns and cause you a lot of trouble. Take a rope and a halter and lead him home. I don't think you'll have any trouble with him. Dean can go along and help you through the gates. When you get him home, put him into the corral and be sure all the poles are in the gate leading to the second meadow and close the gate by the island pasture. You might take a small bag of bran for him to eat to get him moving along. If he tries to run or won't walk, let him smell the bran and you'll have him eating out of your hand. Bill Thomas will help you catch him and get the halter on."

I tried to picture this as a smooth operation, but somehow, knowing Rodney, I didn't think it was possible. Dad headed towards Dillon for his day's work. Dean and I checked out the fence around the corral and found one top rail broken. I cut a new pole to replace the broken one. I nailed it in place while Dean took the broken one to the wood pile. The cows wouldn't try to go over the top of the fence with only one pole off, but Rodney would love the chance to try his luck at jumping over it.

We ate an early lunch, picked up our ropes, and headed towards Bill's Ranch. When we got to the ranch, Bill was nowhere to be found.

Bill had a number of privately owned cabins on his ranch and also owned several cabins that he rented out. We knew a number of the people and went to their cabins to see if they knew where Bill was. Bill didn't drive, so there wasn't a car to look for. Everyone that we talked to had seen Bill in the morning but hadn't seen him since. Someone said he thought he went to Rainbow Lake fishing with some friends.

At first I thought we should go to the lake, but after talking it over with Dean, we decided the best thing to do was to entice Rodney to go into Bill's barn. Then it would be easy to put a halter on him.

Rodney was feeding in a pasture up by the railroad track. The barn was down by Bill's house at least two or three hundred yards from the pasture. Dean opened the gate and ran down to the corral and waited for Rodney to show up. I went into the pasture, carrying a stick about four feet long and started moving Rodney along. We didn't have too much trouble getting him to go into the corral. He walked along, mumbling to himself, and never tried to run in any direction. I don't think he really thought we wanted him to go into the corral or he would have headed somewhere else.

"This isn't going to be any problem after all," I thought, as I closed the corral gate. However, getting him into the barn was a different story! I tried to put the rope halter on him out in the corral, but he wouldn't stand still long enough for me to get the rope over his horns.

After about seven times around the corral he ran into the barn. I rushed up and closed the door before he could come back out. Inside the barn we poured a little bran into a wooden box that Bill used to feed his horses. While Rodney was eating the grain I managed to get the halter on him. I fastened my fifty foot rope on the halter. Dean had been carrying a rope about twenty feet long.

"Dean, I have a good idea what we can do to keep Rodney from running. I'll tie your rope on the end of his front foot. You can walk along behind him and if he starts to run, all you have to do is jerk on the rope and Rodney will fall down."

"Good idea," Dean said. Dean got hold of the end of the rope and I coiled up my rope to where I had about two feet between Rodney and me. I pulled a little on the rope and Rodney followed right along. We went to the corral fence, where Dean let the rope go and opened the gate. Rodney and I walked through the gate and kept on going. Dean closed the gate and hurried up to us. He picked up his rope and tagged along behind.

Rodney stopped several times while we were crossing Bill's meadow. Each time it was hard to get him moving again. One time, when he wouldn't take another step, Dean went up close to his rear end and popped him with the end of the rope. This reminded him that we were taking him someplace else and he hadn't been consulted about the move.

Dean was anxious to try his rope at stopping Rodney, so when Rodney was trotting along, Dean pulled on his rope, holding Rodney's front foot from going forward, causing Rodney to stumble, nearly falling down. Boy, was Rodney mad! He regained his footing and, with his head down, turned around three or four times trying to see what caused him to nearly fall. He sure tangled up our ropes, but he was quite satisfied to stand still while I untangled the mess.

When we got to the fence that went around Bill's meadow, Dean let his rope drop and went around Rodney to open the gate. The fence was of four-strand barbed wire. The gate consisted of four wires and two staves. One stave was in the middle and the other was at the end and would be fastened to the existing post when closed. Dean tightened the gate to release the wire ring that held the stave and the post together. He moved the gate out of the way and Rodney and I walked through.

"Dean, this is going to be a snap," I said, as we went through the gate.

Confidently he replied, "We have him where he can't get away from us, no matter how hard he tries."

I walked a short distance from the gate to allow the rope that was on Rodney's foot to clear it. I held the coil of rope in one hand and the rope that went to Rodney's head in the other. I released two coils of rope, making the rope to Rodney a couple of feet longer to give me a little more freedom, in case Rodney made a few more circles like he had in the meadow. I still held onto the rope about two feet from Rodney's head. Dean pulled the gate around and proceeded to tighten the two poles together. The wires that ran through staples on the center stave made a loud screeching noise as they slid through the staples.

This was the excuse that Rodney was looking for! He took off on a run, tightening the rope around my wrist! When the rope tightened it left seven or eight feet of rope between me and Rodney's head. I kept jumping in the air trying to keep on my feet. I couldn't get the rope free from my wrist. The only way I could get free was to loosen the tight pull Rodney had on the rope. We were going through a sagebrush field and at the end of the field was a small creek called Jug Creek.

Dean fastened the gate and took off after us yelling, "I'm going home and get the rifle and shoot Rodney." I couldn't answer him. I had all I could do to try and keep up! In my mind I was thinking the same as Dean, but at this time I was dodging one sagebrush bush and then another. My life was passing before my eyes! I yelled a few hundred times at Rodney, but to no avail. He had the upper hand now, and he was going to use it to the best of his ability.

Finally, when I could keep up no longer, I fell down, but Rodney kept going! Over the rocks and through the sagebrush we arrived at Jug Creek amidst a great whirl of dust! Instead of going across, he turned and ran along the creek bank. Glancing from side to side as we traveled along, I tried to see how I could possibly slow him down. Suddenly up ahead I saw a huge willow bush rapidly approaching. I thought to myself, "If I go on one side and he goes on the other he will surely lose momentum," but like an astronaut in training I flew over the top!

With my free hand I tried to grab onto a willow branch, but he pulled it right out of my hand. With great speed we exploded from the willows and hit the road that went from Bill's ranch to Frisco! Down the road we flew towards Bill's Ranch and there he spotted Dean out in the sagebrush running as fast as he could and shouting, "I'm going to kill him!"

Rodney cut back towards the creek and when we arrived it was a place where the creek had cut a narrow channel in the ground. It was just a little too wide to jump across so Rodney went down into the creek and stopped to get a drink. Desperately I tried to release the rope from my wrist. I sure did wish I had a knife in my pocket now. I could see that I would have to have some help to free my arm. There were a few willow bushes along the side of the bank, and in the creek. While Rodney was drinking, I managed to get hold of the rope that was tied to his front foot. I quickly threaded it around a small willow clump and made a half hitch in it so I could take up the slack. I pulled it as tight as I dared without causing Rodney to start off again. He stood and drank for some time and then he looked around for a minute, and then took another drink.

I could hear Dean in the distance yelling all kinds of threats. I worked on loosening the rope on my arm, but when Rodney would decide to go on I wanted to be ready for whatever was in front of me. I could hear Dean calling a lot closer now. Rodney looked up and decided that it was time to go. He tried to take a step. The rope held his foot from going forward. He couldn't figure what was going on. He stepped back and tried again to step up out of the creek bottom. Again his foot held him from good footing. I pulled the rope tight that held Rodney to my arm.

Dean called, "Where are you," and I decided I had better answer, even if it would spook Rodney.

"I'm over here," I yelled. Dean came running up and thankfully he had a knife in his pocket. In an instant he cut the rope that held my arm. He grabbed the rope on Rodney's foot, and by this time, Rodney was out of the creek and wanted to leave. Dean gave a great big jerk on the rope and Rodney nearly fell down. Back on my feet, I soon had the rope off my wrist and arm. I grabbed the rope that went to Rodney's head and we started Rodney on towards our ranch. I went right up by his head and held on there, trying to get him to walk along.

Rodney came up with two alternatives that he felt he could present to save face. One was not to move at all and the other was to run. We came to the timber and every time Rodney would try to go faster than a walk I would go around a tree a couple of times and this would stop him dead.

The rope on his foot was a lifesaver! Dean also would pull on his rope every time it looked like he was going to get the best of us. We had made it to the back street of Frisco when along came Dad.

"What is the problem, boys?" Dad asked, and in the same breath said, "You sure are scratched up, are you hurt?"

"I don't think so," I said, as I proceeded to tell him all the problems that Rodney had given us.

"I don't think it is a good idea to have that rope on his foot," Dad said, as he edged closer to Rodney.

Rodney stood still all the time Dad was talking. Dad took the rope off his foot and grabbed him by the halter and started him walking.

We weren't quite halfway home, and after a short discussion, Dad said, "We'll take him back to Bill's Ranch tonight. I think you have had enough for today."

Rodney walked along without a problem till we got to the fence at the meadow. He decided that he wasn't going to go any farther. Dean opened the gate and Dad tried to get him to move. Rodney just stood there. Dad, looking around, spotted a piece of fence stave lying along the side of the fence.

"Dean, bring me that fence stave and Harold come here and hold Rodney by the halter," he said. I held onto Rodney and Dad gave him a great big swat on his north end as he faced south. Rodney got the message. He went through the fence running.

Dad yelled, "Let him go, he can't get away now." I sure was glad to turn him loose! My hand was sore and scratched up. I had a few bad scratches on my face, but my worst problem was my arm and my shoulder, they felt like they had been pulled apart.

Dean ran across the meadow and opened the pasture gate. With a little work we got him in.

Once Rodney was in the pasture we headed back home without stopping to see if Bill Thomas had gotten home yet. At home we were a little late with the milking. Dad was surprised that Rodney was so hard to lead.

Dad said, "Bill Thomas led him all the way from here to his ranch last fall and the bull never gave him a bit of trouble."

"I think we wouldn't have had a big problem with him if he hadn't heard the screeching of the fence when Dean tightened it," I answered.

"Probably," Dad said, "but he does take spells when he is hard to work with. Tomorrow when you go after him, take a couple of good 'persuaders' with you. Don't tie up his foot. This will only make him mad and you could hurt him if he fell just right." (I wasn't worried about HIM!)

"Go in the morning when Bill will be around and he will help you get a rope on him. If you get him going along without a lot of aggravation, I think he will walk along fine."

Morning came and I decided to make a little change in our plans. I got a chain about ten feet long out of the harness room and an extra heavy rope and put them in the pickup. Dean went to the wood pile and cut two poles about three feet long and put them in the pickup. Boy was I stiff and sore! My shoulder and arm still ached and the many cuts I had were all very painful. I could hardly make it to the barn for the morning milking, but after the chores were done I felt fine.

Dean and I got into the pickup and headed to Bill's Ranch. When we got there, Rodney was back up in the pasture by the train track.

Bill said, "I have a heavy duty halter that I'll lend you. I'll go to the pasture and I think I can put it on him with no problem. Give me your rope and I'll tie it on the halter, then I can lead him down to the corral. You boys stay right here."

Bill went towards Rodney and when he got almost to his head, Rodney whirled around and trotted off. Bill made a number of attempts to rope him with the help of language that neither Dean nor I nor Rodney fully understood, but we all got the drift. Wisely, Rodney just kept out of Bill's way.

Finally Bill said, "You boys come over here and we will drive him over into the corner of the fence." Looking at each other, Dean and I spread out and drove Rodney to the corner. He stood still, not seeming the least bit excited. Bill walked up to him and handed him a handful of bran. He sure did like it. Bill was reaching around his head to fasten the halter on him when Rodney decided to leave, knocking Bill down, and ran to the opposite end of the pasture. Bill wasn't hurt, but he sure was mad at the bull.

Bill opened the gate out of the pasture and we drove Rodney out. Once out of the pasture, Rodney ran across the hay meadow to the far end. I said, "Bill, I would like to fasten my chain on your halter and tie him to the back of the pickup and take him home that way."

"Good idea," Bill said.

Bill, Dean and I went out into the meadow and drove Rodney back up to the corral. Once we got Rodney in the corral it wasn't long till we had a double halter on him. Bill fastened his halter on first, and then we made a chain halter and fastened it on him. Bill led him out of the corral and down to the road where we fastened the end of the chain and the rope to the back of the pickup.

Bill said, "Boys, I don't have anything to do this morning, I can go home with you and help you put the bull in your corral, if you will bring me back." This was music to our ears. Any trouble that we might encounter on the way home, Bill would be there to help us.

"I'll not only take you back, but we can eat lunch before I take you home." I drove down the road to the gate in low gear. The bull had to walk fast to keep up. Once or twice he decided to stop, but the pickup forced him to keep on moving. This was a far cry from the trouble that we had yesterday.

When we went through Bill's gate, I slowed to almost a stop when Bill said, "Keep on going, we can close the gate when you bring me back."

I drove as slowly as I could in order not to get Rodney all fired up. Arriving at the highway through Frisco, I stopped and when all was clear I stepped down on the gas but, Rodney had decided to stay where he was and the pickup didn't move! I gave it a little more gas. One wheel started to spin on the gravel, killing the engine. Rodney jerked back, breaking the chain. We all bailed out to see what to do.

Bill had fastened our heavy rope on his halter and also tied it to the back of the truck. However, there was a little slack in the rope. I walked around to see how Rodney was taking it. He just stood there swinging his tail. "I've won this battle," he seemed to be thinking.

We made a new chain halter and tightened the slack in the rope, trying to make both the chain and the rope assume the same responsibility. I got in the truck again and Dean and Bill stayed outside to encourage Rodney to start walking. Once he took a step, his power to hold back was broken and he had to walk along. This was accomplished with one of the sticks that Dean had put in the pickup. When Rodney saw the stick he started to walk before I got the truck in gear. Once across the highway Bill and Dean got back into the truck.

Everything went well until I had a fairly steep hill to go up by the Frisco beaver ponds. About halfway up the hill, we met a lady from Frisco walking her dog. The dog started barking and Rodney, not wanting to be outdone, put on his brakes, lowered his head, and made a pass at the dog. By this time we were stopped. The dog would have been ripped apart had the rope and chain not held the bull from reaching the dog which had moved right up to the back of the pickup for a closer look.

I set the brake and once again we all bailed out of the truck. The lady was scared to death. Anxiously she called and called her dog to come to her. The dog was barking so loud and fast that he couldn't hear her or he realized Rodney couldn't get to him and he wanted to show his authority while he had the chance.

Rodney was moving from side to side at the back of the truck. The rope and chain didn't allow him to move very far. I don't think he was exactly afraid of the dog, but he sure did want to get his two cents worth in while he could.

Dean climbed into the bed of the truck and handed the stick to Bill. Bill yelled, "Lady, get your dog out of here or I will bust him with this club." What a commotion with barking, screaming, and unveiled threats!

I went to Rodney's side and tried to keep him from turning around. Bill chased the dog away from the truck and then the lady grabbed her dog and snapped on a leash. Once we got the lady and her dog out of the picture, we tried to get Rodney going again. This turned out to be quite a job. By this time Rodney discovered that it was hard for us to get the truck moving while on the hillside, and if he didn't move he could hold us there indefinitely. Each time I tried to go up the hill, Rodney would hold fast and I would spin my wheels.

As he got out of the truck, Bill said, "Give me that stick and I bet Rodney will move. Keep on going when you get started. I can catch up to you at the top of the hill." Bill gave Rodney a couple of love pats on his back side. He started to whirl around to fight back when I started up. It was too late now. On up the hill we went and when I got on top I slowed down as slow as I could in first gear. Dean and Bill soon caught up to me. They got into the truck without my quite stopping. We continued on to our gate where, once again we had to stop. Dean got out and opened the gate.

To our surprise Rodney walked right through. I kept on moving and I didn't stop till I got to the corral gate where Dean caught up to us and opened it. Bill and I unhooked Rodney from the truck. Once inside the corral Rodney felt right at home. Dad had told me that we wouldn't turn him out into the pasture for a few days, so I put a couple forks of dry hay in the corral for him to eat.

"Lets go to the house, Bill, and see what Mom has for lunch."

## FIRE IN THE PICKUP

The pickup was my pride and joy and it served many functions. It was our main delivery vehicle for milk as well as short turns around town. Shortly after our tour of duty with Rodney we started having trouble. After I would travel a short distance the pickup would sputter and stop. I was always able to get it home, but it was getting worse. I stopped at the Frisco garage to let Ken Chamberlain look at it.

Ken started the engine and raised the hood and after a minute he closed the hood and turned the engine off.

He said, "Your fuel pump is going out and I don't have one that will fit, but I can call Henry Ashlock and see if I can get one from him." I went into the café and waited till Ken got a chance to call.

After a while Ken came into the café and said, "I found one and they will send it over with a miner headed to Climax in the morning. You can come over and get it any time after seven."

I drove home and the pickup didn't stop till I got right to the spot where we parked it.

When morning came I tried to start it and it started right up so we loaded the milk to deliver. We planned for me to go to Frisco and put the fuel pump on at Ken's garage and head to Climax with the milk. When the milk was all loaded and I was ready to go the pickup refused to start.

Dad said, "Go to town and get the fuel pump and put it on the truck right here. You will save time in the long run."

I looked around to see if a saddle horse was close by to ride to town, but no such luck. I went back to the pickup and tried again to start it. It just wouldn't start. I was just about ready to walk to Frisco for the pump when a brilliant thought entered my mind. Or so I thought!

I could take a half gallon can of gas and fasten it to the dash with a piece of wire. I then could borrow the hose off the hot water bottle and fasten it to the gas line leading to the carburetor and start a siphon from the gas can. This would allow me to drive to Frisco. It didn't take but a minute till I had put these thoughts into action and the truck was running.

I was proud of myself for thinking of such a good idea.

I called Mom and said, "I can make it to town and I'll put on the new pump before I start to Climax." I didn't try to explain how I managed to get the truck going, the only thing that mattered was that it was running.

I got into the truck and headed towards the gate. We had extra milk that morning. I had two crates of milk sitting in the seat on the passenger's side. I locked the door and pushed the crates against the door to give me more room. I rolled the window up and just as the glass got to the top the handle came off. I tossed it on the floor with the door handle that kept coming off.

I decided to have Ken help me with the handles as I would need to open the door for every house stop.

Dad was down by the gate when he heard the truck coming. He laid down his shovel and opened the gate. I slowed down almost to a stop and when I saw Dad opening the gate I stepped on the gas.

Just as he got it open I glanced down at the floor and saw a flame on the hose. Almost instantly the flames shot upward!

I set the brake and grabbed the can of gas and was going to throw it out of the cab, but the wire that I used to fasten it to the choke held it solid. I jerked it several times, trying to free it. When it finally came loose I realized that I couldn't open the door without the handle that was on the floor under my legs and which was now covered with fire!

My clothes were covered with gas slopping from the can. I was reaching for the handle in a blazing fire just as Dad jerked the door open and pulled me out! Fortunately our irrigation ditch that ran along the side of the road was full of water.

Dad yelled, "Hold your breath!" and rolled me in the water. I was afraid he was going to drown me before he let me up. By this time the front of the truck was covered in flames. Dad ran around the truck and grabbed the can of gas and threw it in the ditch. He took off his jacket and started beating the flames which were in the cab and under the hood. There was an empty bucket in the back of the truck next to the milk. I grabbed it and threw water from the ditch on the truck. When I got winded Dad took the bucket and threw several buckets of water into the cab. This put the fire out there.

Dad grabbed a rag and opened the hot hood. The fire had

consumed the spilled gas from the hose and was burning the spark plug wiring. I again took the bucket and threw water on the wiring. The fire was out, but there were some things behind the seat that were smoking as well as the oil that had collected under the engine. Dad grabbed the shovel and scraped the smoking dirt and oil off the bottom of the engine.

With another bucket of water and a few shovels of dry dirt the smoke finally stopped.

Dad grabbed me and walked me some distance from the truck and said, "Puff-puff, I am about out of breath. Are you all right?"

"I think I'm O.K., except my finger hurts where I grabbed the can of gas, but are you all right?"

Dad said, "I'm fine or will be as soon as I can get my breath. As I walked us over here I just thought about the gas tank and how it could have exploded with all that fire and we would have been badly injured or burned to death."

My hand was burned, especially where I grabbed the wire holding the gas can to the choke. I lost the hair on my arms and a little hair on my head. Dad lost the hair on one hand and had a blister on the back of his hand. The truck ... well, it had to have all new wiring, a new seat and steering wheel plus covers for the instruments. Of course a little paint in a spot or two would help. We got help delivering milk for a few days till we repaired the pickup.

Dad said, "You should never try anything like that. Gas is safe only when it is confined to the areas intended for it, but it will only take a second, and I mean a second, to kill you when it catches on fire."

"I didn't realize how dangerous the gas was," I said. "I sure am glad that you were there at the right second to get me out of that fire!"

## GAME WARDEN MOVES LIVE BEAVER

Meadow Creek ran in the west end of the ranch and continued through the middle of the ranch to the lower end where it turned towards the Lusher Place. Most of the creek was covered with beaver ponds, one after another. At the west end of the ranch there was a big beaver dam. It created a small stream that flowed along parallel to the main creek for much of the west quarter of our place. There were also many beaver dams on this stream.

Beaver lived all up and down the creeks. In the late summer they would restore old dams and build many new ones. We were always opening a dam to keep the water from covering our

***Allen Fitzgerald with a Live Beaver***

meadows. We would tear a hole in the dam from one to two feet deep and a night or two later it would all be patched up.

It was against the law to trap beaver in Colorado so Dad called the Game and Fish Commission and asked if they could move some of our pesky beaver.

Allen Fitzgerald was the game warden who was assigned the chore of moving a number of the beaver.

Allen would come to the ranch every morning to check his traps. The traps were big wire cages that would close when the beaver got into them. He was able to relocate eighteen or twenty during the late summer and early fall. He turned them loose on creeks that needed beaver dams to conserve the water. Six of the beaver were taken to Salt Lick Gulch for their new homes. A couple of years after the beaver were moved, there were a lot of new dams on the Salt Lick Creek. We didn't miss the beaver on our ranch and I'm sure that they were pleased not to have to keep rebuilding their homes that those pesky humans kept tearing up.

## You Could Have Heard Her in Denver

One evening I had some things I wanted to do so I got the drinking water from the irrigation ditch below the house instead of going to the spring. It usually took about fifteen minutes to make the round trip to the spring during the summer and a little longer during the winter.

I had just settled down to something more rewarding when Mom said, "You have barely enough time to go to the spring before dinner and get fresh drinking water."

"Mom," I said, "I just filled both of the buckets on the cooking table."

"I know," she said, "but I want spring water instead of ditch water."

I tried to explain that nobody would know the difference, but after a short discussion it was decided that it might be in my best interest to go to the spring for water.

I emptied one bucket of water into the stove reservoir and took another bucket from the milk house and headed to the spring. I put one of the buckets down into the spring and lifted out a nice bucket of cold water and then I got a brilliant idea!

It was late in the fall and the brook trout were spawning. When they were spawning they would swim up the creeks as far as they could. There they would clean off the moss and lay their eggs on the gravel or sandy soil which brought them right up to our spring. We kept a spare bucket at the spring so I took it and went down the spring drainage where it emptied into Meadow Creek and laid the bucket on its side in about ten inches of slow moving water. I picked up several pieces of willow sticks and threw them up stream into the water where the fish were all congregated and spawning.

Immediately, just as I thought, the fish streaked downstream to the outlet. As soon as I heard two or three fish swim into the bottom of the bucket with a bang I jerked the bucket out of the water. I had several fish.

I took three fish around eight or nine inches long out of the bucket and put them in one of my buckets of drinking water. I turned the others back into the spring and headed back to the house.

I set both buckets of water on the cook table as I asked, "When are we going to eat?"

"We'll eat just as soon as we can get the water glasses filled," Mom replied.

Mom took a dipper and lowered it to the bottom of the bucket as if she thought the water in the bottom of the bucket would taste better than that on top.

Suddenly, in the quiet of the evening, there was a terrifying scream you could have heard in Denver as Mom dropped the dipper and left a poor fish flopping around on the floor.

The excitement was too much for Mom. She rushed to the bedroom for a quick change of under clothes while the rest of the family gathered around to see what had happened.

I picked up the poor fish and put him in the wash basin and poured some nice cold spring water in the pan and included a couple of roommates for a short stay. Not too much was said and we all got seated for the evening meal when Mom returned from the bedroom.

She went straight to the wash basin as if drawn there by some magic force. She put her hands into the basin and once again this blood curdling scream pierced the evening quiet. Dad rushed to her side and escorted her to a chair. The drinking water was replaced with milk and the evening meal went fine until I just couldn't hold out any longer and had to laugh.

Then my brother and two sisters joined in and we all had a big laugh till Dad said, "That is enough for one evening."

My folks were pretty easy to get along with and enjoyed a joke, but I thought I had pressed my luck as far as I could for one evening.

## BOSSY ELSIE EATS A WORM

When I went to Breckenridge High School there never seemed to be a dull moment. Each and every day produced an exciting time and if it was a dull day there was always someone who could come up with a little excitement, just to keep anyone from getting stale.

There was a gal named Elsie who was very aggressive, and a very dominating person. She was small for her age. Where she should have had some bulges she didn't. Elsie stood about five feet tall and weighed less than ninety five pounds. She was a 4.0 student and a top athlete. No one seemed to get the best of her.

One activity period, a friend and I went to the side of the field to throw a few fast balls to each other. Here she came with a bat that she had taken away from a kid twice her size.

"Hey you guys, come over here, I am going to bat a few balls to you," she yelled, as she intercepted one of Donald's fastest balls.

"Not a very fast ball," she remarked, "but I will help you correct that."

"Hey," Donald protested, "We want to practice throwing and catching fast balls, and we don't need any help from you."

"Throw me the ball and go over and play with the girls," I said. Just about that time she threw a ball so fast that I was afraid to try and catch it. I stepped out of the way and let it land in the street. I retrieved it and threw a high one towards Donald. I was proud of the height and distance. Donald started running for it. Elsie also ran towards the ball. As the ball came down she pushed Donald out of the way, knocking him down and caught the ball herself. Donald got up and then we had a huddle.

Since we couldn't get rid of her we decided to throw the ball from one to the other in a triangle formation. We set up the rules that when one of us would miss catching the ball, that person would be out till the second one missed the ball, then we would start all over, only the next time we would reverse the direction and proceed the same way. As we spread out, I thought what a dumb thing to agree to.

I remembered when she conned me out of my seat on the bus going to school, causing me to ride from Dillon to Breckenridge on a seat next to a two hundred pound gal who used two-thirds of the double seat.

Elsie had the ball and threw it to Donald. He caught the ball, but he fell down in the attempt. He got up shaking his hand, then he threw the ball to me. I decided that I would throw the ball as fast as I could, hoping to get it somewhere near her. I wound up and let the ball fly. It was a little high, but no problem, she jumped in the air and caught it like a professional. She wound up and threw another fast ball to Donald. He again caught it, but barely stayed on his feet. Donald threw the ball to me and I caught it, making a complete turnaround and threw it to her all in the same motion.

She wound up like she was going to give Donald the works and when she released the ball, it somehow sailed so slow that I wondered why it didn't fall to the ground. Donald was all primed to catch a fast ball and when he recovered from the shock, the ball fell right where he was standing.

"That was a bad ball," he yelled.

"I threw an easy ball and if you were any good you would have caught it," she yelled. Donald retrieved the ball and threw it to me. It was a little outside, but I couldn't believe that I let it go right through my hands. I ran it down and threw a high ball to Elsie. It was high and away off course, but of course she ran, dove after it and made the catch.

"I'm tired of throwing the ball," Elsie said, "Let's do some batting practice."

"Donald, you go down to where Harold's standing and I'll bat you freaks some balls," she said. I stood still, wondering how we would be able to get the ball and keep it. Donald said a few choice words to her and then came down to where I was. She backed up a long way and tossed the ball in the air and swung at it. The ball went high into the air and sailed over our heads out into the street. I ran after it, while Donald argued about hitting it so hard. I threw the ball to Donald and he threw the ball to her. She batted several balls to us and all seemed O.K. when she took the ball and walked off.

Donald yelled, "Throw me the ball, it's not yours."

"I'm going to keep the ball," she yelled. The rest of the period was taken up trying to get our ball back, but to no avail. She kept the ball.

"Don't worry, Donald," I said, "She'll give it back." About a week later at activity period she showed up on the field with the ball. Donald and I immediately went over to where she was tossing the ball in the air and catching it.

"Hi Elsie," I said. "We thought we would throw a few balls, do you want to play with us?" Over to the side of the field we went.

Elsie threw a few balls, first to me and then to Donald. Suddenly Donald caught the ball and ran for the schoolhouse.

Elsie caught on real fast. Donald hadn't gone very far when she caught up with him and tripped him. As he was falling he threw the ball towards me. I chased after the ball and picked it up just in time to be knocked to the ground, but I held onto the ball. Donald rushed over to me and tried to pull Elsie off of me. He got hold of her arm and held on. She had a death grip on my arm with the ball. I tried to pry her hands off, but to no avail. I finally managed to toss the ball a few feet away.

Before you could blink your eyes she had the ball and took off with it. Donald was really getting mad now. He jumped up and ran after her. When he caught up to her he made a flying tackle and they both fell to the ground. I ran to his aid and we finally got the ball from her, but not without some problems. Donald had a nosebleed and a torn shirt. I had a big scratch on my arm and about four or five buttons missing from my shirt.

Elsie didn't seem to have a scratch, or at least nothing showed. Donald and I sat on the grass a minute and got our breath, then joined the rest of the kids as they headed inside at the end of the period.

Donald and I tried and tried to figure how to get even with Elsie. Anything we could think of would only get us into trouble. After days of planning, an idea was finally born. The only thing we figured that would bring our arch enemy to her knees would be to somehow trick her into eating a worm. In our minds this would be the ultimate payback.

HOW? I hadn't figured that out yet. A project like this would take a little time and a lot of planning. I smiled to myself that I had even thought of such a good idea. "Boy, will she ever be mad when she finds out that we tricked her into eating a worm." Days went by and Donald and I worked out several ideas and then canceled them one by one.

We seemed to always come back to the same idea. We will DARE her to eat a worm. The dare part would be the motivating force.

"I'll bet she would eat a worm," Donald said. "I don't think she would pass up a dare, but we want to be sure that she doesn't get the best of us in the attempt."

Finally we arrived at a method to perform this task.

I said, "Donald, I'll dig up some garden worms and some night crawlers and bring them to school." On Thursday I took the worms to school in a discarded aspirin bottle. Between classes Donald went over by where she was tormenting some big guy and asked her if she wanted to see what he had in a match box. This was the right approach. She got all excited and immediately wanted to see what he had.

"It will cost you one dollar to see what I have," Donald said.

"I don't have any money, but please let me see what you have," she begged. Donald walked over to me and slid the box open so I could see in.

"Those are beauties," I said. A couple of other guys got interested in looking into the box. Several girls came over and offered Donald a dollar if they all could see in. Donald didn't take them up on the offer. He insisted on one dollar each. Elsie was now wild with curiosity!

"Donald, if you don't let me see what is in the box, I'll take the box away from you."

"No you won't," I said. "I also have my money wrapped up in that project."

Elsie came over to where I was standing and said, "Harold, loan me a dollar and I'll give you two dollars back next week."

"What have you got to give me to hold as security?" I asked.

"Nothing," she said. "I don't have anything of value, and if I did, I wouldn't give it to you." With this, she walked off, just about ending our attempt for retribution. Class took up, so this project had to be postponed for another time. As we rode the bus home in the evening Donald told me that he had several people offering him a dollar to see what was in the box. Elsie, of course, was on the bus. She pushed the kid that was riding on the seat with her out of the seat into the aisle and invited Donald to ride with her.

Donald immediately saw what she had in mind, "No thanks," he said, "I don't want to mash my box."

I was one of the first kids off the bus. Donald got off right after me. When he got off, he slipped me his match box. Elsie got off and immediately put her arm around Donald and marched him into Pete Lege's store. I think she was still trying to see what was in the box, but then, maybe she was after a free bite to eat before she went home.

Next day Donald and I got together to implement plan number two, which was not yet born. By now I had decided that we had to come up with something in the box, and also figure another angle how to get her to eat a worm. We finally decided that I would draw a green letter "B," about two inches long in the bottom of the match box, using a dark green Crayola. Trying to generate some more excitement I told one kid I thought Donald had a two inch long green bee in the box. This should take care of the interested parties wanting to see in the box, however, I doubted that it was worth a dollar to see a green "B" drawn on the bottom of a match box.

Plan "B" called for a nice apple cut in four pieces and a hole cut in one piece and a worm installed in the hole, then the piece put back over the worm.

I approached Elsie and gave her a big green apple cut in four pieces.

"How come the apple is cut up?" she asked.

"Mom always cuts my apple into four pieces and wraps it in some waxed paper," I said. She removed the paper and took a bite of the apple.

"Not bad," she said, "but I can't see you giving me an apple unless there was something fishy about it."

She ate one piece of the apple and didn't find the worm. A couple of her girl friends came by and she handed each a piece of the apple. I looked at Donald. You could see by the look on his face that he was afraid of what was going to happen any second. They just ate away on the pieces of the apple. Elsie took a bite of the last piece.

"What could have happened to the worm?" I wondered. I didn't think it could have crawled out of the apple without someone seeing it.

All of a sudden one of the girls gave a terrifying scream and threw her piece of apple on the ground.

Donald asked, "Was there a worm in the apple?"

I remarked, "I didn't see any spot where the worm ate his way into the apple." We didn't fool Elsie. She picked up the piece of apple and looked at the worm.

"This doesn't look like an apple worm to me, I bet one of you dummies put the worm in the apple just to see if I would eat it."

"I'm not afraid of a little worm," she continued, as she looked at the worm, who was now trying his best to get out of his abode before something worse happened to him.

Several kids came over to see why Betty was screaming so loud. Chuck had a cup, which I immediately borrowed. I got a cup of water at the hydrant and poured water over the apple that Elsie was holding.

"What are you trying to do, drown the worm?" Elsie asked, as she took her finger and pushed the worm to safer quarters on the apple.

Donald finally came to and said, "Elsie, if you are not afraid of that worm, I dare you to eat him."

"I don't want to hurt the poor little worm," she said.

Chuck entered into the debate and said, "Go ahead and eat the worm, he won't last very long. I see only part of him is there anyway."

With this, Betty gave another terrifying scream and I thought she was going to upchuck right there.

I decided now was the time to push Elsie into eating a worm. "I double dare you to eat the worm," I said.

John, who was standing back and hadn't opened his mouth said, "Elsie I double, double dare you to eat the apple and the worm on it." He continued, "As a matter of fact I got a dollar that says you won't."

I reached into my pocket and pulled out a dollar bill and said, "There you are Elsie, two dollars says you won't eat the worm."

Simp, who was just returning from the far end of the field stepped up and said, "I'll add two more dollars to the pot."

Elsie hesitated a little when Simp spoke again, "I'll put another dollar in the pot making five dollars that says you won't eat the worm."

Elsie couldn't bear to be outdone and she sure did want the money. "Give me the apple and I'll eat the worm." By now Chuck was holding the apple and when he handed the apple to Elsie the worm had vanished. Every one looked for the worm, even Elsie. When the worm, or the back half of the worm, was not to be found Elsie said, "Give me the money, I would have eaten the worm if he hadn't been lost."

Chuck, who was holding all the money, refused. Looking at Elsie I decided she was trying to decide whether she could take the money away from Chuck or not.

I spoke up, "I just happen to have a spare worm. This worm will be as good as the worm that was in the apple," I said, as I reached in my pocket and pulled out a little bottle with a great big night crawler in it. I handed the night crawler to Elsie, who shivered as she took it.

"This night crawler is a lot bigger than that little worm I was going to eat."

Finally she said, "OK, I'll eat the worm, but someone will have to give Chuck five more dollars to hold for me or I won't eat him." It wasn't long before Chuck had the additional five dollars. There were a lot of kids crowded around Elsie and she was really enjoying all this attention. I think she wanted to prolong the snack as long as possible. Someone had to go wash the worm and she also wanted the piece of apple to be cut in two so she could see in it.

She took the two pieces of apple in one hand and the worm in the other hand and held the worm up into the air above her head. The worm dangled a good six inches below her fingers. She stuck her tongue out and touched the worm with her tongue. At least ten girls started screaming. I think I noted a bass tone in the screaming, but at that time I decided I wouldn't make an issue of it. She went through a trial run. She lowered the worm and at the same time made a fast pass at her mouth with the apple. She had John go get her a glass of water and stand by. Now she lifted the worm up again and stuck her tongue out and with a swift swing she put the apple in her mouth and with the same motion she cupped the worm in her hand and pushed it into her mouth with the apple, so it looked like she had fulfilled the dare. She stood there for a minute chewing on the apple when suddenly she grabbed the money from Chuck and took off on a dead run, not stopping for a drink of water.

The comments were, "I didn't think she would do it!" "I'm surprised!" "I knew she would do it!" and "You guys ought to be ashamed of yourselves!" The period was up and there was a mass exit from the area. I picked up the glass of water and as I stood there looking around to see if anything else needed to be picked up, guess what I saw? The night crawler was on the ground and trying his best to get out of sight. I picked him up and put him back into my bottle and went to the next class.

## "I *AM* THE GAME WARDEN"

Russell Mumford had a job in Breckenridge as justice of the peace and custodian at the courthouse and in his spare time he did many different jobs. He gave driving tests and issued drivers' licenses. When hunting season opened he issued hunting licenses to late-starting hunters.

One morning, right after the season had started, Russell was at his desk in the courthouse when a game warden stopped to pick up all the licenses that he had written the last few days.

"How's it going, Russell?" the game warden asked.

Russell leaned over and opened his desk drawer and said, "I have a whole handful of receipts. I had a good run on the licenses the day before season opened, and a couple of stragglers came in here yesterday."

"Good," Paul said, "we have sold more licenses this year than the last two years combined."

They transferred the money and receipts and Paul was about to leave when he looked out of the window and said, "I see a man coming in here and I can see the horns of a big deer in the back of his pickup. I hope the guy doesn't want to see you, but if he does he probably needs his driver's license renewed. I'll wait to see what he wants and then I'd better go."

The man walked into the office and said with a smile on his face, "Howdy, gentleman, I want to buy a hunting license." A concerned frown came over Paul's face.

Russell started to say something when the guy continued, "I got up at daylight and headed towards the goose pasture. Just before I got there, I came around a curve and there were several does and a big buck standing right beside the road. I bailed out of the pickup and before they got a hundred feet I dropped the buck. He sure is a nice four point. It's almost a perfect set. You had better write me up a license before a game warden comes around."

Russell said, "There is a gentleman here who wants to talk to you."

The guy, never guessing who Paul was, said, "What's on your mind?" as he stuck out his hand to shake Paul's hand.

Paul said, "Did I hear you say you shot a buck already this morning?"

"You bet you did," he said. "I have him right out here in my truck. If you wait a minute till I get my license I'll take you out and show you the best set of horns you ever saw. I'll even buy you a cup of coffee after I show you my buck." About this time Russell was about to laugh out loud.

Paul said, "I don't want to ruin your day, but I *am* the game warden. It is unlawful for you to hunt without a license and it is unlawful to have a deer in your possession without one."

The man almost fainted, but managed to say, "I came in here to get a license, then it would be legal. You are not going to arrest me are you?"

Paul said, "I'm afraid I have to."

The man said, "I was just kidding you guys, I didn't get a buck, but I will as soon as I get my license."

Paul walked over to the window and said, "Do you own that pickup out there with the horns of a buck extended above the bed?"

The guy said, "O.K. I sure have a fine buck. Give me a ticket and I will write you a check right now."

The hunter and the game warden walked out to the pickup.

Russell said, "I'll bet that is the last time he pulls a trick like that, but then, who knows?"

Just one of the many stories of life in Summit County.

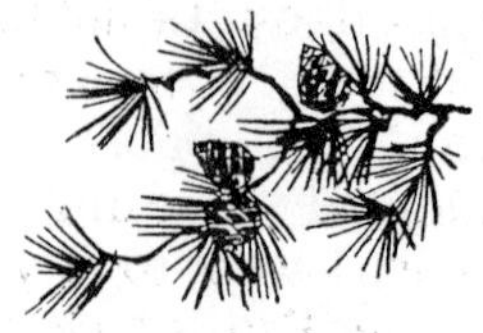

**HALLOWEEN IN BRECKENRIDGE**

It was the last week of October 1942 and things were getting dull. Halloween was only three days away. A party was planned in Frisco: A dance with ice cream and chocolate cake to be served by mid-evening.

It occurred to me that this was too dull for the evening's entertainment on Halloween.

I talked to some friends at school and we decided to take an old 1927 or 1928 model Dodge that was abandoned on a vacant lot in Breckenridge down to Main Street. I suggested we put a sign on it "FOR SALE, GOOD CONDITION, ONE OWNER. Ask for Mr. Schmitz." Mr. Schmitz was our high school principal.

I had seen the old car and talked to my Dad about offering five or six dollars for it. Ken Chamberlain could convert it into a bull rake to use in putting up our hay in the fall. After I described the car to Dad I think he decided to pass it up.

During Thursday's activity period several of us skipped the regular games and met at the back side of the school building to make plans for this great event. We made a quick trip over to the car to see if it needed any work before the trip that it was to undertake in the near future.

A quick survey showed someone had borrowed the steering wheel in times past. Frank crawled up into the front seat and hollered, "Harold, look, no steering wheel."

"No problem, it should still be steerable using a pipe wrench on the exposed gears on top of the steering column. I have a pipe wrench at home we can use for the job," I said.

Frank was a sober, but friendly, chunky kid. He always had his hair hanging down in his face. He wore pants a size too large and his leather belt would go around him twice, but the last lap around was outside the loops just hanging out. He wore a black hat that had the brim trimmed off around the sides and back, leaving a covering above his eyes.

After looking at the gears on the steering column Frank said, "It will work fine, I can drive her anywhere."

The tires were nearly flat, but they would be fine for our endeavor. The windshield also had departed long ago, as had both front doors. The left front fender had taken the place of the bumper which was missing. It looked like the fender had been pushed up against the tire and partially straightened out with a sledge hammer. Also the left front headlight looked straight down.

Jim, a not too tall, skinny kid who always needed a haircut and wore his bill cap turned backward with his hair hanging out the back, walked around to the opposite side and said, "Hey, you guys, come around here and look at this fender and running board."

The running board on the right side was rusted out where it was supposed to be fastened to the fender, which also was badly rusted leaving the end of the running board hanging in the air.

I said, "I can bring some bailing wire from home and tie the running board up."

Jim lay down on his side and examined the underside of the running board and when he got up he said, "The bracket on the bottom is broken, but I can find enough wire around home to tie it up. I'll do it right after supper this evening."

Frank, listening to Jim said, "You may need some help. Give me a call and I'll meet you here when you're ready."

The floor boards in the front were missing. Sitting on the front seat left something to be desired as several of the coil springs protruded out from the seat covering. Looking down you could see the ground beneath the car. There was an indented scrape on the right side about a foot wide that ran from the back of the car to the front of the back door where it disappeared. It looked like the car had been backing up and got too close to a tree. Both back door handles were missing and some wire held one door shut.

At one time the car was painted black. Sometime later someone had painted the back door on the left side a very dull orange using a stiff brush. Frank pulled and pushed on the door but to no avail. The door seemed to be welded in place.

"Harold," he said, "I think the door may have been replaced when the old door had some kind of entanglement with an unknown object." This could be possible as it didn't quite fit right in the opening.

The fabric top showed it had spent many years unprotected from nature's changing conditions. The back seat was missing and the area was filled with scrap iron, rotted shingles and several rusted pieces of corrugated metal roofing, not to mention lots of old rusted cans. The glass in the back and side windows was missing. Looking at the cargo it appeared the car's last effort may have been gathering scrap iron for the Japanese scrap iron drive.

"What do you guys think?" I asked.

Jim responded, "Excellent, I wouldn't mind having it for myself if it didn't have the back seat filled with trash."

Frank, having just finished kicking the tires for the third time, answered, "Harold, it will be perfect for the job we have for it to do."

Our plans called for us to meet at 9:00 P.M. on the vacant lot where the car was stationed, speaking in a whisper if we needed to talk. We didn't want anyone to know who moved the old retired car down onto the main street of Breckenridge.

Halloween night came. Most of the kids got together and terrorized the peaceful community of Frisco and received the usual handouts. Then we went over to the party at the town hall. After our helpings of ice cream and cake our gang headed to Breckenridge. We briefly stopped in Dillon and picked up Jim and continued on to where we parked on the east side of the school where the Dillon bus usually parked. We headed towards the vacant lot.

Everyone had the same thing in mind: Park the car on Main Street without a sound and leave without being seen or heard. All hands arrived about the same time so we immediately positioned ourselves at our assigned stations. Frank climbed in the car with the pipe wrench and positioned himself on the seat to steer with no practice. Jim climbed in and seated himself beside Frank on the front seat with a six foot long steel bar. If the car got to going too fast he would drop the end of the bar down to the ground through the opening in the bottom. This would serve as an emergency brake. Bob had borrowed the bar from a nice family

that lived not too far from where the car was parked. They were not home so he left an IOU note and borrowed the bar for the job at hand. Well, *maybe* he left a note. He was sure they would not object to the loan as it might save someone from getting run over.

Access to the front seat was easy since the doors were gone, as was the windshield; however the borrower of the windshield didn't take the windshield wipers. It was a clear night so I doubted that we would need the wipers anyway.

Darrel (Donkey Ears) was assigned the job of one man power on the right side of the car. This was a perfect job for him as he was a tall, skinny guy with extra big feet (good for emergency braking), short sandy hair and always wore a black stocking cap (which was perfect for night-time assignments), that is if he could find it. After the car started moving he would assist Jim if any emergencies cropped up. With this kind of an operation you couldn't be too sure of anything.

Three guys, Bob, Bill, and Chuck were lined up along the back of the car to do the pushing. Bob was of medium height and weight and was around 16. He was a classy dresser. He was always seen combing his light brown hair and rarely wore a hat. His black shoes were always polished, however, he wore a pair of boots for this job.

Bill was another pusher and was a tall, medium weight, ordinary, jolly fellow. He always wore a big black hat with the sides curled up. He wore bib overalls, and a red hankie around his neck, but in a pinch he could get rattled.

Chuck, also 16, wore glasses, was a stout, sandy haired kid who wore his hair in a crew cut. He exercised daily, but was still a bit overweight. His twin brother said he didn't know when to leave the table.

One more guy had the job of pushing on the left side by Frank, and that was me, Harold.

We had two or three blocks to go on flat ground, then a little over two blocks downhill to Main Street. The three back pushers were to go to the front of the car as soon as it started rolling downhill and hold it back so it wouldn't go too fast.

She started moving, slowly, silently, just what we wanted except for Chuck's laugh that ended up in a cough. In all of our excitement we had not noticed a ditch covered with long grass that we had to cross. The car was moving smoothly and suddenly "CRASH" into the ditch she went, both front wheels buried up to the front axle in water. With lots of chuckles, grunts and much heaving we finally got out of the ditch and once more were headed to the street that heads downhill and to our journey's end.

So far so good and all was quiet except for an occasional chuckle and a grinding noise from one front wheel. She was moving freely now. Frank negotiated a great turn onto the street headed downhill. I was now sure that Frank was the right person to guide this vehicle to its new home.

All of a sudden the silence was pierced by at least ten dogs announcing the car was finally leaving its present abode for new quarters yet to be named. With a few more dogs joining in the racket and several porch lights coming on, the rear pushing crew got the old car moving a little too fast. They had a hard time trying to get to their new stations in front to hold the car back.

About half way down the hill Jim noticed the pushing crew's problem: They lacked the courage to step out in front and try to stop a runaway car going down the hill! Jim decided it was time for the emergency brake. He let the bar drop and, WOW! what a terrifying noise. When the lower end of the bar hit the street, the upper end of the bar hit the dash with a deafening crash, lodging there while the other end continued to drag on the ground.

In all the excitement Frank dropped the pipe wrench, exhausting all hopes of steering the car. Darrel, who was pushing on the right side, decided he couldn't keep up and climbed up on the side with Jim. Sizing up the developing situation, he decided it was about time to abandon ship so he yelled "Let her go," as he jumped off the side. He had misjudged the distance to a ditch of water and landed painfully on a rock pile.

I managed to keep up, but only because there were at least ten dogs just one jump from my rear end and a couple of huge dogs gaining on me. I then had no trouble keeping up. (It wouldn't have surprised me if I had beat everyone to Main Street.)

With three brakemen in front trying to hold her back, dogs barking, a six foot bar nicely wedged into the dash and dragging on the gravel street, Frank yelling, "We're all going to die," two guys on the sides yelling to slow her down, and two large dogs with deafening barks moving in for a close up view, this wasn't the silent approach we had envisioned or anticipated a little earlier!

As we came to Main Street, one front brakeman, Bob, had abandoned ship! Chuck had crawled on the hood and was preparing for a quick exit. The other brakeman, Bill, was trying

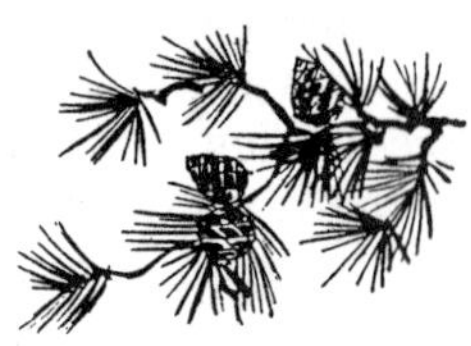

to hang onto a headlight and was wasting all his strength hollering, "Turn down Main Street! Turn down Main Street!" Little did he know that long ago Frank, in all the excitement, had dropped the pipe wrench and there was no turning. He was doing all this hollering and we didn't want to make a sound! (Talk about letting the cat out of the bag!)

Jim, as we approached the main drag, gave one big jerk on the bar and, as nothing seemed to give, made a perfect dive into an irrigation ditch about half full of water.

"CRASH," then soft as a summer rain, glass started falling down. At one time it was a four foot glass window in the storefront. Now it looked like Hattie's garage door when she forgot how to stop her car as she approached her garage. The car plowed through two showcases and came to a stop half way through the store.

Bill must have been saved by his guardian angel as were Frank and Chuck. Chuck didn't know how it happened but he was in the front seat upside down when the car stopped.

With all hands able to walk, although a bit scratched up and a little shaky, we surveyed the damage: Ten feet of wood storefront, two show cases, and one window! Hitting the sidewalk had slowed things down, enabling Frank to guide the car to a smooth stop without anyone's getting hurt.

Bob returned the bar and the owners had not noticed it had been borrowed.

All would have been fine but the Deputy Sheriff found the pipe wrench and took it to Dillon and gave it to my Dad (because it had *Rutherford* scratched on it!) When he handed it to Dad, Dad said, "Good, where did you find it? That's my best pipe wrench!" (We let the cat out of the bag *again*!)

Dad, being a carpenter, took care of the repairing of all the stuff and us guys paid for all the materials, but we had to push the car back up the hill with the Deputy Sheriff watching, inch by inch, all the way back up, across the ditch and back to its former resting place.

We all agreed that Halloween was getting to be just too much fun!

## EPILOGUE

Had I included all the stories I remembered, and the stories friends reminded me of, the book would be a foot thick. More books are planned.

Going to high school was a difficult process for kids in Frisco for years. I went to high school in Frisco, Breckenridge, and finished in Climax. At Climax I stayed in the dorm working swing shift seven days a week, while attending school in the daytime. Most Saturday mornings I caught a ride to Frisco so I could help Dad with the ranch chores, but I had to go back to Climax for the swing shift. Occasionally I would go home on Sunday so I could go to church with the family and have one of Mom's good Sunday meals. When this happened, I had friends who would lend me their car for the day or go with me. This was rare, however, as gas was rationed during the war.

Shortly after I graduated from high school I joined the Navy. In February, 1946, with the war over, I got an honorable discharge. I was also the proud father of a girl born the last day of 1945. When spring arrived I went to Frisco hoping to acquire a ranch somewhere in the area. This didn't work out so I moved to Denver where I spent most of my career in construction work.

On July 4, 1950, my brother Dean, lost his life on a Naval rescue mission out of Adak, Alaska.

With health and age becoming a problem, and none of the family in a position to buy the ranch, Dad decided to sell. He felt he couldn't spend another winter waiting for the Dillon Dam to be built. After anticipating the project for so many years, little did we know that within a year the work would finally start and the ranch would become very valuable.

Helen Rutherford Davidson and her husband make Sandpoint, Idaho their home. Their family of five children and their grandkids all live in the northwest.

Mildred Rutherford lives a few blocks from the author and spends much of her time keeping in touch with many friends and relatives, near and far. For the last few years, she has been working on genealogy as well.

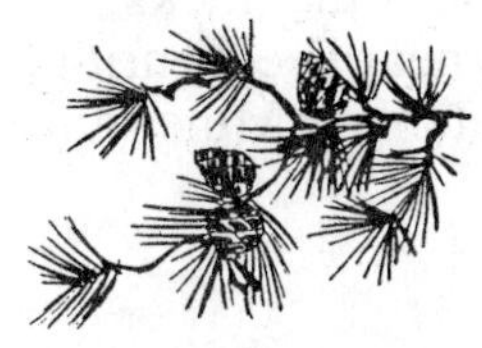

## PHOTOS & GRAPHIC ILLUSTRATIONS

**Page No.**

### PART I



### PART II



### PART III

**Page No.**

## PART IV



## PART V



## PART VI

**Page**
**No.**

## PART VII

## MORE ABOUT THE AUTHOR

Harold Rutherford is a Colorado native and spent his early life on the plains in Eckley, Colorado. At the age of eleven he moved with his family to a small, vacant ranch at Frisco, Colorado.

Harold inherited his gift of storytelling from his mother. He recalls many of the funny stories his mother told and the songs she taught them as the family was growing up. His mother always saw the best in everything and his childhood was filled with laughter and enjoyment.

The poverty, dust storms, and cyclones in Eastern Colorado and the rich ranch life in Frisco provided him with a wealth of material to write about.

Harold makes his home in Denver, Colorado, with his wife, Lois. He has been blessed with a daughter, two sons, seven grandchildren and four great grand-children.

Harold likes to hunt and fish and enjoys telling and writing stories. He enjoys wearing his kilt to Scottish Festivals during the summer and fall.

He is currently working on several books.